Trevor Beeson
and Jenny Pearce

A VISION
OF HOPE

*The churches and change
in Latin America*

FORTRESS PRESS   PHILADELPHIA

First published in the United Kingdom by
Fount Paperbacks, London.

Copyright © 1984 by Trevor Beeson
First Fortress Press edition 1984

Library of Congress Cataloging in Publication Data
Main entry under title:

A Vision of hope.

    Includes index.
    1. Christianity—Latin America—Addresses, essays, lectures. 2. Church and
social problems—Latin America—Addresses, essays, lectures. I. Beeson, Trevor.
II. Pearce, Jenny.
BR600.V57   1984   278   83–48927
ISBN 0–8006–1758–4

K463I83   Printed in the United Kingdom   1–1758

Contents

Preface

This book offers an account of obedience to God in societies largely controlled by extreme and repressive regimes. Its main concern is to describe the life and witness of the churches in Latin America through the eyes of Christians who have taken sides with the poor and given voice to the cry for justice and basic human rights. This can be a dangerous vocation, as the life and death of Archbishop Oscar Romero and countless others bear witness.

In November 1980 the involvement of the Church in the struggle for social change in El Salvador was given prominence in a film screened at the Assembly of the British Council of Churches in London. The response to the film and subsequent debate is recorded in the following resolution:

> The Assembly, aware of the critical social, political and economic conditions prevailing in some countries of Latin America, declares its deep concern for the peoples and churches, both Catholic and Protestant, of Latin America, calls upon its member churches and member bodies of the Conference for World Mission to give higher priority to the Latin American situation, and welcomes the proposal that the Division of International Affairs conduct a study project, with the co-operation of other divisions, leading to a background and policy document on Latin America . . .

A Vision of Hope is part of a response to that resolution. As members of the study project working party, we interpreted our brief as a description of the churches' mission in the context of these 'critical social, political and economic conditions'. With many years of Latin American experience between us, we thought it essential to give adequate space to an analysis of these conditions in order to explain the emergence of a theology of liberation in the churches, before going on to describe their role in social and political change. We are of course fully aware of the controversial

7

nature of liberation theology and the criticism it evokes both inside and outside Latin America; but the response to it, however expressed, indicates its crucial importance in the contemporary Latin American scene. In varying degrees we share the perspective of liberation theology, but this does not imply that no other expression of Christian faith possesses validity or interest for us. This study is therefore offered as just one contribution to an understanding of the vast field of Christianity in Latin America, the great complexity of which is sketched without any attempt at comprehensiveness. Time and space have not permitted us to describe the situations in Bolivia, Colombia, Ecuador, the Dominican Republic, Haiti, Panama, Uruguay and Venezuela.

Thanks are due to a number of specialists who have contributed background papers, but who cannot of course be held responsible for the final result of their use: William Bell, José Miguez Bonino, Nestor Bonino, Sue Branford, Eduardo Crawley, Sue Cunningham, Clare Dixon, Roberto Espindola, Manuel Gaxiola Gaxiola, George Gelber, Tony Hill, Andrew Kirk, Steven Mackie, John Medcalf, Andrew Nickson, Jenny Pearce, George Philip, Arthur Robinson, Jan Rocha, Jackie Roddick, Emily Ryan, Maurice Sinclair, Jean Stubbs, Derek Winter.

We are also grateful to the following advisers: Alan Angell, Sylvia Beales, Leslie Bethell, William Cook, Clare Dixon, Brian Duckworth, Colin Harding, Luke Holland, Walter Hollenweger, Philip King, Mildred Nevile, Hugh O'Shaughnessy, John Rettie, Alonso Roberts, Maurice Sinclair, Luis del Valle, Ann Zammitt. And to Gabriela Gelber and Stella Maris for their help in translation.

Finally we also wish to thank Trevor Beeson and Jenny Pearce for their perseverance throughout an inevitably long and arduous programme of writing, and Emily Ryan for her invaluable help as secretary of the working party. Jane Gibbons has typed complicated and much amended manuscripts and we are grateful to her, too. We hope the result of their labours will foster an understanding of the conditions in which Christian faith is celebrated and share in the communities of hope in Latin America, and will stimulate reflection on an appropriate response.

Michael Rose, Steven Mackie, George Gelber,
Andrew Kirk, Derek Winter, Paul Oestreicher,
Julian Filochowski

Chapter 1

Introduction

Latin America comes to Britain in a series of well-worn images: military dictators, guerrilla fighters, Amnesty International reports, revolutionary priests and the vanishing Indian tribes of the Amazon basin. In 1982 the continent became headline news for some months when Britain went to war with Argentina over the Falkland Islands (known in Argentina and the rest of Latin America as the Malvinas). But this was unusual prominence for a continent which until this war, and the more recent events in Central America, received very little attention from the British press. Beyond the foreign pages and the colour supplement there are reports of bank loans, export orders and an occasional brief tour by a junior government minister drumming up business for Britain. It is easily forgotten that Britain was once a major economic power in Latin America, sufficient to turn Argentina into 'The Argentine' and the Rio de la Plata into 'The River Plate', with passenger and cargo ships paying regular visits to the major ports of the region. Weakened by two world wars and long years of economic decline, however, Britain has long since been replaced by the United States as the dominant economic power in Latin America, and now lags behind other European countries in trade and investment.

Yet, behind the popular images, and the ignorance they mask, Latin America is assuming an importance which reaches beyond the Americas and which cannot be ignored. The world has become more complex. Many Latin Americans, especially those of the centre and left – in power, in opposition or in armed rebellion – look to Western Europe for understanding and support. Even right-wing regimes are uneasy with the interventionist policies of the United States and wish to decrease their dependence on their powerful northern neighbour. Nevertheless, it is in Central America that the Reagan administration has decided to draw the line against

'Communism', importing Cold War attitudes and language into the region and setting the scene for a possible confrontation between East and West. At the same time, influential sectors in the Latin American churches, particularly the Roman Catholic Church, have begun to stand by the poor in their demands for social and economic justice and they look to Christians in the West for moral and practical support. Nowhere has this stand been taken with greater courage and determination than in Central America. Archbishop Romero and the other murdered priests of El Salvador and Guatemala are a symbol of the Church's solidarity with the poor. In Nicaragua, the involvement of the clergy at the highest levels of government shows the willingness of priests to accept the responsibilities of power as well as protest.

Within the United States, there is growing revulsion amongst ordinary people at simplistic, hardline anti-communist policies that lead to support for brutal dictatorships which for decades have suppressed dissent and blocked reform. Some of this opposition within the United States is the direct result of pressure from American churches, other is based on a wider fear of American foreign adventures after the Vietnam debacle. Domestic public opinion is therefore an important factor that President Reagan and his advisers must now take into account as they chart their policies towards Latin America. The current war in Central America raises a particular issue for Europeans as both the United States and the opposition forces in the region appeal to them for support. But the oppression and poverty which led to that war exist throughout Latin America. This book looks at the continent as a whole and attempts to give some account of its diversity, with case studies of half of its twenty republics, and of the history and new directions of the Latin American churches which lay special claim to the support of European Christians.

Many learned writers have wondered if it really makes sense to talk about *Latin* America. The term was invented by the French to justify an imperial adventure; the Spanish, to this day, stick doggedly to *Hispano*-America or at most *Ibero*-America (which allows for the incorporation of Portuguese-speaking Brazil). Political leaders like Nicaragua's Cesar Augusto Sandino and Peru's Victor Raul Haya de la Torre unsuccessfully tried to impose *Indo*-America. In the English-speaking world, popular parlance still tends to come up with *South* America, as distinct from *America* on its own, which is of course reserved to the United States.

When *Latin* America became the officially adopted name for the region in the newly-founded United Nations, it referred to twenty republics stretching from much further north than the main cities of Texas to the rim of the Antarctic circle – approximately 4,500 miles from North to South, 3,000 miles from East to West. It was once even larger – about half of Mexico's original territory has been absorbed by the US. Some 320 million people live presently in those twenty republics. In eighteen countries the official language is Spanish, in one (Brazil) it is Portuguese, and in another (Haiti) it is French. All but one of the Latin American republics (Haiti) are classified by the World Bank as 'middle income countries'. Only 5 per cent of the land area of Latin America is under cultivation, and about 30 per cent is unused or unusable. About 50 per cent is forest. The interior is still difficult to live in, or even to cross, and most of the population live within 200 miles of the coast in cities, towns and mainly villages, and very few in between. The Andes mountains extend from one end of the continent to the other without a break, constituting a western wall some three to four miles high, 500 miles wide in Bolivia, where 73 of the 150 towns are over 12,000 feet above sea level, and 120 miles wide in Ecuador. The Amazon basin is almost as large as the United States, and the Amazon river itself is longer than the distance between Liverpool and New York – seven of its tributaries are over 1,000 miles long, one of them, Mamoré-Madeia, being about 3,000 miles long.

Within this vast territory there is great diversity. Some nations are huge, with large and rapidly growing populations, like Mexico with its almost 1.2 million square miles and close to 65 million people, or Brazil with its 5.1 million square miles and more than 117 million inhabitants. Others, like Argentina, are vast and empty, with only about fifteen people per square mile. And at the opposite end of the scale, there is tiny El Salvador, its mere 8,000 square miles each crammed with 600 people. Income per capita in the wealthiest country, oil-rich Venezuela, is more than ten times higher than in the poorest, Haiti, and about seven times higher than in Honduras, which the World Bank also classified as a 'middle income country'. In these statistical terms, Venezuela ranks behind Israel and Greece, but ahead of Hong Kong, Yugoslavia and Turkey, while Honduras is roughly in the same league as Ghana, and Haiti lags behind Uganda and Lesotho.

Diversity is also the hallmark of Latin America's ethnic make-up. The original inhabitants were Indians but in Argentina, where they were hunters on the huge Pampas, the Indians were annihilated by the army in the nineteenth century, leaving only a few remnants on the fringe, in Patagonia to the south, in the Andes to the west, and in the Chaco to the north. The position is different in the Andean countries, Peru, Bolivia, and Ecuador, which were dominated by the Quechua-speaking Incas before the arrival of the Spanish. Here, where the Incas were settled and skilled farmers, millions of Quechua speakers survive, relegated to a degraded subsistence agriculture. The same is true of Guatemala where the descendants of the Maya Indians form a majority of the population. Between 1500 and 1850 many millions of Negroes were brought from Africa as slaves (under a relatively humane Spanish law), and their descendants are to be found in all parts today, especially in Brazil. Though the languages of the European colonizers have been established for centuries, many of the original tongues have survived: Quechua in Peru and Guarani in Paraguay have even been accorded some official standing. But absence of official recognition has not been an obstacle to the survival of Guatemala's 23 indigenous languages, of Mapudungu in Chile or the myriad Tupí-Guaraní dialects in Paraguay and Brazil.

Statistically, Latin America is misleading, for beyond the geographical divisions that inspired the title of Marcel Niedergang's important book, *The Twenty Latin Americas* more than four centuries of history have given each republic a complex structure of class and power. On average, Latin Americans appear to be healthier, better fed, better educated and better paid than their peers in most of Asia and Africa. But among the poorest sectors of Latin American societies, the discrepancy narrows and the common problems of underdevelopment emerge just as clearly as elsewhere in the Third World. The existence of these internal divides explains two apparently contradictory, incompatible discourses on Latin America. There is the Latin America where rapid development is recorded, where urban mores and manifestations of culture resemble those of the industrialized North, and where standards of living justify the World Bank's description of 'middle income countries'. And there is also the Latin America of underdevelopment, of hunger for land and food, of high infant mortality, endemic diseases and low life expectancies. The first is the Latin America familiar to bankers and tourists, comprehensible through national accounts and exchange rates, industrial growth statistics and balance of payments figures. The second is more frequently referred to by social reformers and political radicals, and provides the basis for the language of exploitation and deprivation.

Both are Latin America. Neither has a greater claim to authenticity, for they are twin products of the same past. They meet violently in history books and political manifestos where the clash between them is recorded as wars between liberals and conservatives, *colorados* and *blancos*, protectionists and free-traders, and as massacres, uprisings and strikes. They meet when the causes of underdevelopment are discussed, when talk shifts from degrees and rates – of investment, of literacy, of urbanization and so on – to power and domination. Then the diversity of Latin American reality begins to recede in favour of what the region has in common: its colonial past (the moment and style of its colonialization); the time and fashion of its accession to nationhood; its linkage to the world economy and the patterns of external domination it has endured; its experiences of economic, social and political reform. The differences do not vanish completely, but they begin to appear as variations on a common theme, which in many key aspects is the same theme as that of the Third World as a whole.

The colonization of what is now known as Latin America began in the fifteenth century. Spaniards and Portuguese began to carve up the hemisphere long before the first English settlers landed in the present territory of the United States and much earlier than the colonization of South Asia and Africa. It began as a commercial gamble, soon to be transformed into a joint effort of conquest and evangelization. Not surprisingly, there are two contradictory versions of these early years: the 'black legend' which sees it as a greedy, heartless experiment in genocide and plunder, and the 'rose legend' which concentrates on the free mixing of races, the enlightened legislation of Indies and the uninhibited transfer of Iberian cultural achievements. The Spaniards arrived in pursuit of gold and silver, of land and of souls in need of salvation. The methods of conquest were harsh, often cruel, but no more so than those of their adversaries, as contemporary accounts remind us. Superior military technology helped, but the exploitation of political disaffection in the Aztec federation and the Inca empire were far more crucial to the success of the campaigns of Cortes and Pizarro. The contempt in which the native population was held and the brutality with which it was treated after the conquest led within a few decades to the complete annihilation of the Indians in the Caribbean and parts of Central America. In the Andean countries the Quechua and Aymara populations were decimated.

The *conquistadores* did not take their womenfolk with them, which soon made for the appearance of a new, mixed-blood *mestizo* population that was destined to become the dominant influence in Latin America. Exploitation of the aborigine was extreme in the mining centres. Elsewhere the *encomienda* system, by which the *conquistador* received a huge grant of land and the right to raise tribute and use the services of the Indians who lived on it, often reduced the Indian to a status somewhere between slave and serf although the *conquistador* was also 'entrusted' with their spiritual welfare. Conditions were far from uniform, and the humanity of some churchmen and administrators gave rise to a vast body of legislation aimed at defending the rights of the native population. The kings of Spain, however, had no way of enforcing such legislation, and for the colonials it was an annoying irrelevance to their overriding concern which was to milk the continent of its mineral wealth. It was during these early days of Empire that the foundations were laid for a pattern of land ownership that persists in some areas to the present time – the huge *hacienda* or estate, worked by semi-feudal peasants, which in colonial times provided the food and hides needed by the mines. Peninsular Spain maintained a monopoly of trade to Latin America, prohibiting its colonies from trading with any other power. This monopoly, maintained for most of Latin America's colonial history, is the origin of many of the structural features the continent carried into later independent life. It was policed by special courts, the Spanish viceroys and the Spanish fleet, and ensured that Spain was the prime beneficiary of the colonial empire. Vast territories were restricted to a handful of easily controllable gateways to the outside world. Trade between the colonies themselves was long banned, and local manufacturing was either prohibited or actively discouraged. Domestic, inland economies were geared to subsistence, mainly in the hands of those of Spanish descent but native-born. On the other hand, commerce and finance, dominated by the *peninsulares*, became closely associated with political power, and from this split there emerged later the two-party division, usually in the form of liberals (the mercantile élite) versus the conservatives (the ranchers and their followers). This division dominated most of Latin American political life until well into the nineteenth century.

Britain made two major attempts to break by force the Spanish stranglehold on the continent: Horatio Nelson's Nicaraguan expedition of 1780 and the invasion of the River Plate in 1806. Both were dismal failures. But through smuggling first, and active support for Latin American revolutionaries later, Britain's commercial interests became interwoven with the struggle for independence and with the emergence of the new Latin American nations. It was not until 1823 that an assertive United States proclaimed the Monroe Doctrine, with its motto 'America for the Americans' (meaning 'Europeans Out!'), declaring Latin America to be an American sphere of influence. And it was not until 1890 that the new power was able to put any military muscle behind this position, inaugurating an era in which Latin Americans would cynically rephrase the Monroe Doctrine to read, 'America for the North Americans'. Meanwhile, three centuries of Spanish colonial rule gave Latin America highly developed forms of urban life, including a number of renowned universities, sitting atop a vast, undeveloped hinterland where most economic activity was either extractive or aimed at feeding and clothing the local population.

The Napoleonic Wars were the European backdrop to the independence of most of Latin America, and it was the weakening effect on Spain of these wars that enabled independence to be won during the early part of the nineteenth century. The pro-independence forces aimed to throw off the economic domination of Spain and establish 'modern' constitutions which reflected liberal ideas then current in Europe. So the nineteenth century was the period of 'national organization' for most of Latin America and, in a sense, the nation state is as old in Latin America as in much of

15

Europe. There were early dreams of a single, huge federation of Latin American countries, a counterpart of the English-speaking United States in the North, and when this failed to materialize, there were several attempts at regional federation – for example, the Gran Colombia that stretched across the north of South America, and the United Provinces of Central America. But these were short-lived experiments. Indeed the dominant trend throughout the first half of the nineteenth century was towards ever greater subdivision and – apart from Brazil, which expanded – none of the large political units created by the colonial administrators survived intact. While it would be simplistic to ascribe the whole of this process to any single motive, it is evident that English and US diplomacy deliberately pursued what nationalist writers have described as a policy of 'balkanization' of Latin America. Protracted and violent civil strife accompanied the establishment of new centralized national authorities. The scaffolding created by 300 years of colonial life dictated the form of the new power structures, and the ownership of land and control over the new republics' commercial and financial outlets became the twin keys to social dominance.

Sometimes it is asserted that the Iberian colonial heritage was largely responsible for the fact that the Industrial Revolution passed Latin America by: the metropolis had discouraged local manufacturing and technological development in order to protect its own industries, and the colonies had grown used to importing all the manufactured goods they required. After independence, taking advantage of free trade embraced by the continent's new ruling élite as a reaction to the previous 'closed' system, England and much later the United States, took over the role of suppliers of manufactured goods to the new Latin American republics. There is some substance to this argument, but it is significant that the opening to world trade of the new Latin American countries, their independence and national organization, and the spread of the Industrial Revolution, were all taking place at the same time. It was in the second half of the nineteenth century and beginning of the twentieth that Latin America was made to fit into the new pattern of international relations created by the Industrial Revolution, and the role it assumed was that of supplier of raw materials and importer of manufactured goods.

This formula worked well for the ruling élites of Latin America; their countries' resources were plentiful and, apart from certain foreign-owned mining enclaves and banana plantations, were owned by the élites themselves. Moreover, most of Latin America's rural population lived beyond, or on the margin of, the market economy, so the fruits of this linkage with the outside world did not have to be shared among many. It was however a formula that led to much internal upheaval and even greater lopsidedness in the structure of the Latin American economies. The fencing of the prairies in Argentina, and the introduction of the plantation system in Brazil and Central America, constituted the first major 'agrarian reform' of the region. The best and most accessible lands, appropriated by force or legal chicanery or both, became export-oriented enclosures. The peasantry, which hitherto had freely rotated their subsistence crops there, were ejected and forced to eke out an increasingly precarious existence from marginal terrain, or surrender to the option of miserably paid employment. In other words, it became a formula for malnutrition, exploitation and desperate migration from the countryside to the cities. At the other end of the scale, the huge incomes generated by the export of Latin America's natural resources began to be spent by the elites on the external trappings of progress, European style. Urban services became more sophisticated; the cities tried to look like Paris and the railways like little Englands. Money was spent conspicuously on mansions, mistresses in Paris, and financial and real estate speculation. It is sometimes argued that the prevailing pattern of international economic relations prevented the investment of this wealth in the introduction of modern technologies and the development of local industry, but contemporary evidence from elsewhere in the world suggests that the limits imposed by the system were hardly strict. There was no lack of politicians who argued for protection and the local development of industry, but the groups who benefited from the free trade system were sufficiently strong to thwart any attempt to change it.

Exchanging raw materials for manufactured goods and the externals of progress for a few was a delicate balancing act. Populations were growing rapidly and were swelled in Argentina, Uruguay and Brazil by massive immigration from Europe. Within these populations, the numbers of underpaid wage-earners and of landless peasants were also increasing. And the needle of the balance – the power to determine the prices for what Latin America had to offer – was beyond the control of Latin America itself, in the hands of the industrialized nations of the North. Conservatives tend to look back to that period with yearning as a 'golden age', but it was remarkably short-lived. Its demise was already foreshadowed by the world crisis of the 1890s, and its collapse was manifestly under way in the early decades of the twentieth century.

The first major explosion of the old formula took place in Mexico in 1910. Under the banner of 'Land and Liberty' the peasant masses rose in a revolution that expropriated the great landowners and led to the creation of the *ejido*, communally-held units that could be passed on from father to son, but not sold. Later, in the 1930s, Mexico was to pioneer oil nationalism, taking over the foreign-owned oilfields – which in the short run earned the country a punitive economic blockade by the great powers, but which also, over half a century, laid the foundations for the Third World's oldest, and ultimately successful, experiment in the autonomous development of an oil industry. The First World War also exposed the weakness of the old formula. Exports of manufactured goods from the belligerent nations of the North, long taken for granted in Latin America, were reduced to a trickle. Virtually for the first time, the need for an industrial base of their own was accepted by the ruling groups in Latin America. The first, important, spurts of industrialization, particularly in the larger nations of South America, date back to this period. But all the conflicting elements of the primary exports/manufactured imports formula did not come together until the Great Depression of the 1930s (which heralded a continent-wide wave of military takeovers) and the Second World War. First, prices for Latin America's commodities plunged, dramatically slashing their purchasing power and their ability to service their burgeoning foreign debts – and sowing the seeds of recession, unemployment and inflation. The 1930s saw an increasing flow of resources from export-oriented mining and agriculture into protected industries, creating two new, powerful pressure groups – local industrialists and an urban, industrial working class. In Chile, in 1928, their joint interests helped a Popular Front government to power. Next, war again interrupted the flow of trade to and from the North, setting the scene for the appearance of the region's large populist movements, of which the most notable were associated with Getulio Vargas in Brazil and Juan Domingo Perón in Argentina.

Given the background of the conflagration in Europe and some of the visible features of the populist movements, it was not altogether surprising that the movements in Argentina and Brazil should have been seen from the North as 'native' versions of fascism. Yet most serious students of Latin America agree that the label does not quite fit. Three elements came together in the rise of populism: (1) the demand for social justice and effective political participation by masses which had been excluded or 'marginalized' economically and politically by the ruling elites and which, save perhaps in the case of Chile, had not developed an affinity for European-style socialism or Communism; (2) the emergence of a class of local industrial entrepreneurs, whose interests clashed to some extent with those of the traditional landowning oligarchies; and (3) the growing conviction among the military that national security needed solid foundations which could only be provided by industrialization. The Second World War also consolidated the position of the United States as virtually the sole outside influence on the whole of Latin America. Almost to the end of the nineteenth century the United States had not felt able to put teeth into its claim to regional supremacy *vis-à-vis* the European powers. Through pursuit of its 'Manifest Destiny', the US had wrested from Mexico the territories of Texas, Upper California and New Mexico, even though it had been unable to prevent the joint English-Spanish-French intervention which briefly installed Maximilian as Emperor of Mexico. The Spanish-American war of the 1890s (which gave independence to Cuba and led to the virtual annexation of Puerto Rico by Washington) signalled that the US was finally ready to impose its will, at least in its Caribbean and Central American 'backyard'.

The first decade of the twentieth century witnessed US military intervention and the installation of puppet regimes in most of the countries of this neighbouring area, as well as the spread of North American economic domination of the local economies. These were the days of the expansion of the United Fruit Company, which came to be known as *El Pulpo* (The Octopus) and as *Mamita*

Yunay (Mother Yunay – a phonetic rendering of *United*); the days that gave birth to that lasting North American stereotype of Latin America – the 'banana republic' with operetta generals in charge. These were the days in which Washington created Panama out of a province in Colombia, in order to construct and control a canal across the Central American isthmus. United States influence then spread southwards along the Pacific to Ecuador, Peru and Chile. All new mining investment was American. Britain, weakened by the First World War and then by the Depression, hung on to its outdated railways and public utilities – the glamour stocks of an earlier age. Only in Argentina, where Britain still controlled commerce, banking and foreign trade, could the North American challenge be resisted. But the Second World War left Britain without resources, and its holdings in Latin America were rapidly disposed of. Domination by the US was complete.

With Europe bankrupted by war, industrialization through import substitution proceeded apace in a number of Latin American countries, especially in Argentina, Brazil, Colombia and Mexico. Once again however economic development was lopsided. The new industries were almost exclusively inward-looking, aimed at the domestic markets. Foreign exchange continued to be generated by the primary sector – agriculture in some cases, mining in others. Industry grew rapidly, creating a new demand for foreign exchange (to purchase fuels, machinery and intermediate products), and with labour-intensive agricultural exports not only growing more slowly, but also subject to the vagaries of the world markets, the new formula seemed almost designed to lead to balance of payments crises. Indeed in the more industrialized Latin American nations it led, long before the developed world had found a name for it, to the phenomenon now known as stagflation. The economic woes of Latin America in this period of transition were interpreted in the light of European and North American economic wisdom. The main obstacle was seen as the insufficiency of capital, compounded by a lack of financial discipline. Right and left were not far apart on this reading, though they differed in the proposed solutions: the former advocated attracting capital from abroad on a large scale, the latter preferred the path of state-directed domestic savings; the former favoured stimulating private enterprise, in the hope that the wealth thus created would 'trickle down' to all strata of society, the latter proposed modifying the structure of ownership, particularly of the land.

The early 1950s witnessed some important attempts at radical reform. In Bolivia, following the 1952 revolution, the *Movimiento Nacionalista Revolucionario* (MNR) led by Victor Paz Estenssoro, with its power base among the miners, nationalized the holdings of the tin-mining oligarchy and embarked upon an agrarian reform that created a new class of small peasant farmers. The impetus of the reform, however, was soon defeated; financial constraints and the rightward shift in the MNR led its leaders to accept the orthodoxy dictated by the United States and the international financial organizations. In Guatemala, the government led by Jacobo Arbenz included the takeover of US-owned plantations in its agrarian reform programme. But in 1954 the United States engineered an invasion by CIA-backed Guatemalan dissidents which overthrew Arbenz and ended that country's only experiment in reform this century. These events were followed in 1959 by the Cuban revolution, which went further than any reform-minded government in Latin America had ever dared. The United States, where Cuban policy was dictated by the powerful sugar lobby, refused to countenance the economic reforms that were the goal of the revolutionary government. In response to this hostile reaction, the Cuban government took over US holdings, expropriated its oligarchy and initiated a far-reaching agrarian reform. The Cubans went on for a time to preach that armed popular insurrection was the only effective way to achieve and defend these reforms against the resistance of the local ruling classes and of the United States. They were soon able to prove the second part of their doctrine by successfully resisting a US-organized invasion in 1962. Yet this very success brought other forms of pressure and intervention. The United States used all the power at its disposal to isolate Cuba diplomatically and economically from the rest of the region, ultimately pushing Castro into an alliance with the Soviet Union. Preventing 'another Cuba' became a prime objective of US policy, and gave birth to the 'Alliance for Progress' – a much-publicized, continent-wide investment and aid programme which was intended to accelerate Latin America's economic and social development and to get rid of some of the region's more anachronistic features such as the huge estates, dubbed as feudal or traditional by the

American advisers. It was hoped that a moderate agrarian reform would undermine the discontent that fuelled revolutionary movements. The United States also set about strengthening the Latin American military, whose role increasingly came to be seen as that of gendarmes charged with preventing 'Communist subversion'.

In spite of these and other frustrations, the 1950s were a decade of hope. Dictators like Ubico in Guatemala, Gómez in Colombia, Pérez Jimenez in Venezuela had been overthrown. A revolution in Costa Rica (in 1948) had led to the establishment of a democratic regime which took the unusual step of disbanding the army. And in the last year of the decade a guerrilla army headed by Fidel Castro had ejected Batista from Cuba. Trujillo continued to rule in Santo Domingo, Gómez was succeeded by the autocratic rule of Rojas Pinilla, the Somoza dynasty survived the assassination of its founder, and the military still held sway over several nations, but the prevailing mood of the 1950s was that democracy was on its way, with social reform not far behind. The 'Alliance for Progress' was matched, from within Latin America, by the spread of 'developmentalism' – the notion that massive foreign investment in key sectors of the economy would bring about the much-awaited take-off, and that improved social conditions would inevitably follow. The Latin American Free Trade Association was created, initially to promote trade by lowering tariff barriers, but with the ultimate aim of establishing a Latin American Common Market by the 1980s. The later regional organizations, such as the Central American Common Market and the Andean Group, were variations on the same theme. All this promoted a burst of economic growth throughout the region. Countries became more industrialized and trade between Latin American nations multiplied quite dramatically. Yet the lopsidedness continued. Most of the agrarian reforms planned by the Alliance for Progress did not take place. The changes that did take place benefited almost exclusively the manufacturing and service sectors of the Latin American economies, and far from spilling over, or trickling down, to the poor and marginalized, the gap between them widened. This was so even when the actual income of the poor was modestly increased. Moreover, those best equipped to take advantage of the incentive offered by governments were the foreign-owned and transnational companies; indeed the larger, complementary markets created by the regional trade organizations suited them perfectly. Foreign dominance of the Latin American economies increased, syphoning out wealth through the repatriation of profits, payment of royalties and often exaggerated payments made to parent companies for services and components. To make matters worse, the larger industrial sectors were still mainly geared to the local market and did not export, thus leaving the Latin American economies still prone to periodic payments crises, only more quickly, on a grander scale, and with a cumulative effect as countries entered the game of rolling over their indebtedness in order to keep afloat.

The Cuban path of rural guerrilla warfare was attempted again and again, without success, in several countries throughout the 1960s. In 1967 the death in a Bolivian jungle of Che Guevara, the best-known advocate of this strategy, seemed to mark the end of such attempts. They were succeeded by a number of bids to take guerrilla warfare into the cities, the very heart of the 'modern' sectors of Latin American societies. In Brazil, Uruguay and Argentina this strategy also met with failure, for not only had methods of repression, with considerable help from the US, become much more efficient, but there was no response from the masses to the call of the gun-bearing revolutionary élites. Yet the obsession with 'preventing another Cuba' went far beyond quashing attempts at armed insurrection. It came to include opposition to any far-reaching programme of social and economic reform, even when pursued through peaceful, electoral means. The most clear-cut and dramatic illustration of this was provided by the 'destabilization' and eventual overthrow of Salvador Allende's socialist regime in Chile, which had been voted into office in 1970. Just as the Cuban revolution had become a landmark in one direction, the overthrow of Allende in 1973 signposted another.

In the mid 1960s the Brazilian military had already heralded the dawning of the era of the 'national security state', which brought the military into political life virtually on a war footing. The enemy was 'Marxist subversion', a category extended far beyond its literal meaning, to embrace political expressions that in other latitudes would be described as liberal or reformist. The rationale of earlier years, that subversion was best thwarted by attacking its root causes, namely, social injustice, was abandoned in favour of a policy of harsh repression. The military governments in Chile,

Uruguay and Argentina took this even further, attempting the total annihilation of the adversary. The methods included deprivation of civil rights, mass arrests, clandestine executions and 'disappearances', and the systematic use of torture, not only as a means of exacting information, but as an instrument of terror. In Chile, Argentina and Uruguay, the establishment of the 'national security state' went hand in hand with the adoption of radical monetarist economic policies and the 'opening' of markets to outside competition, which in effect meant the dismantling of the policy mechanism used since the 1940s to promote local industrial growth. The cost of these policies has been massive unemployment, depressed earnings for the wage-earners and harsh repression of trade union activity. Although initially the strategy of promoting non-traditional exports enjoyed some success, it could not survive the deepening of the world recession, and by 1982 all three countries were in a serious economic crisis.

If 1967, the year of Che Guevara's death, marked the end of the first wave of rural guerrilla attempts, it also marked the beginning of a new era in the life of one of Latin America's oldest institutions, the Church. Meeting at Medellin, Colombia, in 1968, the bishops of Latin America startled the world with a remarkable document. 'Latin America', they said, 'still appears to live under the tragic sign of underdevelopment, which makes it impossible for our brothers not only to enjoy material goods, but also to fulfil themselves. Despite all the efforts that are made, we are faced with hunger and poverty, widespread disease and infant mortality, illiteracy and marginalism, profound inequalities of income, and tensions between the social classes, outbreaks of violence and a scanty participation of the people in the management of the common good.' The bishops also candidly examined the Church's own position *vis-à-vis* this situation: 'Complaints that the hierarchy, the clergy, the religious are rich and allied with the rich also come to us. . . . The great buildings, the rectories and religious houses that are better than those of the neighbours, the often luxurious vehicles, the attire, inherited from other eras, have been some of the causes. The system of taxes to support the clergy and maintain educational institutions has become discredited and has led to the formation of erroneous opinions about the amount of money received. To this has been added the exaggerated secrecy in which the finances of high schools, parishes and dioceses have been shrouded, favouring a mysterious atmosphere which magnifies shadows to gigantic proportions and helps to create fictions.' The bishops' response to the general situation of Latin America, the characteristic feature of which they described as oppression, was a commitment of the Church to *liberación*. Their answer to the criticism of the Church's own ambiguous position was a commitment to become, in fact as well as in theory, 'the Church of the poor'. In Latin American political circles it had long been taken for granted that the Church almost automatically aligned itself with the powers that be, invariably repeating the rulers' defence of private property and the denunciation of subversive forces. Colonization itself was a venture that combined the sword and the Cross, and evangelization provided the ideological underpinning for the conquest of Latin America's indigenous people. Thus the Church inevitably appeared as the justifier of the atrocities committed by the *conquistadores* and the later serfdom of the Indians.

Yet for all this, the Church's record is far from totally black. The record of the great Friar Bartolomé de las Casas (1474–1566), and his untiring defence of the Indians, is recognized by all as a sign of a more widespread authentic concern for the Church's new American flock. The vast Jesuit missions, a virtual empire covering Paraguay, part of Argentina and the south of Brazil, were models of social organization, and while they lasted protected the Guarani from the Portuguese slave hunters. As official educators in officially Catholic countries, the churchmen moulded much of Latin American culture. None the less, the colonial Church became wealthy and powerful. In Mexico, for example, it was for a long time the only countrywide banker and also one of the largest landowners. And in spite of the fact that it was a priest, Father Hidalgo, who set in motion the movement that made Mexico independent, the identification of the Church with the rich and the powerful was such that the Mexican revolution acquired a markedly anti-clerical attitude. Indeed, Mexico is to this day the only country in Latin America where, according to law, clergymen may not wear clerical garb outside their churches. Close association with power also involved considerable involvement in politics. Clergymen were prominent in many of the first post-independence governments, and the Church retained its influence on education and civil legislation, particularly where this affected family life. All over Latin America, in the second half of the nineteenth century and the first half of the twentieth, the Church supported Conservative parties against Liberals and free-thinking Radicals. Open support from the Church was instrumental in securing a majority vote for Argentina's Perón in 1946; his confrontation with the Church was a key factor in his overthrow in 1955.

Even today the extreme right continues to bid for the support of the Church, arguing that only Conservative politicians are really prepared to defend the values of Western Christian civilization against atheistic communism. As however the fortunes of the Conservatives have waned, so in some countries, the Church – or at least prominent figures within the Church – has, since the 1950s, given its backing to Christian Democrats – parties who, drawing their inspiration from the Catholic thinker Jacques Maritain, preach a third way between capitalism and Communism. Before the late 1960s it was rare for the Church or many of its representatives to be found to the left of Latin America's political spectrum. The Medellín Conference and its adoption of *liberación* as an aim and of the 'option for the poor' as its means, has changed all that and caused a major upheaval both within and beyond the confines of the Church. When the Latin American bishops met again in Puebla, Mexico, in 1979, they said, in a document criticized as too soft by the more radical liberationists, 'Between Medellín and Puebla ten years have gone by.... If we focus our gaze on our Latin American region, what do we see? No deep scrutiny is necessary. The truth is that there is an ever-increasing distance between the many who have little and the few who have much.... We discover that this poverty is not a passing phase. Instead it is the product of economic, social and political situations and structures.... Hence this reality calls for personal conversion and profound structural changes that will meet the legitimate aspirations of the people for authentic social justice. Such changes either have not yet taken place, or else they have been too slow in coming in the concrete life of Latin America.'

This introduction deliberately stops short of events that are still unfolding. The last decade has witnessed a number of major developments which could be held up as vivid and significant illustrations of the diversity and complexity of Latin America, rather than of its essential unity. In the latter half of the 1970s the Southern Cone witnessed the emergence and consolidation, in Chile, Uruguay and Argentina, of the most savage autocracies recorded in Latin American history. But it also saw a move towards relaxation of the military grip on Brazil, the predecessor of the 'national security state'. The move which began further north, restoring democracy after long periods of military rule to Ecuador (1978), Peru (1981) and Bolivia (1982), spread after the Falklands/Malvinas war to Argentina, Uruguay and Chile. Also in the 1970s, the emergence of OPEC on the international scene suddenly projected oil-rich Venezuela to new heights of economic potential and political influence. Moreover, it drastically altered the development of Ecuador's economy, and created the conditions under which the discovery of new giant oilfields in Mexico – not a member of OPEC – would put financial power behind that country's traditionally independent foreign policies. Two years into the 1980s, the oil glut produced by recession in the industrialized economies seemed to dash all this to the ground, and the names of Venezuela and Mexico became synonymous with mammoth debts rather than with oil wealth.

In Central America the 1970s came to an end with a sudden escalation of the revolutionary struggle in Nicaragua, which in 1979 brought down Latin America's longest-lasting dictatorial dynasty, that of the Somoza family. And it saw the appearance in El Salvador of new mass-based political alliances which challenged the military who ruled the country as proxies for the landowning oligarchy. Amid predictions of a revolutionary 'domino effect' spreading from Nicaragua to all of Central America, the 1980s began with the escalation of political strife in El Salvador to a full-fledged civil war. This coincided with a change of government in the United States. The new administration, headed by Ronald Reagan, intreprets events in Central America as a local chapter in the wider confrontation between East and West, and its policies (which include funding the military efforts of anti-Sandinista forces based in Honduras) have aroused fears of the kind of US intervention that followed the Cuban revolution – and even of outright war in the region.

Many things have changed since Fidel Castro came to power in Cuba in 1959. The economic presence of the United States in Latin

27

America may be stronger, but Washington no longer holds the same kind of political sway over all Latin American governments. In the intervening years, it has had to face the increasingly independent action, and at times the open hostility, of the avowedly anti-Communist military governments of Brazil, Argentina and Chile. Attempts to win over the Argentines foundered in the wake of the South Atlantic war. Later attempts to use debt-rescue packages as leverage to swing around Brazil, Venezuela and Mexico have had little noticeable effect. Mexico feels it is in a position to constrain US actions in the Caribbean basin; Venezuela has clearly signalled that its acquiescence cannot be taken for granted.

On the other hand, in order to sustain their growth during the 1970s, and in some cases pay greatly increased import bills, almost every Latin American country resorted to heavy borrowing from private international banks. The region's debts, particularly those of the most industrialized countries, Mexico and Brazil, are now so huge that a failure of either of those countries to repay would cause a crisis throughout the international financial system. And the repayment of even the interest on the debts is such a burden on Latin American economies, particularly at a time when world recession has reduced demand for the region's exports, that the region will be skirting a serious economic crisis throughout the 1980s. This may limit some of the capacity for independent action *vis-à-vis* the United States which some countries were beginning to embark upon in the 1970s.

The picture is a difficult one to absorb. The range of political and economic situations is staggering, and they come in many different combinations. It seems to add up to more than twenty different options for twenty different Latin Americas. Yet the threats, the causes for despair and the hopes are all phrased in the same language, with the same words. In a way, that is what makes it Latin America.

Chapter 2

Mission in Conflict

Religion has always had a central place in the consciousness of the Latin American people. The situation prior to the arrival of the Spanish and Portuguese *conquistadores* in the fifteenth and sixteenth centuries has been vividly described by Professor Frank Tannenbaum:

> At the time of the discovery the American Indian was a profoundly religious and mystical human being. A great part of his daily existence was bound up in religious rites, in propitiating his many gods, in finding grace, justification and peace. Every act had its religious significance, every wind, every change in the colour of the moon, every appearance of the unexpected, had its religious portent. In such highly developed cultures as the Aztec and the Inca, a large priesthood served to interpret the will of the gods. A mystical philosophy, a questioning of the essence of human existence, informed and disciplined the attitude of the Indian toward life and death.
>
> (*Ten Keys to Latin America*, p. 53)

The outward manifestations of these deeply religious cultures were eventually made impossible by the European invaders, and the values and dualistic beliefs of Indian civilization became completely undermined in the long and bitter conflict. But of course religion is rarely, if ever, eliminated by external action, however ruthless. The missionaries of the Roman Catholic Church who followed the *conquistadores* simply provided a new channel through which the religious needs of the indigenous people came to be expressed. The early missionaries built their churches on the sites previously occupied by the old temples and at other recognized holy places. Catholicism, with its cult of saints, its use of symbolism, and the sense of mystery surrounding its sacramental system, evoked a remarkable response from the Indian who was spiritually and culturally disorientated by his loss of contact with the past and with life's supernatural dimension. Hence the conversion of millions of Indians to Roman Catholic Christianity in a very short period of time.

What is still far from clear, however, four centuries later is how deep was the conversion to Christianity. Mass movements carried forward by political and cultural factors rarely produce pure forms of religion. For most Indians the addition of another deity to their polytheistic world view was not greatly disturbing. In many Indian villages today it is difficult to discern whether there has been a genuine Christian baptism of the ancient religious cultus, or whether the old beliefs remain, covered only by a veneer of Christian practice and always ready to break through when needed. The position is further complicated by the fact that the slaves who came during the colonial period brought their African religions with them and there is much evidence of the persistence of animism, spiritism and voodoo. Throughout Latin America there is an ambiguity about the true character of popular religion.

This said, it is a plain fact that historically, culturally, statistically, Christianity is everywhere visible in Latin America. Eighty per cent of the population declares itself Roman Catholic in the censuses and most of the remainder are affiliated to other churches, mainly Protestant (or 'evangelical', as they call themselves). As the twentieth century advances, however, the religious situation becomes less clear. Prophetic voices in Catholicism have been warning for some decades that a rapid process of de-Christianization is eroding an already fragile grasp of the Christian faith by the Latin American people, and that the continent has to be seen as 'a mission field'. During the 1970s, seminary enrolments dropped, monasteries and convents became empty and had to be used for other purposes, the number of active clergy declined sharply. Conflicts and tensions mounted within the churches – an already fragmented Protestantism became prone to further division, while traditionally monolithic Catholicism was severely shaken. Some of these dramatic developments are now less evident in some countries due to a repression that muffles all sounds except its own. But beneath the surface the same critical factors are present and at work today.

The Christian churches have never been so visibly in the news as in these last years. Bishops, synods and assemblies make headlines denouncing injustice, repression and torture; priests and laymen are identified with revolutionary movements and many of them have been accused, persecuted, imprisoned or murdered. Theological literature – once almost unknown in Latin America – appears now in the windows of all bookstores and sells in thousands of copies. The poor, the persecuted, Indians and trade unionists turn to the churches for support. In Argentina, Catholic youth movements count their numbers in the hundreds of thousands. Hence the uncertainty: Is Latin America witnessing the dissolution of the last bulwark of 'massive Christianity'? Or is it on the threshold of 'a new breed of Christian'? Or both?

The two main Christian confessions took root in Latin America in close relation to the two basic epochs in the region's history. Roman Catholicism was brought by the Spanish *conquistadores* in the sixteenth century as a part of the colonial order. Protestantism was introduced by English and American missionaries and European Protestant immigrants in the nineteenth and twentieth centuries. This was part of what was once called the process of 'modernization' introduced by certain liberal élites. More and more indigenous Pentecostal movements later increased the spread of Protestantism among the poor urban or semi-urban populations, and grew with the economic and social changes in the 1920s. Folk religion or folk Catholicism, one of the products of the ambivalent mass evangelization of Latin America from the beginning, sometimes only loosely connected with the official institutional life of the Church, and occasionally even opposing it, continues to hold the majority of the poor population, particularly in the rural areas.

The collapse of the colonial order during the first part of the nineteenth century had a profound effect on the Roman Catholic Church which was symbiotically related to the colonial structure. Then, slowly, Rome regained control of the Latin American Church and re-launched the missionary movement. During the second decade of the twentieth century a vigorous programme of mobilization of the laity under the direction of the hierarchy – Catholic Action – began to relate the Church to the modernizing and democratic forces in society. Catholic universities, a Catholic labour movement, the Christian Democratic parties, were the practical instruments in this attempt to build 'a new Christendom'. Since the middle of the present century, the Catholic episcopate has gained a certain regional unity (expressed in its Latin American Episcopal Council, CELAM) and, following the Second Vatican Council, a relative autonomy. Protestantism, on the other hand, became established in the space opened by the victory of the 'modernizing project' in the second half of the nineteenth century. It was seen by the modernizing élites – and it understood itself – as an ally in the struggle against the colonial order, a support for democracy, liberal education, personal initiative and social progress, and freedom from the clerical control of society.

Both the Catholic and Protestant churches are now caught in the crisis of the post-colonial order brought about by the continuance of economic colonialism and the emergence of the movement of the poor as an influence in public life. For the Roman Catholic Church the crisis has many aspects. It is, for example, now felt by some of the hierarchies to be essential for the Church to express its 'presence' in terms that are relevant to and show solidarity with the aspirations of the masses of the poor. This, in turn, seems to threaten the traditional relation of the Church to political and economic élites. And the two elements together raise serious questions about the vertical, hierarchical structure and functioning of the Church: conflicting ecclesiologies become apparent. Consequently, right-wing governments become impatient with a Church which can no longer simply support 'law and order'. Some bishops, on the other hand, become alarmed by priests who identify with popular revolutionary movements and with theologians who undergird this option. Thus the crisis for the Catholic Church is both external and internal.

Inevitably, the Protestant churches have been affected by the same crisis. In the nineteenth century, Protestants were identified with liberalism, free trade, scientific and technological progress, democracy and capitalism; now there is a growing awareness that their role was more ambiguous than they had realized. While many cling to traditional religious practices and roles in the community, tacitly identifying themselves with the social and political status quo, others now realize that they may have been unconscious instruments of a North American or European cultural and economic domination which actually requires repressive, anti-democratic regimes throughout Latin America in order to survive. Protestants once saw themselves as the avant-garde of a new order, dispelling inertia, scholasticism and traditionalism. Now some of them have been co-opted to provide support for foreign penetration, conservatism and vested interests. Many Protestants, who through social mobility have attained a middle-class status, are caught in the crisis of their class. While neglectful of the condition of the poor they are themselves being progressively impoverished and demoralized by the present political and economic conditions. Caught between the demands of the Gospel and their position in the class structure, their crisis of identity shows up as a crisis of conscience or an escape into highly spiritualized expressions of Christian faith.

At stake in all this is the nature and demands of the Church's mission in the late twentieth century. Here the 'spirits' part their ways, for Christians are dealing not merely with contrasting theological and ideological positions but with a conflict involving complex economic, political and social factors. The significance of Christianity in the history of Latin America and its strong implantation in the conscience of the people make religion an important force in society; consequently there are strong and divergent efforts, both within sectors of the Church and from different strata of society, to shape and direct the life and action of the churches to serve particular interests. An understanding of what the Church is in Latin America requires not only a reflection on the Gospel but also on the coming together of several factors derived from the history of the churches – from their relation with the economic and political interests that hide behind 'integristic' (conservative) conceptions of the Church, or that find expression in the hopes and actions of Christians engaged in revolutionary movements. Some political and even religious leaders are ready to channel the expressions of popular religion: sometimes in an other-worldly direction, sometimes in a revolutionary direction. Though disrupted by the *conquistador*, the Indians' gods survive in a close and dynamic relationship with saints and biblical figures, enabling the people (particularly the Indians of countries such as Bolivia and Peru, Central America and Mexico) to give expression to their original roots as well as to their age-long oppression. The interrelation of indigenous folk religion and Catholicism and Protestantism in the present situation makes Christianity in Latin America a faith with both one face and many faces, like the continent itself. For this reason it becomes difficult to define the impact of churches as a whole. The limits cannot be drawn simply according to the different types of worship, and preaching. It is also necessary to consider what the different members of the churches do, how they do it, in what circumstances and also from what social position.

Within all this complexity Latin American Christians are now trying to find some guidelines for an understanding of what God is calling the churches to be and to do in the present situation. For example, in recent years the question of human rights has become a focal point for Christians in their understanding of the Church's mission, and the special situation in Latin America has given the subject a peculiar relevance. How is the value and significance of human life to be affirmed? How is meaning to be given to the lives of millions who scarcely survive in unimaginable, appalling conditions of misery? How can Christians affirm the civil and political rights of the people (democratic freedom, the rights of the individual) if they do not in the first place affirm the right to the basic means of life – food, shelter, and work? What are the political dimensions involved in the Christian's stand for life? The answer to these questions in countries subjected to violent repression, under a 'national security' state, cannot be just a verbal statement: a commitment to change is required. This is not something new in Latin America. Since the time of the Conquest there have been priests who have fought in defence of the Indians and some of them even took up arms to join the struggle for independence. What is new is that this has become of major importance in the Church, not least at the level of the hierarchy. In the Roman Catholic Church the clearest demonstration of this position was given at the Second Assembly of the Latin American Episcopate, which took place in Medellín, Colombia, in 1968, and which has become a decisive historical landmark in Latin American Christian life. For the first time a body of bishops, in many cases drawing on their personal experience and on the experience of hundreds of lay people and priests from different parts of the region, and making use of social and economic data, produced in detail an 'option for the poor'.

Thus, on the relation between sin and unjust social structures, the bishops said:

> The lack of socio-cultural integration in most of our countries has resulted in one culture being superimposed on another. At the economic level, systems were imposed which only take account of the possibilities of those sectors with high acquisitive power. This lack of adaptation to the possibilities and nature of our population produces in time frequent political instability and the consolidation of purely formal institutions. On top of that there is the lack of solidarity which, both at an individual and a social level, leads to real sin, the form of which is clearly exemplified in the unjust structures which distinguish the Latin American situation.
>
> (Medellín, Secc. JUSTICE, para. 1/2)

This analysis is followed by a call for the participation of the ordinary people in the construction of a new society. In another document the denunciation of institutionalized violence is strong and precise:

> If a Christian believes in the fertility of peace for the achievement of justice, he must also believe that justice is the unavoidable condition of peace. One can't help seeing that in many parts of Latin America there is a situation of institutionalized violence, because the actual structures violate fundamental rights, and this situation demands global changes of a bold, urgent and deeply new kind. We should not be surprised that 'the temptation for violence' arises in Latin America.
>
> (*idem*, PEACE, para. 2/2/2)

Statements of this kind precipitate all sorts of different and contradictory reactions affecting the whole of Christianity in Latin America. This 'new' Catholicism has become a dynamic factor for all the churches, partly because its statements go together with a greater ecumenical openness, and partly because it challenges other expressions of Christianity to take a stand about the problems of the continent. The dynamism is generated because there is freedom in the majority church for the development of radical movements among the clergy which, in the recent past, have taken even bolder positions over social change, for example, 'Third World Priests' in Argentina, 'Golconda Group' in Colombia and 'The 80' in Chile. In this way, the issue of the Church's political participation is raised sharply, because many of these groups took a clear political position and adopted a militant stance. Some sectors of the Church have participated in revolutionary movements – regarding it as 'putting faith into practice' – and a few have even enlisted in the armed struggle (as did Camilo Torres in Colombia in the 1960s). Others have sought to express this 'option for the poor' from more moderate, though still socially critical, positions.

The reaction to all this was inevitable. Certain social sectors within and outside the Church felt threatened, and a strong conservative movement arose in the late 1960s and became sharper in the 1970s. In the Church the most progressive commissions of CELAM itself have been changed to favour this more conservative approach. The more critical positions inspired by the Brazilian Episcopate have been replaced by attitudes of compromise more compatible with the interests of conservative governments and regimes. But the reaction does not come only – or principally – from within the Church. Repression is frequently launched by economic and political interests and carried out in many cases by military governments which, appealing to the doctrine of 'national security', spare no efforts to put down all forms of opposition. There are many Christians, priests, lay people, bishops and religious, who are paying for their commitment to social and political change with imprisonment, exile or their lives. The organizations of clergy have been dispersed (except, perhaps, ONIS in Peru, which performs exceptional pastoral work in the poor areas of the country).

In spite of opposition, however, the grassroots communities (*Comunidades de base*) generate and feed a living faith committed to the poor sectors of the population. In certain areas where injustice and repression have reached appalling levels, particularly in Central America, the repression has provoked greater response and – in cases like those of Nicaragua, El Salvador and Guatemala – more or less open civil war. In other places (especially in some countries of the Southern Cone) the repression has been so violent and cruel that it has shocked the conscience of even the conservative sectors of the Church, which have felt morally obliged to act in defence of life and individual and collective rights. Throughout the 1970s the Episcopal Conferences were particularly outspoken, as the following statements indicate:

So, even at the risk of being misinterpreted or persecuted for it, the Church can't do less than raise its voice when injustice takes over society. It can't be silent when human rights are violated, whether in an institutionalized way or in particular cases like those mentioned above. The denunciation, in our case, does not spring from desire for revenge, nor are we interested in favouring those who protest for purely personal reasons. It comes as a commitment to HIM who denounced the sin wherever it was.

('To fight for justice does not mean to play politics', Episcopal Conference of El Salvador, March 1977. The first signature on this declaration is that of Bishop Oscar Arnulfo Romero, murdered while saying Mass on 24th March 1980)

*

The outbreaks of violence and the subsequent response of institutional and political repression, deeply affects not only our churches but the country itself, for the property, honour, freedom and even life of the people are at risk! It particularly affects the Church, as an injury to Christian feelings, an abuse of the Church's good name and a threat to, and limitation of, its freedom.

We want to state briefly the configuration of facts which make this a time of testing for all Christians and good citizens. They are:
- Indiscriminate repression and detention of students and peasants.
- The practice of torture has increased and in very many cases people have been arrested, murdered or disappeared in unclear circumstances.
- Intrigue and the denunciation of people, as well as violence, are publicly and deliberately promoted.
- The Church suffers through intervention in its colleges, and the political ransacking of its seminaries, apostolic institutions and colleges.

- Priests, seminarists and staff of church institutions have been arrested and are kept totally incommunicado.
- Many priests of the Society of Jesus have been expelled from the country in a degrading and arbitrary fashion.

('Christianity and Violence', Episcopate of Paraguay, June 1976)

*

In the face of this situation (the need for social change and the eagerness of the dominant groups to preserve their privileges), some options for the oppressed emerge from the Christian community, identifying itself with their problems, their struggles and aspirations. Many Christians see their commitment illuminated by a theology which, starting from faith, interprets this reality as a situation of sin, and as a denial of God's plan, and which moves therefore to a commitment to liberation as our reply to our Lord who calls us to build history. So the Church discovers the inevitable political implications of its presence, and that it cannot announce the Gospel in a situation of oppression without stirring consciences with the message of Christ the Liberator. It sees in its evangelical poverty the expression of its solidarity with the oppressed, and denounces the sin of a society oppressed by consumerism which creates artificial needs and superfluous spending. It perceives the urgency of becoming open to the problems of the world in order to be true to its mission, for in the past, and even now, it has tended to confine itself to internal problems, and it runs the risk of failing as a sign if it becomes isolated from the pain and afflictions of men.

('The Church should promote Justice',
Peruvian Episcopate, 1972)

These quotations indicate both the situation which the churches have to face, and the nature of the denunciation and call they make. On the same lines statements have been made on kidnapping and disappeared people (Argentina, Chile, El Salvador), on the freedom of unions and freedom of expression (Chile, Brazil, Paraguay), on the marginalization of the indigenous people (Bolivia, Peru, Ecuador, Brazil), on the need for land reform, and even on subjects such as the doctrine of 'national security', which has encouraged and often been used to justify the extreme political and economic repression in Latin America (statement of the Brazilian and Argentinian Episcopates, and the Third Assembly of the Latin American Episcopate in Puebla).

Perhaps the most significant fact in the history of the Christian faith in Latin America is that the 'breath of the Spirit' has not only swept over the ecclesiastical authorities, but has also awakened a new life in the people. Thus the grassroots communities have been formed and number millions of participants, particularly in Brazil, but also in Central America, Chile, Peru, and in lesser numbers in nearly all countries. They are centres of community Bible study and of involvement in the life of the secular communities in which they exist. They are made up of lay people – men and women – who share everyday experiences in the light of the Bible, often under the guidance of priests and nuns, but otherwise of lay people; in some places non-Catholics take part. Here the trade unionist, the housewife, the university student and the peasant all meet and the result is *concientización*, a term coined by the Brazilian educationist, Paulo Freire, for 'making aware' – creating awareness of the possibilities of wholly liberated people, and hence of the obstacles that stand in the way of achieving that liberation, namely oppression and economic injustice. The contribution they have made, not only to the community but to the whole life of the Church, moved the Brazilian theologian Leonardo Boff to entitle his book on the communities *The Grassroots Communities Re-invent the Church*. These communities maintain in most cases a fluid relationship with the 'normal' structure of the Church. They are accepted by the hierarchy and in some places very much supported and promoted by it – though sometimes they are regarded with suspicion – but at the same time they preserve a certain freedom and autonomy. In some ways the grassroots communities have created a new role for the Catholic laity who traditionally played a passive part in church life. Moreover, by providing the Church with a solid, conscious and active base in the poor population (to which the majority belong), they have enabled it to free itself from (or at least to resist better) the pressure of sectors of the oligarchy to which it used to be too closely bound. Church leaders have been able to listen to the voices of the ordinary people, with their simple but committed interpretation, and in so doing have been helped to hear the Word of God anew.

The voice of the people has become audible in the Church in other ways, for the new dynamic has made the people feel that the Church belongs to them. With all other natural channels of communication closed by political repression, the churches have become recipients of the needs and worries of those who, not permitted to express themselves, expect the Church to speak for them. So, for example, the Argentinian bishops have been constantly asked to answer the calls of the relatives of those who have disappeared for political reasons and who demand that 'their priest should also keep vigil for them'. Trade unions, politicians, local communities have also joined in the call for the Church to become 'their church'. Thus, the Church in many places has felt obliged to distance itself from regimes which might previously have expected unconditional support from the ecclesiastical institutions. This does not mean that the Roman Catholic Church has become a political force. It has however begun to play a new political role, and it is gradually becoming a moderate, but audible, critic of the repression and economic injustices which ruthless governments – linked to international interests – have implemented for their self-preservation.

Protestantism has never been more than a minority faith in Latin America. Today the members and adherents of the mainstream Protestant churches and the sects number about ten million, or three per cent of the total population. During the sixteenth and seventeenth centuries small French and Dutch enclaves in Brazil were the scene of some Calvinist activity for a few years until the Portuguese regained control. A permanent Protestant presence had to await the arrival of Scottish Presbyterian immigrants in Argentina in 1826, and these were followed, in Argentina, by a number of sheep-farming Welsh Anglicans. Among the Italians who settled in Uruguay in 1850 were some Waldensians, and later German Lutheran farming communities were established in Argentina, Chile and southern Brazil. Anglican chaplains were sent to minister to British communities in most of the major ports. Prior to 1850, Protestantism was confined to European ethnic groups, but the foundation of the Patagonian (later South American) Missionary Society in 1844 by a former British sea captain, Allen Gardiner, saw the beginning of modest missionary work among the Indians of Patagonia, southern Chile and the Chaco, in the north of

Argentina. During the second half of the nineteenth century a small, but increasing, stream of Protestant missionaries came from the United States, reflecting the growing American influence in the region, and by the beginning of the twentieth century there were about 50,000 Protestants in Latin America. The rapid increase in this century to the present figure of ten million has been largely due to the growth of Pentecostalism among working people in the urban areas of Chile, Brazil, Guatemala, Mexico and Haiti, and it is estimated that the number of Pentecostals in Latin America is now of the order of nine million.

In Latin America, as elsewhere, the separating lines between Christians are no longer defined by confessional borders but run across them. The real division – and the real unity – is discovered and expressed in attitudes to the Church's mission, to poverty and oppression, to political and economic dependence, and to the cultural manipulation of the people. Among Latin American Protestants a growing number see ecumenism as sharing in the common struggle to overcome the conditions that lead to the oppression of the people. Confessional and ecclesiastical differences are not regarded as significant in this broader context, and the emphasis of ecumenical theology is on *working* together rather than on *coming* together. Those who have adopted this position are however faced with certain problems raised by the very characteristics of Protestantism in Latin America. There is for example the personally traumatic realization that Protestantism, in one of its social functions, allowed itself to become a vehicle for what can only be described as alien cultural penetration and domination. Then there is the difficulty, created by the often middle-class composition of the Protestant churches, of finding the means to relate to the working class and to participate in their struggles. Yet, in spite of these problems, a real 'conversion to the poor' has taken place, as illustrated by a statement from the (Protestant) Latin American Council of Churches in 1980:

The big gap dividing a small minority of powerful and oppressing rich people and a great number of people who are suffering misery and oppression is one of the biggest offences to our Father. For this reason, many of our Brothers are engaged in a prophetic work, denouncing injustice, the sin of avarice, discrimination and oppression. We have also heard of those who love justice often being imprisoned, tortured, assassinated, or persecuted day and night in order to silence them. Many of our countries keep corrupt and dictatorial governments in power (St Matthew 20:25), in order to become richer at the expense of the labour of our brothers (Nehemiah 5:1–13), and accumulate riches and power ignoring the real needs of the people (Isaiah 5:8).

(Letter to the Latin American Churchés
from the Latin American Council of Churches, 1980)

Behind this statement there are different interpretations, ranging from those calling for reform to those taking revolutionary positions, but there is a common recognition of the situation and the will to relate to the demands it makes in the life and testimony of the Church. Many Evangelical churches have created inter-denominational and ecumenical organizations which are characterized by works of conscientization, defence of human rights and community development – such organizations as CEPAD in Nicaragua, CEAS in Brazil, MEDH in Argentina, and many others.

Other sections of Protestantism have, however, reacted against attempts to bring about change in Latin America, objecting even to the activities of their own radical minority groups. It is evident that some of the immigrant communities, and also a number of autonomous churches, do not wish to commit themselves to the struggle for change. They have adopted a policy of retrenchment, of withdrawal from the process of change, preferring to concentrate on their own cohesion and the internal life of the Church, trying hard to cultivate their doctrinal and historical identity. They avoid positions which might provoke confrontation with the authorities, although at the same time they try to avoid identification with the secular powers. There is also, especially amongst the Evangelical middle-class churches, an attraction to charismatic movements. These satisfy needs of expression and religious habit, but at the same time they represent a turning away from what is seen as a complex and dangerous environment.

Then there is the uncompromisingly conservative section, mainly directed by missions based in the United States. Because they are not concerned with the problems of this world, they regard themselves as 'non-political'. Protestants of this tradition, whose attitudes are sometimes unconscious and sometimes deliberate, serve as nothing less than a channel for the interests of the United States. Not surprisingly, such groups are given support and privileges by governments, since they are considered to have an ideological affinity with them and to be a useful means of countering social protest. This conservative element is offered facilities to carry out evangelistic campaigns and, unlike the other churches, given free access to the media. With the aid of large financial resources provided by international organizations, dazzling propaganda campaigns are mounted through the media to discredit other Christians, often accusing them of being Communists, heretics – or both.

Yet another movement is now discernible among the Protestant churches. During the last fifteen years, the Latin American Theological Fraternity, an independent group of theological teachers and writers as well as leading Christian thinkers from other disciplines, has been actively promoting theological thought related to the complex reality of Latin American life from an evangelical perspective. It has organized a number of regional and continental conferences, publishes a regular bulletin in both Spanish and English, and has produced a number of books. It has also been highly active in making known the concerns of Latin American evangelical theological thought on the world scene. A number of its spokesmen, in particular Orlando Costas, Samuel Escobar, Rene Padilla and Pedro Savage, have become recognized and influential figures in Christian circles in many parts of the world.

Christians within this movement are critical of those who remain unmoved by social injustice and try to live in a spiritual ghetto. They understand very well the social and political situation which has given rise to liberation theology, and they are concerned that this dimension should be part of the curriculum of theological education. None the less they are not uncritical of some of its presuppositions. They claim that over half a century before the emergence of liberation theology, the Gospel brought by evangelical missionaries was a liberating force for thousands of Indians and other marginal groups, as well as among the middle class, faced by a conservative and oppressive clericalism. Attempts to characterize the two main Christian movements, in the sixteenth and nineteenth centuries, as two movements of a single process of political and cultural colonialism, are therefore to be seen as pouring history into a Marxist mould, and fail to do justice to the real sense of personal liberation which the 'evangelical' expression of faith has brought to many people. These Protestant theologians are also uneasy about the claim, which they consider to be inherent in liberation theology, that the only adequate interpretation of Scripture is of commitment to liberation as defined by a class-based analysis of history. This can, they say, lead to a forced interpretation of Scripture, though they also admit that evangelicals have not escaped the pitfalls of an ideological exposition of Scripture which pictures Jesus as the embodiment of the American way of life. The most positive feature of this stream of Protestant thinking is that, while distancing itself from some of the answers of liberation theology, it agrees that the right questions are being addressed, and it is responding in an open way to the Catholic renewal taking place in the grassroots communities. Thus there is the beginning of freedom from fear that a positive evaluation of Catholic faith may be a threat to Protestantism's own *raison d'être*.

> Latin American Protestants are being challenged to consider the possibility that the evangelization of Catholic Latin America may take place ... within the Catholic Church, and to search for ways in which Protestantism can relate to this phenomenon.
> (Bill Cook)

It is more important to realize that, although each of these four positions outlined may be more characteristic of one denomination than another, each of them can also be found in almost all the mainstream Protestant churches, and that the emphases within a particular denomination may vary from one country to another.

Special mention must now be made of Pentecostalism, which since its beginnings in the continent in the 1920s has become the most important religious force after Catholicism. In some countries, Chile and Brazil for example, it has the allegiance of a considerable percentage of the national population (sometimes as many as 10–15 per cent). Latin American Pentecostalism has a greater affinity with the independent African churches than with the charismatic movements in the USA or Europe. It is a form of Christianity that takes root in indigenous culture, and expresses itself in an oral theology of song, story and dance, prayer for the sick, exorcism and speaking in tongues. A typical Pentecostal gathering for worship in Latin America is characterized by its vitality, the people's sense of the divine presence, the ability of the preacher to communicate with the people, and the strong feeling of solidarity inspired by a closely-knit community. In cities like Santiago and São Paulo, worship takes place in huge barn-like cathedrals; but to the worshippers it is much more the 'cathedral of sound' arising at Pentecostal services – wherever they are held – that announces: 'God is here'.

The Pentecostal churches are unique in Latin America for their rapid and substantial increase in active membership – mainly among the poor slum dwellers, particularly those who have removed from rural to urban areas. No other denomination measures its increase in millions during the last two decades. One factor contributing to this growth is the approach adopted towards selection and training of leaders. More than half of all Pentecostal pastors currently serving have had only primary education and 79 per cent are quoted as being first-generation evangelical believers. The academic sophistication of most theological seminaries would be totally foreign to them, and the training most actually receive is entirely local and functional. There are many variations in the pattern but an aspiring Pentecostal pastor passes through an apprenticeship in which he learns by 'doing'. He approaches a series of tasks and can only graduate to the next when he has successfully completed his present one. He may start as a street preacher, go on to be a Bible class teacher, then take charge of a new preaching point. If effective in winning converts and establishing believers in these situations, he will be accredited by the annual conference and set to work to plant a new congregation. When, and only when, this congregation grows to become self-supporting is the promising Pentecostal leader given the title of Pastor. Ordination is thus a seal on effective ministry already undertaken, rather than a mark of transition from academic study to pastoral work, which may or may not prove fruitful. The Pentecostal trainee also belongs to the social group within which he will minister. He is not uprooted from

45

his neighbourhood, nor from his congregation; neither is he placed in an entirely separate category. Moreover, every Pentecostal church member is encouraged to pursue at least some of the tasks carried out by pastors. In this local setting theological education by extension can be very effective.

The question of how Pentecostals relate to other Christian traditions in Latin America is of great importance for the future of Christianity in the continent. It is arguable that they have already exercised a considerable influence on the Roman Catholic Church, not only in the charismatic movement within Catholicism, but also in terms of the populist methodology of the grassroots communities. Their oral culture, with its emphasis on spoken word and prophetic action, was developed long before it became a feature of the Catholic communities. Yet on the whole the content of Pentecostal culture, with its emphasis on the transcendent, tends to reinforce an other-worldly and apolitical expression of Christian faith, and a lack of solidarity with the aspirations of the social class with which its members are most identified. A fruitful dialogue with theology of liberation will never take place while the exponents of that theology retain the language of Western academic sophistication. Argument does nothing to persuade Pentecostals that the coming of Christ has anything to do with building a better world. But when they see a community they recognize as Christian engaged in the struggle for a more just society, that carries conviction. In extreme social and economic situations some Pentecostalists have adopted critical positions and begun to be aware of sins inherent in extreme individualism and in society's social structures. Many supposedly conservative and non-political Pentecostalists participated actively in the revolutionary movement in Nicaragua in the late 1970s, and became involved in the struggles for change in El Salvador and Guatemala. There has been in recent years a growth in ecumenical participation, and several Pentecostal churches are members of the World Council of Churches. They now represent more than 30 per cent of the 113 affiliated churches in the Latin American Council of Churches.

In Latin America – perhaps more than anywhere else – theology has always been closely linked to pastoral practice and to the different conceptions that churches have had of their mission. There has been no development of an 'academic' theology within the universities: theology has developed in seminaries closely linked to church life or in the churches themselves where the missionaries have held together reflection on preaching, pastoral work, and social action. Even so, Latin American theologies have for the most part been reproductions of theologies from Europe and North America imported by the missionaries. It is only in the past 25 or 30 years that a desire has arisen among Latin Americans to reflect on theology for themselves and to develop a distinctive response. This development coincided initially with the crisis in Catholicism in the 1950s of the 'new Christendom' theology of Jacques Maritain and other French theologians. The different currents of thought which were renewing Catholic theology in Northern Europe (critical biblical scholarship, the liturgical movement, and new trends in social thinking) began to challenge the post-Tridentine Roman theology which until then had dominated Catholic seminaries and literature in Latin America. And at the same time, a third generation of Latin American Protestants began to look for new horizons beyond classical fundamentalism and liberal theology. The challenge of Barthian theology came as a liberation to liberal Protestants, yet retained the strong emphasis on the Word of God, so dear to the heart of Latin American Evangelicals.

These currents of renewal could not stop at this stage. Circumstances increasingly challenged both Catholics and Protestants into social and political action designed to improve the human lot. Those who had adopted such a commitment urgently needed a theological articulation adequate to their new understanding of Christian obedience – hence the development during the last fifteen years of different forms of 'liberation theology'. Its practitioners do not however regard themselves as belonging to a new theological school, for it is not 'a new theology' which has been discovered, but 'a new way of doing theology' in the Latin American context – in the context, that is, of the struggle for liberation. The primary fact is that a growing number of Christians all over the continent have engaged themselves in the struggle for the political, social, economic, cultural and spiritual liberation of their people. They do not require from the theologians a 'justification' for this choice; rather they want to deepen and purify their commitment, and at the same time analyse it critically, in order to make it more accurate and more effective. This task of critical reflection must be grounded in the sources of the Christian faith – in the Christian tradition and, especially, in Scripture. As Gustavo Gutiérrez puts it, in his seminal work, *A Theology of Liberation*: 'It is a critical theory, worked out in the light of the Word, accepted in faith and inspired by a practical purpose.' Liberation theology is not just for theologians. It is a theology for all committed Christians, designed to help them strengthen their commitment and to invite others to participate in it.

For this reason liberation theology cannot be understood apart from the life and experience of the Christian grassroots communities (sometimes known as 'base communities') and of other Christian groups engaged in the liberation movement. The liberation theologians are deeply involved personally in a pastoral and prophetic ministry in the urban slums of Lima and Recife (Gustavo Gutiérrez and Dom Helder Camara), or in serving the basic communities caught up in political conflict in Nicaragua (Ernesto Cardenal) and El Salvador (Jon Sobrino). Their theology is based on this experience – as Sobrino explains in the first chapter of his book on Christology. Indeed its purpose is to serve the new kind of Christian community which is being created: 'the Church that is being born of the people'. Hence its most significant writings may not be scholarly volumes translated into many languages and studied all over the world, for they are designed, like those of the New Testament, for particular people in particular situations. Equally important are the Sunday School courses, the catechism classes, the courses of instruction for lay readers, often written by the same authors, and intended to communicate theology to the poor, in the language of the poor. The liberation theologians are seeking to articulate this theology themselves and they argue that it is the Christian community as a whole that should be doing theology, not merely the experts with their academic training. But there is no doubt that within the grassroots communities, among ordinary Christians who have the biblical text for the first time in their own hands in their own language, theological reflection is in fact taking place and is being expressed in poetry, in worship, in life-style and in social and political action. Cardenal's *Love in Practice: The Gospel in Solentiname* provides a vivid insight into this theological process. His poetry and his Nicaraguan Peasant Mass are expressions of liberation theology of equal importance, and probably of greater influence, than the scholarly works of

Gutiérrez, Segundo or Sobrino. Other significant expressions are to be found in the novel of A. Perez Esclarin, *Jesus in Gramoven*, and in the poetic meditations on the *Way of the Cross – Way of Justice* by Leonardo Boff. A popular theology and a spirituality of liberation are beginning to develop alongside the more discursive theology which is better known abroad. But in all these forms and at all these levels liberation theology has certain characteristic tasks and priorities.

The first of these is an indissoluble relationship between theory and practice. Theology is not conceived of simply as theory, based on deductions from Scripture, from the dogmas of the Church, or from philosophical presuppositions. It is seen rather as a reflection, in the light of the Scriptures and of Christian tradition, on the contemporary life of Christians and of their communities (particularly those engaged in the struggle for liberation). This means, therefore, that the theologian must himself have a relationship with Christian and social practice, and that he is responsible for his theological work to the Christian community and the people. The whole subject matter of theology may be considered, but priority is given to those themes which are considered urgent for the movement for social change. Thus, in the works of Boff, Sobrino and Vidales, a Christology has been developed based squarely on the historical ministry of Jesus, considered in the light of his death and resurrection. The preaching of Jesus about the Kingdom of God is seen as of particular relevance, especially in view of the similarity between the political and social pressures of first-century Palestine and of twentieth-century Latin America. Attention has also been given to the Church as the People of God, emphasizing the community and its eucharistic celebration, its meditation on the Gospel, and its commitment to act as light and salt within society.

From the beginning, liberation theology has sought to articulate a methodology for theological reflection. To achieve this, and with the help of recent biblical research, the nature of truth has been rethought. Truth is something that is done. In the first place it is what God does, and therefore also what the believer does if he lives in relation to God. For this reason, 'orthopraxis' – the correspondence between human actions and the demands of God – is at least as important theologically as 'orthodoxy' – the conceptual expression of that relationship. The theologian is not only responsible for the rightness of his opinions, but also for his actions, and for the life and actions of the Christian community. When contrasted with other contemporary theological trends, liberation theologians are in no sense heretical, rather do they express a somewhat cautious orthodoxy. The discrepancy is at the level of praxis; and from the Latin American perspective it is not liberation theology but Western theologies that should be labelled heretical because they ignore or distort the biblical correlation between the demands of God and the actions of Christians.

At this methodological level also, emphasis is laid on the social sciences as a necessary element in the theological enterprise. If theology corresponds to liberating action – to concrete struggles against poverty, oppression and injustice – it is essential to understand the social, economic, political, cultural and socio-psychological mechanisms which operate in society. Theology cannot exist in a vacuum: it must reflect on the actual historical process. The social sciences provide the analysis, the categories and the vocabulary for this reflection. Since theology has traditionally used the categories and the vocabulary of philosophy, this represents a new departure. And because in Latin America the most critical sociology, and in the views of many Latin Americans the most helpful analysis, has been Marxist, it is Marxist categories which have on the whole been followed. It is important however to distinguish between the widespread, though by no means universal, acceptance by liberation theologians of certain Marxian tools (a class-based analysis, a dialectical method, and a commitment not just to understand society but to change it), and the diversity of their political judgements in specific situations.

In fact, liberation theologians adopt a more dispassionate approach to Marx than is sometimes visible outside Latin America. They are not afraid to remove him from the pedestal where some would place him, nor to drag him up from the hell to which others would consign him. They place him where he belongs, among men and women in history. Hence they accept Marx where they find that he speaks to their condition, and reject him where his concepts are inappropriate to their world. To the charge that a ride on the tram of his social and economic analysis inexorably carries them to the terminus of dialectical materialism, they reply simply 'We have not found it so'. They would rightly observe that much of Marx's invective against religion was directed to the social function of the religion that existed in nineteenth-century Britain and Europe, rather than an attack on the essence of Christian faith: indeed, they join him in unmasking that expression of religion that makes 'lyrical calls to social harmony', arguing that when the Church ignores the fact of the class struggle it tacitly supports the system that perpetuates the privileges of a minority, at appalling costs to the majority of Latin American people. But they are more realistic about human nature than Marx, and while denouncing sin in the structure of society, they understand it as a reality of the human condition, not a phenomenon peculiar to one social class or nation. With Marx, they see great significance in human history, and in the current irruption of the poor into the history of Latin America; but for them it is a history whose ultimate meaning is found in the presence among men and women of God's kingdom, inaugurated by Christ and to be fulfilled in his coming. A Christian-Marxist dialogue is seen as an urgent task, although 'Christian' and 'Marxist' are accepted as overlapping categories. The Cuban revolution is widely recognized as a creative social experiment; but in general, liberation theologians see themselves as Latin American Christians committed to a *socialist* rather than a *Communist* project of liberation (see J. Míguez Bonino, Assmann, etc.).

Finally, in the field of hermeneutics, it is the relation between text and context that is seen as important. Liberation theology claims to be a biblical theology, and it takes very seriously the results of critical biblical scholarship. Some of the liberation theologians (J. M. Miranda and S. Croatto) are primarily biblical scholars, and others (G. Gutiérrez, L. Boff, J. Sobrino) base their theology on the discussion of certain biblical passages. They are concerned to look for biblical interpretations which respect the biblical text, but which at the same time make possible a reliving of the history of salvation in the contemporary historical situation. This requires more than a mere intellectual updating of the text. It calls for a careful study of the part played by the text in the situation for which it was written, and also a critical look at the intellectual presuppositions and social prejudices of later interpreters. Both J. L. Segundo and J. Míguez Bonino have discussed at length how such a rereading is possible, and how text and context can question each other and lead contemporary Christians to forms of concrete obedience which are both liberating today and in continuity with the liberating message of the Bible, and the liberating activity of Christians and Christian communities in the past.

Liberation theology is essentially ecumenical, though naturally it involves more Catholics than Protestants. It was influenced in its origins by both Catholic and Protestant authors, and today both Catholics and Protestants feel they are engaged in a common task – that of reinterpreting their own history, and reflecting critically on their current pastoral practice and their future destiny. Popular forms of Christian piety, Catholic, Protestant and Pentecostal, are taken very seriously.

Liberation theology is, then, at the centre of the theological debate in Latin America. But for all its growth, it remains a minority concern in the Latin American churches. Equally, for all the formal commitment of the Roman Catholic bishops to liberation, national hierarchies remain deeply divided over concrete situations. The majority of El Salvador's six bishops side unequivocally with the US-backed government. In post-revolutionary Nicaragua there is a barely patched rift between the bishops and the churchmen who have taken positions in the new regime. Even Brazil's hierarchy, renowned for the number of its 'progressive' bishops, has its divisions. Moreover, the considerable publicity given to the Catholic Church's swing towards *liberación* easily creates a wrong impression. It tends to exaggerate the extent of the changes in the Latin American Church since 1968. In a projection of the Church's previous association with power, it sometimes suggests that Latin America is in for more of the same, only with a new, more left-wing slant. In many countries ruled by military autocrats, the Church since Medellín has certainly become the only spokesman for a silenced opposition. In more, it has become an insistent spokesman for the majorities that tend to get overlooked by the rhetoric of 'development'. In a few, a considerable segment of the Church – clergy and laity – has committed itself to revolutionary struggle. It is tempting to recall Che Guevara's forecast that if the Christians of Latin America ever became revolutionaries, the revolution would be unstoppable. But taken as a whole, the Christians of Latin America have not yet become revolutionaries, and the ultimate direction and impact of the potent force unleashed since Medellín is still a matter for speculation.

Chapter 3

Cuba

The triumphal entry into Havana of the guerrilla fighters from Sierra Maestra on New Year's day of 1959 marked the beginning of dramatic changes in Cuban society. But more than that, it signalled a major landmark in the history of Latin America and the Caribbean. An understanding of the Cuban experience is essential to any analysis of the processes of change and conflict in the rest of Latin America. The Cuban revolution has inspired emulation by some, fear in others and created a myth for most. Objective evaluation is rare.

The immediate impact of the Cuban experience owed much to the disappointment felt by many Latin Americans when their hopes that a new, just social order would emerge in the post-war period failed to materialize. Corrupt and repressive governments continued to block avenues for democratic change throughout the region. So the determination and eventual success of the Cuban revolutionaries inevitably made a profound impression. Many who did not approve of their methods nevertheless respected the guerrilla fighters' commitment to more egalitarian forms of social organization.

Social and economic development have also earned the respect of many Third World nations which have disagreements with other aspects of Cuban society and political life. These achievements – in health, education, housing – and the evident commitment to meeting the basic needs of the majority of the population make a great impact on visitors to Cuba. Questions about the methods by which they are accomplished cannot be, or at least ought not to be, avoided and are of critical importance to revolutionary and reforming groups in other parts of Latin America.

Cuba was the last colonial outpost of Spain in the Americas. Following the Spanish-American war of 1898 it achieved nominal independence but simultaneously became an unofficial dependency of the United States. The monolithic character of its economy imposed by the colonial system remained unchanged with independence. On the eve of the revolution, in 1958, sugar constituted an average of 84 per cent of her export earnings, the rest was accounted for by tobacco, tourism and nickel. Two thirds of Cuba's trade was with the United States, whose annual quotas and sugar prices virtually controlled the country's economic performance. The Cuban ruling groups also found the United States a more attractive haven for their investments than their own country, and by the 1950s these investments amounted to more than US $ 400 million. Unemployment and underdevelopment were endemic, and aggravated by the seasonal nature of work in the sugar sector. During the 'dead season' (May to December) the proportion of the labour force employed in sugar dropped from 25 per cent to 5 per cent, the majority of the sugar workers joining the ranks of the 16 per cent of the labour force who were unemployed all the year round. In spite of the close proximity to, and economic integration with, the United States, living conditions for most Cubans were appalling, with average incomes amounting to less than a third of the lowest registered in the United States. Only half of school-age children attended school, illiteracy was as high as 50 per cent in rural areas, malnutrition, grossly overcrowded housing, lack of sanitation and health facilities – these were the characteristics of a Cuba that was never seen by the tourists and was ignored by the mainly urban upper class. Under the dictatorship of Fulgencio Batista who was in power from 1940 to 1944 and again from 1952 to 1959, not only did the majority of the population live in conditions of poverty and misery, but the country had become a byword for repression, torture and corruption.

Historians agree, however, that the Cuban revolution was not the result of a popular uprising against exploitation and misery, but a political reaction to a dictatorship universally regarded as illegitimate, which sought to keep itself in power through corruption and terror. On 26th July 1953, Fidel Castro, then a student leader, led an ill-prepared band of 150 young men and women in an attempt to take the Moncada barracks in the eastern city of Santiago. Only a hundred actually took part in the attack; the others lost their way and failed to rendezvous with the rest. The attack was beaten off easily: many were killed in the fighting, or later in the prisons and streets. Only 30 survived, Fidel Castro among them, and at his trial he made a defiant speech which began, 'History will absolve me'. Student and worker unrest continued. Batista responded savagely with torture, assassination and terror, but in 1955, in a gesture of appeasement, he released Castro and the remaining survivors of the Moncada attack. They went to Mexico and immediately began to organize their return to Cuba. In November 1956 the motor yacht *Gramma* returned with 82 men on board. It was blown off course by a hurricane, and arrived two days late on the wrong beach. The 'invaders' were strafed by Batista's air force and lost their provisions, weapons and boat; there were twelve survivors. This group, with Fidel Castro and 'Che' Guevara, became the nucleus of the victorious army which entered Havana on 1st Janaury 1959.

Castro declared in April of that year: 'Without social justice there can be no such thing as democracy, for people are then slaves to poverty. That is why we have said that we are one step ahead of both right and left, and that ours is a humanist revolution. It takes away nothing essential to man, but makes him its major object. Capitalism sacrifices man; the communist state because of its totalitarian nature sacrifices the rights of man. That is why we can take neither side. Every people must develop its own political pattern to suit its needs, a pattern neither imposed from outside nor copied from anyone else. Ours is an autonomous Cuban revolution – as Cuban as our music.' The government's initial programme was not in fact particularly radical. The land reform, for instance, expropriated only the very largest estates. Two years were to pass before any Communist was given an important government post. But the wealthier groups in Cuba opposed any curtailment of their privileges and property rights. At the same time the United States insisted on seeing the nationalist desire for socio-economic development, greater economic independence and social justice in Cold War, anti-communist terms. The US began to exert considerable pressure on the country, refusing to give aid except with very stringent political conditions attached. During the next two years the new government began to shift from a broad-based commitment to fundamental reforms, to an open avowal of Marxist-Leninist principles and the formation and eventual predominance of a Marxist-Leninist ruling party.

The consolidation of this party was gradual and difficult, and there is no evidence of long-term conspiracy behind its formation. It came into existence as the result of an amalgamation of the 26th July Movement (the group of young radicals from traditional parties) with Christian activists and members of the Communist Party which had existed before the revolution. In 1965 this became the Communist Party of Cuba, but with a membership which still reflected a coalition of forces; it was not until 1975 that it felt strong enough to hold its first Congress. The transition from the idealistic pluralism of 1959 and 1960 to the formation of a one-party state was neither easy nor inevitable. The CIA-inspired Bay of Pigs invasion of 1961 was for the Cuban leadership evidence of the continued hostility of the United States. In the event, the failure of the invasion greatly strengthened Castro's prestige and influence. The blockade imposed by the US, which had exercised almost total technological, commercial and financial control over the island for the greater part of the twentieth century, also imposed enormous problems. And the most enduring challenge to the Cuban leadership was how, in the face of the impoverishment and dependence of the island, to reorganize the economy along socialist, centrally planned lines and make it work. Many of Cuba's skilled middle-class technicians and professionals had left the country in search of an easier life in the US. It was in this desperate situation that Cuba moved to greater and greater reliance on the Soviet bloc countries, although the distances involved meant that the cost of supplies was almost trebled by freight charges.

Faced with these enormous problems, the leadership appealed to the Cuban people for further sacrifices and effort. This 'heroic' phase of the revolution was symbolized by the sugar harvest of 1969–70, for which a target of 10,000,000 tons was set, to be achieved by massive mobilization of the nation's resources and by voluntary effort. The failure, by a wide margin, to reach the target marked the end of this period and it became clear that the path towards economic diversification and industrialization would be long and difficult. The early 1970s were years marked by a spirit of pragmatism and consolidation. Slow but steady progress was made on the economic front, aided – for once – by the high price of sugar on the international market. With the reins now firmly in their hands, the Cuban leadership embarked on the task of setting up mechanisms for political decision-making and renewal which would ensure institutional legitimacy for the revolutionary government. The method chosen was 'popular participation' (People's Power), formalized in the new Constitution promulgated in 1976.

All recent analyses of the Cuban political system, whether they are the sharply realistic reports produced by commercial banks or the hostile assessments circulated by the United States Central Intelligence Agency, agree that it is very stable. Visitors to Cuba remark on the degree of popular support for the government, and the genuine appreciation of Cuban citizens for the achievements of the past twenty-four years. These are considerable. Thirty-four per cent of the total Cuban population are now enrolled at different levels of education. Illiteracy has been eradicated, and by 1979 all members of the economically active population had completed at least six years' formal education. Achievements in the field of health place Cuba ahead not only of Third World countries but also of many Western industrialized nations. Life expectancy at birth is estimated at 73.5 years; there is a medical doctor to every 520 inhabitants. Moreover there are 2,513 Cuban health workers – of whom 1,400 are doctors – currently participating in health programmes in twenty-six Third World countries. The provision of food and consumer durables has not been neglected by the government, which is trying to respond to the rising expectation of a population anxious to see some material reward for its sacrifices. Those who are familiar with other Latin American countries also note the absence of heavily-armed police in the streets. At the same time it is evident that many Cubans hanker after the benefits of the consumer society, of which they are kept fully informed by relatives visiting from the United States and radio and TV programmes beamed from Miami. The Cuban government is sensitive to complaints, usually voiced through trade unions or People's Power representatives, about the prices and availability of consumer goods or the quality of services, and tries to monitor the potential demands of the population, planning to set up a specific research institute for this purpose.

In a context of economic austerity and blockade by the United States, internal support and legitimacy are essential both for the maintenance of the Cuban socialist system and for continued economic development. Participation and ideology are central elements in this legitimacy. Thus, after an experimental period in Matanzas province, the People's Power assemblies came into operation. Their purpose is to provide structures for political participation at the municipal, provincial and national levels, as well as to introduce a degree of decentralization in the management of the local economy. Representatives to the municipal assemblies of People's Power are elected by popular vote on the basis of candidates put forward by the different neighbourhoods of a municipality, which have chosen from a shortlist drawn up by the local mass organizations. These representatives are subject to recall and are accountable to three-monthly neighbourhood meetings. The municipal and provincial assemblies of People's Power are entrusted with the management, in co-operation with the relevant ministries, of all the services (hospitals, garages, schools, cinemas, etc.) and industrial and agricultural production units within their territory, except those of a strategic or central importance to the economy, e.g. oil refineries and international tourist hotels. Through the municipal and provincial assemblies, every four years, a national legislative body – the National Assembly of People's Power – is elected. This National Assembly elects from its members the national executive bodies, the Council of State and the Council of Ministers. More than half of those elected to the municipal assemblies in 1976 were not members of the PCC (Communist Party of Cuba), although this proportion falls markedly among members of the provincial and national assemblies. It is significant that the expression of complaints and grievances through these channels is seen as legitimate. In the debates of the National Assembly, which are televised, a complaint made by a delegate about inefficiency or bureaucratization in a particular service, requires an immediate reply from a minister in front of the cameras.

An important role is played by mass organizations such as the CDRs (Committees for the Defence of the Revolution), trade unions and the FMC (Federation of Cuban Women), as well as the PCC. The CDRs are one of the best-known features of the Cuban revolution; they were created in the period prior to the Bay of Pigs invasion, when acts of sabotage and terrorism were still common, organizing guard duties and support for the revolutionary process in each residential block. They still have that function; every night two of the families in a CDR take turns at patrolling their block and looking after their local shops (workers undertake similar tasks in their work places). In other words, they undertake functions which in most contemporary societies belong to the police, whose main duty in Cuban cities is traffic control. Later on more tasks were given to the CDRs: they now control the supply of food and consumer durables to their local shops, distribute ration books, organize sports, voluntary work, inoculation and vaccination campaigns, and community support for the old, the bedridden and the families of workers and soldiers who are abroad. Every three months, the CDRs of a district organize an assembly of neighbours to discuss the services in their area.

The FMC also has a geographically-based structure, and although it does not have such an active membership as the CDRs, it has played an important role in pressing for legislation concerning the family and the place of women in society. The Family Code promulgated in 1975 gives explicit legal recognition to the equality of women. Legislation by itself, however, is not enough. Women in Cuba share the same complaints as women everywhere: that they are still assigned the traditional role, with its concomitant tasks, of home-makers, and are seriously under-represented at the managerial and decision-making levels of society – a fact often recognized in Castro's speeches.

Trade unions provide the other main channel for participation. There are eighteen national unions organizing all the workers within a sector of the economy, regardless of their trade or specific occupation. Organized along vertical lines, their basic unit is the union section, bringing together the workers of one economic unit (e.g. factory or office). In 1979 there were 2,413,055 workers affiliated to union sections; membership is voluntary, but there are peer group pressures to join and 95.4 per cent of the labour force (excluding the regular armed forces and the police) are affiliated. Trade unions are organized nationally into the Central Organization of Cuban Trade Unions (CTC), which represents the eighteen national unions and their municipal and provincial federations. Union sections organize regular meetings (production assemblies) in which all the workers in their unit meet with management, to discuss targets and performance. They are also in charge of the organization of voluntary work, of housing arrangements, as well as of the distribution of consumer durables to all workers, regardless of whether they are affiliated or not. Salary scales, production targets and their application are discussed at every level, starting with negotiations between the relevant ministry and the national leadership of the union.

Unions do not have the confrontational role which characterizes their relations with employers in some Western countries. Many of their leading members are also members of the Cuban Communist Party, and this applies also to those with whom they negotiate. In such a system there is an ever-present danger that the union leadership will be used to impose party decisions on a reluctant work force. Nevertheless, the Marxist-Leninist ideology of Cuba affords workers a favoured place in society and there can be no doubt that what they say is taken seriously. Many unionists from other Latin American countries would be happy indeed if they had been able to achieve similar benefits, in terms of pay, social security and stability of employment, for their own members. One of the dangers inherent in centralized economies such as that of Cuba is, however, bureaucracy and its attendant ills, and in recent years, especially in December 1979 and early 1982, the Cuban unions have been outspoken in their criticism of management inefficiency and of bureaucratic habits in government ministries.

Ideology is the other mainstay of modern Cuban society: it emphasizes Cuban nationalism, tracing a direct line of descent from the nineteenth-century campaigns against the Spanish colonial regime to the successful guerrilla fighters of the Sierra Maestra. It stresses national dignity and independence, contrasting the present with the servility of pre-revolutionary governments towards the United States. It depicts Cuba today as one national community. The aim is to distinguish it from the divided nation which existed before the revolution, with its affluent urban sector looking to the United States, and an impoverished rural sector with a plantation and peasant economy unchanged for decades.

One of the most distinctive features of the Cuban ideology is its presentation of Cuba as a nation under attack. Its language, linked with the pre-1959 guerrilla campaigns, is military, transforming a medical team into a brigade and a graduating class into a contingent; education or health campaigns become battles or offensives. A whole generation has grown up in Cuba accepting the active hostility of the United States as a permanent fact of life. Cubans too have become accustomed to their own response, a Marxist-Leninist revolutionary language which often sounds strident to uninvolved foreigners. This has had an effect on Cuban society: dissent from the revolutionary process as defined by the Cuban leadership is regarded as desertion. Dissent therefore is expressed about specific policies or individual functionaries and not about the goals or general directions taken by the country.

In such circumstances, the CDRs and other mass organizations have come to exercise informal, but nevertheless effective, social control. This is one aspect of Cuban life which people out of sympathy with the government find most irksome and which foreign critics describe as totalitarian. Individual dissenters are often tolerated, even good-humouredly, by their local CDRs or unions, but any form of organized dissidence provokes an immediate reaction. In the summer of 1980 thousands of Cubans pressured the government for exit visas by occupying the Peruvian Embassy in Havana. Approximately 114,000 Cubans were able to leave through the port of Mariel. Many were attracted by the prospect of an easy life in the United States and there were a good number of petty criminals and ne'er-do-wells among them, some of whom were specially released from prison in order to embarrass the American government. The number of *Marielitos* shocked the Cuban leadership, however, since it revealed a hitherto unsuspected level of dissatisfaction.

The second major feature of the Cuban ideology is its high moral tone and the depiction of Cuban society as actively pursuing basic ethical values. This was even more marked in the 1960s when Cuba was said to be 'creating the New Man', who would function in a society without material incentives. Less was said about the New Man in the pragmatic 1970s, but the ethical thrust remains: the rejection of material consumption as the main goal in life; human solidarity; the vision of work as an essential element in human dignity; the emphasis on co-operation rather than competition; the pursuit of equality. Concern is expressed when younger Cubans, who have grown up with the revolution, take for granted its bread-and-butter achievements – health, education, housing and so forth.

The censorship, limitations on ideological debate, travel restrictions, social control – with prison sentences as the ultimate sanction for those who step out of line – are, however, often regarded as the 'cost' of Cuba's achievements in social and economic welfare. Whether or not the cost is acceptable depends, of course, upon the ideological standpoint of the observer. The debate normally centres on the number of political prisoners and their treatment. An Amnesty International mission to Cuba in December 1977 was told that between 1959 and September 1977 up to 23,000 people had been detained for political offences at one time or another. Not all of these prisoners qualified as prisoners of conscience: some had been members of organizations which had advocated or used violence against the Cuban government or had actually taken part in violent acts. At the time of the Amnesty mission there were 3,200 political prisoners. During 1979 the Cuban government undertook a special programme which resulted in the release of some 3,600 prisoners, reducing political prisoner population to its present level of approximately 250. No complaints have been made about torture, although Amnesty International has received complaints of harsh treatment.

The majority of these political prisoners belong to a group known as the *plantados* (the unmovable ones). They are prisoners with long sentences who refuse to wear prison uniform, obey prison regulations or co-operate in rehabilitation programmes. Amnesty is particularly concerned that, since 1977, at least fifty prisoners have had to serve or are still serving additional sentences after the completion of their original sentences, apparently as a punishment for non-co-operation in prison. In the case of the long-term prisoners it seems that the Cuban authorities have adopted a vengeful attitude, keeping them in prison long after they have ceased to be any sort of threat to the present government. Cuba maintains the death penalty as an optional punishment for several crimes other than murder, such as sedition, crimes against the security of the state, robbery with violence, and rape. There are no official figures for the numbers of executions, although Amnesty International's reports indicate that death sentences carried out do not reach double figures in a year.

Cuba, like most Third World countries, is attempting to achieve economic development, to reduce external dependence and to obtain greater equality in the internal distribution of goods, services and opportunities. The Cubans have often been judged over-optimistic for trying to achieve all these objectives simultaneously.

But they argue that these goals are intimately linked, and the postponement of egalitarian goals in favour of economic growth alone can undermine and finally block economic achievements, as experience in other Third World countries has shown.

Economic development is an objective frequently expressed in terms of growth and diversification of production. On both counts the recent Cuban achievements have been considerable. During 1981, when the average rate of growth in Latin America was of the order of 1.2 per cent and the highest rate of growth in the industrialized West did not go beyond three per cent,* the Cuban economy grew by twelve per cent. This was a somewhat artificial figure inasmuch as growth in 1980 was only about four per cent, a third short of the projected target, due mainly to pests and diseases which blighted the sugar and tobacco crops. Even so, 1982 brought further evidence of positive trends when the growth rate reached 5.5 per cent in the first six months – well exceeding the modest forecast of 2.5 per cent. Industry has contributed to this growth, having doubled its contribution to the national income. This relatively good performance has not, however, protected Cuba from the effects of the world recession. In March 1983, Cuba successfully renegotiated part of its Western currency foreign debt of US $ 3 billion, but at the cost, familiar to so many Third World countries, of agreeing to restrict growth in incomes and to postpone development programmes.

The real progress towards economic development and a more egalitarian society undoubtedly makes the Cuban experience attractive to Third World countries – and for the nations of Latin America and the Caribbean in particular. But questions must be asked about Cuba's continuing external dependence on the Soviet Union and COMECON (the Council for Mutual Economic Aid – an association of Soviet-oriented communist nations founded in 1949 to co-ordinate economic development, etc.). To what extent does this high level of external support, which would not be available to Third World countries in general, make Cuba an exceptional and unique case? The most frequently quoted figure for Soviet bloc aid to Cuba is US $ 8 million a day. However, this is an artificial figure. It represents the cash equivalent of the subsidy on

*In 1981, France, Great Britain, Italy and West Germany experienced 'negative growth'.

Soviet oil supplies to Cuba (compared with world market prices) together with the difference between the price which Cuba's sugar would fetch on the world market and the price which COMECON actually pays for it, about four times as much. This cash equivalent accounts for approximately 87.5 per cent of Soviet bloc aid to Cuba. This favourable treatment, it should be added, is no more than the policy urged by the Brandt Report on all developed nations in their dealings with Third World countries and demanded, so far unsuccessfully, by the poorer nations. One American critic has also pointed out that the United States gives more in federal aid to Puerto Rico, a smaller island with only a third of Cuba's population, than the Soviet Union gives to Cuba.

The question of dependence cannot be adequately examined without looking at the nature of the Cuban economy as a whole. Cuba's real misfortune is that it is still so heavily dependent on sugar. Although it was thought in the eighteenth century that only countries with a tropical climate could produce sugar, extracting it from cane, most countries have now found alternative sources. Europe is one of the largest exporters of sugar obtained from sugar beet, and Japan has even been able to manufacture a sweetener extracted from rice. The international market has been parcelled out by different protective agreements – the Sugar Protocol attached to the Lomé Convention regulating quotas and prices for former European colonies, the Sugar Act regulating quotas for the US market, and the EEC policy on subsidies and prices for its own producers. Producers in the Third World are dependent on price and quota decisions made in the industrialized countries, and are subject to dramatic price changes: the world market price has dropped from its record level of US $ 0.54 per lb in November 1974 to its present level of less than 7 cents per lb.

Cuban dependence on sugar is still overwhelming. In 1975 sugar accounted for 90 per cent of Cuban exports, but this has now been reduced to about 75 per cent. The long-term agreement with COMECON has protected Cuba from the deterioration in the terms of trade caused by the fall in sugar prices, but she still has to export three times as much sugar to the West as was exported in 1980 in order to import the same level of goods and services. Not surprisingly, Cuba is trying to reduce the importance of sugar as an export, and with some success: in 1975, sugar accounted for 87 per cent of all exports to the West, and in 1982 (first six months) for 59 per cent.

Just as COMECON support is a unique advantage for Cuba, so the United States blockade is a unique problem. The United States, with Florida only ninety miles north of Havana, is Cuba's natural supplier and market, but since 1960 the United States has been enforcing a unilateral economic and financial blockade against Cuba. This includes not only direct American exports to and imports from Cuba, but also affects firms in other countries that import from Cuba and export to the United States. Countries using Cuban sugar, such as Canada and Switzerland, have been threatened with a 'secondary blockade' on any exports to the US market which might possibly contain any sugar imported from Cuba. Firms from six Western countries interested in purchasing Cuban nickel have been forced to suspend negotiations and even to cancel contracts owing to the threat of American retaliation. The blockade has been intensified by the Reagan administration, which has reversed the gradual moves towards relaxation initiated by the Carter government. It has recently been calculated that this embargo has cost the Cuban economy US $ 9 billion, or the equivalent of 243 per cent of the Cuban foreign debt in hard currency.

Cuba maintains substantial contingents of combat troops in Ethiopia and Angola (11–15,000 and 15–19,000 respectively, according to United States estimates). In Ethiopia they are fighting the Somali-backed independence movement in the Ogaden; in Angola Cuban troops, rushed to Luanda in November 1976, helped push back a South African invasion and have stayed ever since, helping to contain the South African-supported UNITA guerrilla army. There are Cuban military advisers in Nicaragua helping to organize the army and advising on the conduct of the campaign against the marauding 'Contra' rebels. This military activity is frequently cited in support of the accusation that Cuba is using military might to spread its influence in the Third World and is acting as a Soviet proxy. The Cubans argue, however, that their presence in these three countries is defensive. They have found unexpected support for this view from Mr Wayne Smith, who was Director of the US State Department's Office of Cuban Affairs, 1977–9, and chief of the US Interest Section in Havana,

1979–82. Smith maintains that the American government, under both Carter and Reagan, but particularly under Reagan, has consistently turned its back on any possibility of normalizing relations with Cuba and, in order to justify this position, has tried to present Cuba as a communist aggressor.

The problem of Cuban-American relations goes back to the revolution itself. The Bay of Pigs invasion and the CIA's support for armed Cuban exile groups made relations bitterly hostile in the 1960s. The missile crisis of 1962, when the Soviet Union tried to install nuclear missiles in Cuba, signalled not only Soviet opportunism but Fidel Castro's intention to resist any American attempts to overthrow his government by force. At the same time, President Kennedy's apparent willingness to go to war to prevent Soviet missiles being based in Cuba set parameters for relations between the two countries: the Cuban leadership would go to any lengths to resist United States pressure, while the United States made clear that it would use its overwhelming military might to eliminate or forestall a genuine threat to its own security.

Cuba's own foreign policy has not remained static. As in other spheres, Cuba has moved from heroic revolutionary stands to more cautious and pragmatic policies. During the 1960s Cuba certainly lent its support to several armed revolutionary movements in Latin America. None of them succeeded. Che Guevara's ill-starred attempt to bring revolution to Bolivia in 1967 showed clearly the futility of trying to force open conflict on an unwilling people, however impoverished and exploited. This policy was abandoned in the early 1970s. Revolutionary leaders have continued to find a discreet welcome in Havana, but such hospitality falls short of the active espousal of armed revolution. Cuban solidarity with revolution now expresses itself more in support for governments, and is marked by realism. Fidel Castro has insisted that revolutions are made by the people themselves and are not imported or exported. His most important contribution to the Sandinistas before their victory was to stress the importance of unity – commonsense advice which most revolutionary groups, in Latin America as elsewhere, have failed to heed. Now Cuba provides diplomatic, moral and technical support, civil and military, to the Sandinista government in Nicaragua. Some support was given to the Salvadorean guerrillas prior to their 'general offensive' in January/

February 1981, but after the failure of this effort Cuba indicated its desire to discuss the Salvadorean situation with the Reagan administration. There was no response from the US State Department. The Cuban government is also keen to enhance its standing with other Third World countries, particularly with the Non-Aligned Movement which it chaired from 1979 to 1983, and which understands Cuba's defence of an Ethiopia threatened with fragmentation and an Angola under attack by South Africa.

In all this there is a clear awareness on the part of the Cuban leadership that its first priority must be the welfare of the Cuban people. No imprudence in foreign policy will be allowed to threaten it. Cuba voted with the Soviet Union on Afghanistan, but it is impossible to tell whether Fidel Castro really believes that the Soviet Union was right to commit troops there. What is clear, however, is that economic dependence on the Soviet Union narrows policy options. Tension and the possibility of war in Central America is now placing Cuba under increasing pressure. Pragmatic foreign policy is matched internally by revolutionary rhetoric and genuine, deeply felt feelings of solidarity with Nicaragua. If Nicaragua were to find itself at war with Honduras, then Cuba would find it difficult to sit by and let the Sandinistas fight alone. For this reason, Cuba now seeks to promote a negotiated solution in El Salvador and dialogue between Nicaragua and Honduras. Cuba's vulnerability makes it a fervent apostle of detente but this is not the same thing as détente at any price.

Cuba is officially a Marxist-Leninist society led by its Communist Party. Nevertheless Cuba shares with the West a common Christian and humanist inheritance, and it is in this tradition that its most senior leaders, including Fidel Castro, were brought up and educated. The Cuban constitution guarantees the freedom to practise any religion or none and, with the exception of the Jehovah's Witnesses (banned in 1979 for a long record of what were considered anti-social activities), the Christian churches, Catholic and Protestant, survive in Cuba. The official ideology, however, takes an orthodox Marxist-Leninist view, regarding religious belief as something that will die out with the spread of education and improvement in social conditions. The Programmatic Platform of the Communist Party of Cuba, produced in 1979, states:

> Among the forms of social consciousness, religion is characterized by the fact that it is a distorted and fantastic reflection of external reality. According to the Marxist conception, religious manifestations and ideas can be overcome by transforming the world that they erroneously reflect, by eliminating the social causes that engender them and by developing educational work based on the scientific conception of nature, society and thought.

The Cuban education system reflects this view and makes clear that those who persist in practising the Christian religion are swimming against the tide of history.

Three main religious currents flow in Cuba – Roman Catholicism, syncretic cults and Protestantism – and their origins can each be traced to a particular period in the island's sociohistorical development: Spanish colonialism, black African slavery and US ascendancy. While Catholicism, introduced at the time of the Spanish Conquest (Dominican missionaries arrived in 1512), continued to be the official religion until the revolution, the growing influence of the US in the late nineteenth century coincided with an influx of Anglican and Protestant missionaries. Anglicans from Britain had held services as far back as 1741 but the first permanent priest did not arrive until 1871. He came from the USA and was soon followed by a number of Episcopal laymen. A resident bishop was appointed in 1906 and the first Cuban bishop in 1967. Two Cuban Methodists, who had been converted as refugees in Florida, returned to Havana as missionaries in 1908, and an autonomous Methodist Church was established in 1964. The Baptist Convention of Cuba was also created from the missionary work of returning Cuban exiles, and during the latter part of the nineteenth century a Cuban started the Presbyterian Church. By 1958 about 6 per cent of the population professed to be Anglican or Protestant, the majority of the latter being Pentecostalists. Both Catholic and Protestant churches, however, tended to cater for a minority drawn from the middle and upper classes, while the mass of the poorer, largely non-churchgoing people developed a fusion of quasi-religious, quasi-mystic beliefs which coloured their daily lives. Major cults developed in the form of Santería – a blend of Yoruba cults with Christianity, fusing saints and gods of each, combining Catholic symbolism and elements of nature; Akabúa – originating in the Carabali of Western Nigeria and organized into all-male sects with secret rituals; and Palo Monte – of Bantu origin and more akin to witchcraft. Spiritism also became quite widespread and mixed with other religious elements.

There is therefore no period in which the churches in Cuba can be described as commanding the loyalty and allegiance of the large mass of Cuban people. In 1959 they were still perceived as foreign in origin and to a large extent in leadership. The Roman Catholic Church retained strong links with Spain and many of the priests and nuns were Spanish, while the Protestant churches derived their leadership from the United States. The Anglican bishop was a US national. The people who attended Mass or services were always a minority, and religion and spirituality were expressed, not by liturgical means, but in other ways which included much that in Europe is called 'folk religion'. Pilgrimages, worship at sanctuaries, and rites of passage drew much larger numbers than Sunday worship.

The ties binding the Roman Catholic and Protestant churches to the urban upper and middle classes had roots in their historical alliances: in the one case with Spanish interests and the dominant descendants of the original *conquistadores*, and in the other with the penetration of US influence. Although the Catholic Church was not a landowning church – being economically dependent on gifts from the faithful, on income from urban properties bequeathed to it and from its fee-paying schools – none the less it was politically the establishment church. The Protestant churches, on the other hand, relied on the financial support of parent churches in the US and were closely identified with 'the American Way of Life'. It may not be true to say that the churches in pre-revolutionary days showed no concern for the poor of Cuba, but this concern was expressed by a middle-class church in traditionally institutional terms – the setting up of schools, medical facilities, etc., among the poorer sectors of Cuban society. Its effect was limited to alleviating some of the worst injustices of the system. Neither did the traditional character of the churches' theology offer any challenge to their identification with the middle classes. In 1959 the Roman Catholic Church had yet to experience the impact of Vatican II or the subsequent theological radicalization at the conference of bishops at Medellín. The Protestant churches, traditionally favouring the separation of Church and State, had likewise no theological resources to support a sharing in the revolution.

In consequence, the churches as institutions did not share in the struggle which led to the overthrow of General Batista by Fidel Castro and the 26th July Movement. Nevertheless, many individuals from the different denominations involved themselves in the revolution, and not a few of the leaders came from religious upbringings – Fidel Castro had a Jesuit education; student leader José Antonio Echeverría (assassinated in the 1950s) was a prominent Catholic; Frank Pais, who organized Castro's urban support network, was a prominent Baptist. The lay organization Catholic Action was active in the cities during the 1950s, and visitors to the El Cobre Church of the Black Virgin can still see the many amulets left for her by Rebel Army fighters. Neither the Catholic nor the Protestant churches opposed the victory of Castro in 1959. Initially at least, the overthrow of Batista was greeted with general rejoicing, even euphoria. It was a honeymoon period in which the churches, along with most other sections of society, welcomed the new leadership. In those days 'even the cat was a revolutionary'. But as soon as the direction of the revolution became clear – and this was before Castro declared the government to be Marxist-Leninist in 1961 – deep divisions began to appear within the churches. Some leaders, particularly those who later founded the Cuban Ecumenical Council, were positive in their response, believing they ought to share in the reconstruction of society. Others, including the bulk of the hierarchy, the clergy and members of the Roman Catholic Church, moved into strong opposition to the government.

The reasons for the hostility were partly ideological, partly economic. At the ideological level, there was the association of Marxism-Leninism with atheism. Fifty per cent of the Catholic Church's 800 priests were Spanish, and many of them remembered the Spanish Civil War as a time of persecution of the Church by the Republican side, and saw in the revolution a possible repetition. At the economic level the pressure came from a mainly middle-class membership whose position was threatened by the redistribution of wealth and other reforms of the revolutionary government. The consequences of this hostility between Church and State were alarming. A number of Christians were imprisoned for their political opposition, and 136 Catholic priests, including the auxiliary bishop of Havana, were expelled. The present Anglican bishop, Emilio Hernández, spent ten years in prison, having been found guilty of conspiracy. Whole congregations of Protestants left for Miami as relations with their parent churches in the United States became increasingly difficult. Roman Catholic priests, including the present Archbishop of Havana, worked in forced labour camps, 400 left the country and a further 100 were expelled for counter-revolutionary activities.

In the late 1960s and early 1970s, however, relations between the churches and the regime began to improve, reflecting changes in attitude on both sides. A group more emphatically aligned with the revolution emerged within the Protestant churches. The impetus of Vatican II and Medellín introduced a new and positive theological direction for all the churches, and in 1969 the Roman Catholic hierarchy moved significantly in condemning the US blockade of Cuba. For the regime the stimulus was provided by the visit of Fidel Castro to Allende's Chile in 1972. Here for the first time he encountered a Catholic Church capable of taking a detached and even benevolent view of a left-wing government. Castro had a long interview with Cardinal Raúl Silva Henríquez, the Chilean primate who used to sit on the presidential dais beside Allende on the 1st of May. While in Chile, Castro made a seminal speech in which he spoke of a 'strategic alliance' with the churches in bringing about social change.

Now, after a period of steep decline in churchgoing, there are about 200 Roman Catholic priests in Cuba, compared to the 800 in 1959. The Protestant denominations have a combined membership of about 45,000. Depending on whose estimates one believes, the total number of churchgoing Christians is between 100,000 and 150,000, as compared with a membership of the Communist Party of approximately 200,000, in a population of ten million. The Catholic Church has two seminaries, while among the Protestant denominations there are seven schools for training pastors and ministers and where children can receive religious instruction.

There are official restrictions on Christian observance, the most important of which is the rule that any religious gathering must be held in licensed church premises. This means that the Cuban churches are tied to a pattern of religious practice which is being abandoned elsewhere, as the churches attempt to diffuse themselves more in the community. Christmas and other religious festivals falling on weekdays do not qualify for holidays, and prior to 1972 Christmas was transferred to July in order to avoid clashing with the sugar cane harvest in December. Individual Christians discover that some avenues of promotion are closed to them, they cannot enter certain social science faculties in the universities, and, although they are able to participate in People's Power and other mass organizations, they cannot become members of the Cuban Communist Party. There is no persecution of the Church as such, but instances of harassment by petty officials do occur; these can often be put right by complaint to a higher level. Representatives of the Cuban government are quick to criticize harassment, although the churches themselves say that the government has failed to give a lead by making a public declaration on the subject.

If formal religious observance is now constrained by regulations, and reduced in numbers to a small minority, this does not mean that religious sentiment has been eroded from Cuban society by socialist ideology. Formal religion was always a minority affair for the Cubans, compared to the far more popular Afro-Cuban cults. Today, Santería remains strong in the rural areas of Cuba, and being 'popular' religion is treated with respect by the authorities. At the same time the strength of traditional Christian practice and belief is evident in the large number of married couples who still have their children baptized and in the massive attendance at the shrines on patronal feast days. One Roman Catholic observer told a British group that 200,000 people made their way to the shrine of St Lazarus outside Havana on 17th December – a journey involving a bus ride and a seven-kilometre walk. Even when allowance is made for possible exaggeration, the numbers involved are considerable. No mention of this, or of similar events, will ever be found in the Cuban mass media.

Attitudes to the revolution within the institutional Church still vary considerably, but there is a growing trend towards dialogue with the government and commitment to exploring what it means to be a church in a socialist society. The Roman Catholic Church, under the leadership of its bishops, is edging towards greater contact with the regime and has become involved in, for example, voluntary agricultural programmes as a way of developing its pastoral ministry. While some Protestants adhere to spiritual and religious values demanding a rejection of official ideology, others wish to press beyond the stage of 'peaceful co-existence' to a relationship variously described as reconciliation or solidarity. The leaders of the Cuban Ecumenical Council have always been in the vanguard of this movement and, since its foundation in 1977, the Council has grown more outspoken in condemning US attitudes, including the blockade of Cuba, and has supported the revolution at international gatherings. It has been attempting, theologically and politically, to help Christians understand how their role has changed. Much of its thinking begins with self-criticism: they acknowledge that in the past they turned their backs on the social conditions of the majority of Cubans and maintain that the best way to evangelize Cuban society is to show that Christians can be exemplary revolutionaries. As one member expressed it in a conversation with a British visitor in 1983: 'Socialism is much closer to the Gospel of Jesus Christ in its values and ideals than capitalism. To put together Christianity and capitalism is impossible.'

The witness of the Church in other parts of Latin America continues to influence the interaction between the Cuban churches and the regime. Those within the churches seeking a Christian participation in the revolution find hope in the part played by the churches in the struggle for justice in other parts of the subcontinent. Conversely, with the success of the Sandinistas in Nicaragua, backed by both Catholics and Protestants, and the continuing guerrilla war in El Salvador, where the guerrilla forces and their supporting political movements maintain an explicitly Christian inspiration, the Cuban Communists are increasingly open to dialogue with the churches. With international opinion so polarized against it, the Cuban government does not want to add the Christian community to the list of its enemies, particularly in cases such as the United States where the church lobby has exerted consistent pressure for a more open attitude towards Cuba and has sought to demythologize the 'communist threat'. It is unlikely, however, that there will be any dramatic change in the immediate future. If certain sectors of the Latin American Church are witnessing a commitment to social change, there are others whose role in this context is less positive. The churches and religion have come to be seen by many – Christians and non-Christians alike – as a battleground of ideological confrontation. In this situation, the Cuban government is moving with the greatest caution. Substantial improvement in relations, based on greater autonomy and freedom for the churches in Cuba, will have to wait for a real and long-lasting reduction of tension in the international sphere.

Chapter 4

Brazil

Brazil is the largest, the most heavily populated and the most economically and militarily powerful state in Latin America. Covering over three million square miles, it is the fifth largest country in the world, ranking after China, the USSR, Canada and the USA. The Portuguese-speaking population numbers over 120 million, 70 per cent of whom live in urban areas and the vast conurbations of São Paulo and Rio de Janeiro. When Portuguese explorers first sighted land in 1500, between two and three million Indians belonging to hundreds of different tribes inhabited the forests, valleys and riverbanks of Brazil. Today, the remnants of those tribes, probably no more than 100,000 people concentrated in the Amazon basin, are fighting a losing battle to retain the reserves still left to them. With less than half Brazil's population in rural areas, it is not pressure of numbers that is threatening them, but the advance of big landowners, the mining companies and the highways of modern development.

In 1500 the Portuguese found a land whose endowment of natural resources was a potential source of considerable wealth. Besides limited quantities of gold and diamonds, there were great forests and vast stretches of land which, if put to use, could be prime farming land. To cut the timber, till the land and later extract the precious metals, cheap labour was needed. The Indians, who had welcomed the white man and readily embraced Christianity, were the obvious source. Armed expeditions set out to hunt and capture them in their thousands. The Jesuits calculated that within 130 years of discovery the Portuguese had killed or subjugated two million Indians. But the Indians made poor slaves, and the Portuguese soon turned to the apparently endless supply of African slaves from across the Atlantic. Between 1550 and 1850, when the traffic was stopped, an estimated three and a half million slaves were brought to Brazil, where their average life span was only

75

10–13 years. Slave revolts and escapes were commonplace; those recaptured were cruelly punished, while the few who escaped set up free territories called *quilombos* in remote, inaccessible areas.

Brazil gained its independence in 1822, but slavery was not abolished until 1888. Following the abolition of slavery, an effort was made to attract European immigrants to Brazil to provide the labour force for the coffee farms of the São Paulo region and for the early industries. In the ten years between 1890 and 1900 over one million Europeans, mostly Spanish, Italian and Portuguese, but with handfuls of Germans, Poles, Swiss and Irish, landed in Brazil looking for a new life. Some, especially the Poles and the Germans, were offered land and financial aid in the south. Many of these founded prosperous farming communities. The feudal land system in the north had no place for immigrants. Some came as contract labour to work on the coffee farms that were being set up in the state of São Paulo. Many of these left as soon as they could escape from the near-slave conditions.

While the wave of immigrants from Europe continued, thousands of Japanese settlers came to Brazil in the first few decades of the twentieth century. Many Arabs, mostly from the Lebanon and Syria, also came and scattered through the vast country, working as travelling salesmen and small traders. These waves of immigrants brought with them their cultural habits, food and religions to add to the basic Brazilian mixture of Indian-African-Portuguese. Today Brazil is often seen as the model of a genuinely multi-racial society, but this is a superficial view. It is true that in social intercourse an open and relaxed attitude to race relations prevails, and such a richly varied human mix can only evolve through a long history of unprejudiced sexual relationships between people of different races. But in terms of jobs, housing, education and health care, nearly a century after emancipation, blacks are still at the bottom of the social heap.

As well as contributing to Brazil's present-day racial mix, the 350 years of a slave-based economy has left a lasting legacy in the organization of wealth and power in the rural areas. A semi-feudal land system predominates in which land is regarded as a symbol of wealth and political power, and physical labour as slave's work and therefore demeaning and shameful. This has produced a patriarchal pattern of society in which the relationship of peasant to *patrão* or boss is one of deference, dependence and extreme exploitation. Through the years of Empire (1822–89) and even after the establishment of the Republic, the dominant figure in Brazilian society was the local *Coronel*, usually a large landowner who held de facto political power in his own area and maintained his hegemony by strong-arm methods. All these factors have helped to perpetuate an extremely unequal society in a country which had enough land and natural resources to provide everyone with a reasonable standard of living. Partly because of the marked social injustices in the society, popular discontent has long been simmering beneath the surface. From the end of the nineteenth century until the 1950s, there was a series of localized popular revolts, often led by messianic figures promising salvation on earth. These religious rebels set up communities which, because of their communal life-styles, were seen as a threat to the status quo and were persecuted and disbanded. The most famous of these revolts was at Canudos in the North-East, where at least 30,000 peasants, led by a mystic called Antonio Conselheiro, fought off successive army expeditions with guerrilla tactics until they were overrun and massacred in 1898. On the whole, however, these episodes made little impact on the established order.

During the second half of the nineteenth century Brazil experienced an important period of economic growth when coffee came to represent 60 per cent of its exports. Coffee production was in the hands of a small oligarchy, the coffee magnates of São Paulo. But as the world price for coffee began to drop at the end of the century, the agrarian export economy entered a period of crisis which was to shift power away from the coffee oligarchy. The period from the end of the First World War until the 1950s is marked by the collapse of the old export economy and the systematic expansion of industry. Brazilian industry had its beginnings in the late nineteenth century, and developed considerably during the presidency of Getulio Vargas in the 1930s and early 1940s. The National Steel Company was officially founded in 1941 and the first steel mills built soon afterwards. Petrobras, the Brazilian oil company, was set up in 1951. However, it was not until the 1950s that the economy really 'took off', during the government of Juscelino Kubitschek (1956–61), the builder of the new capital, Brasilia. Kubitschek offered generous financial incentives to attract transnational companies, particularly car manufacturers, to Brazil. Thus began a long period of rapid economic growth under the domination of foreign capital. For the next thirty years Brazil was to grow at an average annual rate of 5 per cent. As a result, it has set up Latin America's most sophisticated industrial sector, and its GNP, standing at about US $ 120 billion, now ranks eighth in the non-Communist world. Moreover, Brazil has managed more than any other Latin American nation to set up the whole industrial process inside itself. Endowed with considerable mineral wealth, Brazil mines its own ore, processes the metal with its own machinery and sells the finished product at home and abroad.

These developments have only been achieved through great effort. In the 1950s and 1960s Brazil was producing increasingly sophisticated consumer goods such as cars, washing machines and TV sets. However, despite its wealth of iron ore, it still depended heavily on imported steel and machinery to produce these finished goods. To break out of this dependence, in the early 1970s the Brazilian government undertook what it called the 'second phase of import substitution'. At enormous expense, it greatly boosted local production of steel, aluminium and other metals, and expanded the base for a local capital goods industry. In 1960 Brazil produced only 1.7 million tons of steel; in 1980 it produced 15.3 million tons and had become a net steel exporter. The expansion of the capital goods sector had also been meteoric; output was worth only US $ 350 million in 1970, but by 1979 it had risen to US $ 3.6 billion, accounting for about a quarter of total industrial output. There were, however, hidden costs of this spectacular economic growth, one of them being that Brazil has become increasingly dependent on transnational companies. Foreign investment is heavily concentrated in the 'dynamic' area of the economy, such as chemicals and petrochemicals, electrical and electronic equipment, mining and capital goods. Brazil's economic future depends therefore to a large extent on the performance of these sectors. This foreign penetration has occurred even in sectors such as telecommunications and computers, where the government has taken firm measures to defend local manufacturers and to set up a 'totally national' industry. For, while the equity may be in the hands of local companies, the transnationals still control the essential technology.

The only local power that can in any way challenge the supremacy of the transnationals is the state sector. Huge state companies, such as the oil giant, Petrobras, and the mining conglomerate, Companhia Vale do Rio Doce, have emerged over the last twenty years. These companies have generally entered areas of the economy which are either unattractive to the transnationals, such as steel manufacturing, or have in some way been defined by the military rulers as 'areas of interest to national security'. Though the state sector has always treated the transnationals with great consideration, the very existence of this powerful sector has undoubtedly placed limits on the exploitative action of the transnationals. It is not by chance that the sectors of manufacturing where Brazil has most successfully built up its own technology and broken away from transnational control are the aircraft and armaments industries. This has occurred because more than a decade ago the armed forces singled out these sectors as crucial areas from the point of view of national security and since then have directly supervised their development, sparing no expense. The military-backed enterprise, Engesa, has become a leading exporter of armoured cars, sending them to Africa, the Middle East and other Latin American countries. Embraer, the state-owned aircraft manufacturer linked to Brazil's air force, has had some successes with aircraft designed and produced in Brazil.

The second – and equally serious – drawback to the Brazilian 'model of development' has been heavy reliance on foreign financing. The gross foreign debt rose from US $ 5.3 billion in December 1970 to US $ 64.2 billion in December 1981. In the early 1970s, when Brazil began to borrow more and more heavily from abroad, this option was attractive, for interest rates on the international money market were low and exports were growing by about one third each year. Some economists have recently suggested that the decision to rely heavily on foreign financing was taken to some extent on the grounds of convenience. The local banking system was backward and inefficient, and it would have required considerable effort to generate local savings. In contrast, the international banks were at that time queuing up to lend to Brazil.

The disadvantages of this system only became fully apparent in the late 1970s, by which time Brazil had been badly hit by the world oil crisis. The whole economy had been built on the assumption of an endless supply of cheap oil. Agricultural products and minerals were brought to the factories by lorry. Steel plates were taken to the car factories by lorry. Agricultural and manufactured exports were carried to the ports by lorry. The motor industry had become the country's showpiece, while the railways had been seriously neglected. Despite considerable effort, Petrobras had never made large discoveries of oil in Brazil, and about three-quarters of the oil consumed was imported. As a result, oil imports shot up from US $ 469 million in 1972 to US $ 10.2 billion in 1980.

By squeezing imports and encouraging exports, Brazil could probably have faced up to the oil crisis with considerable success. But the situation was made much worse by the extraordinary increase in interest rates on the international market in the late 1970s. By 1981 Brazil was paying out US $ 8.5 billion annually in interest payments on its foreign debt. Together with amortization payments, the foreign debt cost Brazil that year an unprecedented US $ 16.5 billion, or about 13 per cent of GNP. Through an enormous effort, Brazil achieved a US $ 1.2 billion surplus in its trade that year. However, this feat was wiped out by the toll imposed by the foreign debt, and Brazil ended the year with the record deficit of US $ 10.5 billion on its current account.

The third disadvantage of Brazil's type of economic development is its social cost, for the pattern of economic growth has led to a steady deterioration of the quality of life for well over half the population. In the industrial sector workers have been obliged to work longer hours to compensate for the reduced purchasing power of their wages, obliged to travel longer distances to work as they are pushed to the periphery of the cities by the rise in property values, and deprived of a minimum standard of nutrition, sanitation and health care for their families. In Sao Paulo the infant mortality rate rose by 45 per cent in the very decade of the economic miracle. A carefully researched report, published a few years ago by the Roman Catholic archdiocese of Sao Paulo, speaks of the 'scandalous misery of the many which sustains the luxury and privileges of the few'. The economic model has been equally disastrous for the rural poor. It has been estimated that the Brazilian government spent about US $ 8.9 billion on export incentives in 1982 in order to ensure the sale of goods in the world market. If this money had been spent on a rural development scheme for peasant farmers, the living standards of hundreds of thousands of families would have improved. Equally, it could have provided electricity, water, sanitation and health care for many of the urban poor.

Yet another indirect, but highly important, consequence of Brazil's type of economic development is its impact on migratory patterns. Throughout the 1950s and 1960s, millions of poor *nordestinos* (inhabitants of the huge, backward North-East of Brazil) poured into São Paulo and other cities in the industrialized 'triangle'. At any time of the day or night, visitors to São Paulo's modern bus station, with its dazzling fluorescent lights, could see families of bemused *nordestinos* clambering out of buses, clutching all their possessions in sacks and bags made out of blankets. The sophisticated, capital-intensive manufacturing sector of the industrialized South-East region provided employment for only a small minority of these migrants. In the early years those who obtained jobs accepted very low wages and poor working conditions, thankful that they had at least found employment. The second generation of factory workers is, however, proving very different. Throwing off their parents' submissive attitudes, these young workers are developing into a tough and independent labour force, and one which is rapidly becoming an important political force, too.

The big cities have offered very little to the majority of the migrants. Some have stayed in the *favelas* (shanty towns) which surround all Brazil's cities, scratching out a living from selling trinkets on street corners or collecting and selling newspapers or old bottles. In São Paulo, industrial wages are so low that many of the *favelas* are inhabited by workers from the local factories. Brazil's poor have shown amazing ingenuity in finding new ways of recycling waste material, from worn-out tyres to burnt-out electric bulbs. Living standards have certainly fallen for many of these migrants. Whereas in the countryside they could usually cultivate their own food, they have often gone hungry in the cities where everything has to be bought. Moreover, the chaotic way in which the cities have grown has created serious health risks. Few of the shacks on the outskirts of the cities have sewerage or running water, and all too often the well dug in one plot has been contaminated by the open lavatory in the plot next door. Small wonder that infant mortality has been chronically high. By 1981, about one million people were living in the shanty towns in São Paulo, while another two or three million had settled in *loteamentos*, or precarious housing estates, usually without public services, where the families get together to build their own homes. As there is so little control by the government, the so-called owner of the land often does not possess valid land titles himself. All too frequently the families build their simple houses and are then evicted for illegal occupation.

The provision of public services to the poorest areas has always lagged far behind demand, not so much for the lack of resources (as the authorities usually allege), but because without political power the poor are simply ignored. Priority is given instead to motorways, flyovers and other improvements for middle-class car owners. Recently, however, things have begun to improve slightly, because residents in these poor areas have started to form their own associations and to demand street lighting, running water, crèches, bus services and so on. Life for the city's poor is also violent. The police frequently raid shanty towns looking for criminals, and anyone whose documents are not in order or who they believe to look 'suspect' is picked up. Many innocent people have been injured when the police have shot at suspected criminals. The Catholic Church's newspaper, *O São Paulo*, reported in 1982: 'Two unarmed and helpless adolescents were killed in Pirituba. Soccer fans were savagely beaten. Two innocent citizens were chased and tortured for the death of a policeman, a crime committed by another policeman. A drunk workman was beaten to death. A few days ago a group of young people who had escaped from a juvenile delinquents' court were massacred. All this by military policemen.'

Some of the migrants eventually move back to the countryside. But rather than return to the North-East, where there are few opportunities, they have gone to the new farming areas which have been opened up in recent decades. During the 1950s the state which attracted most migrants was Paraná, to the west of São Paulo. Thousands of peasant families moved in to cut down the virgin forest and then to cultivate their own plots or to work on the coffee plantations which were being set up. By the late 1950s, however, land began to run out. To deal with the shortage, the families started to subdivide their plots among their children and to take on tenant farmers. As a result, the proportion of farms in Paraná covering less than 26 hectares rose from 3.5 per cent in 1950 to 12.5 per cent in 1960. By the 1960s the new families reaching Paraná had little option but to pack their bags once more and move on. Many migrants decided to push north, moving either to Mato Grosso and Pará or, increasingly, to Rondonia and Acre. The population of Rondonia rose from 37,000 in 1950 to 110,000 in 1970 and to about 450,000 in 1976. Peasant families were also reaching the Amazon region where land ownership is often uncertain. Terrible conflicts have taken place as peasant families, landowners and *grileiros* (land thieves) have fought over the land. All too frequently the landowners and land thieves have won by bringing in *jagunços* (gunmen) to clear the peasants from the land. No one knows how many peasant families have been illegally evicted in this way, but a member of the government made an unofficial (and confidential) estimate that about 20,000 families were evicted from plots in the Amazon region in 1978. The rate of expulsion may have fallen slightly since then.

The government has taken little action. Some ministers have thrown up their arms in apparent helplessness. In 1971 Colonel Jarbas Passarinho, then labour minister and now a senator for the pro-government PDS party, confided to Dom Alano Maria Pena, Bishop of Marabá, 'I'm beginning to think that the land situation in the south of Pará is so difficult – because of legal anomalies, the overlapping of land titles and other irregularities – that there is no possible solution.' Other ministers have taken a much more cynical attitude. Antonio Delfim Neto, then finance minister and now planning minister (but economic supremo in both periods), commented in 1973: 'The Amazon is still in the bandit stage. It is only later that the sheriff will be required.' Many transnationals have invested heavily in land in these 'frontier' areas, thus adding to the pressure on migrant rural workers and the beleaguered Indian population.

Brazil's political system today is a strange hybrid in which the military, in alliance with an élite of civilian technocrats, runs the country, but in which an elected congress has limited power. Recent years have seen a return to relative freedom of expression in the press, and political parties are now re-emerging. This situation has arisen as the result of *abertura*, the process of political liberalization through which the military leaders claim to be guiding the country back to some form of democratic government. But the basic power structure has not changed. The military seized power in 1964, with the support of the broad mass of the urban middle class, leading state governors, some members of the church hierarchy – and the USA. The 1964 coup followed a period of increasing political instability under President João Goulart, who came to power when President Janio Quadros unexpectedly resigned in August 1961 after just eight months of government. Goulart had attempted for some time to hold the country together in the face of mounting inflation and growing economic problems. In 1963 he resorted to increasingly left-wing rhetoric to maintain the support of the masses, but, although he never presented a coherent socialist plan for the country, his populist gestures scared right-wing military leaders who feared that Brazil would be pulled into 'Communism'. Goulart's overthrow put an end to a twenty-year period of relatively democratic and fairly open government which, although ineffective and inadequate in many ways, nevertheless represented the most serious attempt in Brazil's history to develop a party system, open to popular interests and influences and working through a freely elected president and congress.

The early years of the military dictatorship, when the military rulers still enjoyed a degree of popular support from the middle classes who had been greatly alarmed by Goulart's left-wing rhetoric, were not characterized by great repression. Though the old political parties were banned, the regime still tolerated a certain degree of criticism, particularly from the established press. The regime's main policy became the ruthless pursuit of rapid economic growth, regardless of the social consequences. The armed forces saw it as their role to guarantee for the planners and the technocrats the political stability regarded as essential for the achievement of this goal. The downward spiral into increasingly authoritarian rule began in 1966 and 1967 when some sectors of society, particularly students and industrial workers, began to challenge these assumptions. It gained momentum at the end of 1968 with the closing down of Congress (which had been functioning in half-hearted fashion with the participation of two artificial parties), the suspension of *habeas corpus* for political offences and new, severe restrictions on the press. In 1969 the government passed a harsh security law which allowed it to persecute even the most moderate opposition figures for allegedly 'subversive' acts.

The hardening of the regime coincided with an outbreak of guerrilla activities, largely undertaken by young, left-wing idealists – mainly students. The groups carried out several spectacular kidnappings in the cities, including that of the US ambassador, Charles Elbrick, in 1969. A small group also started a rural guerrilla offensive in the Amazon region in the early 1970s, and, although it is believed to have had less than a hundred members, it was only crushed with the deployment of over 10,000 soldiers.

The escalation in violence at both ends of the political spectrum led to thousands of arbitrary arrests and the widespread use of torture by the political police and army units. In 1972 Amnesty International published a fully-documented report in which it listed the names of 1,081 people who claimed to have been tortured. The National Confederation of Brazilian Bishops (CNBB) accused the government of 'unimagined violence, murdering students who marched peacefully in the streets and workers who organized strikes for higher wages and the return of their rights'.

The cautious move back to a less authoritarian regime began in the mid-1970s. The guerrilla movements had been completely wiped out by the early 1970s, and for a few years the regime enjoyed relative tranquillity, with rapid economic growth and little social unrest. In 1974, General Ernesto Geisel took over as President from General Emilio Garrastazu Medici, thus bringing the *castelistas* (supporters of General Castelo Branco, the first military president after the 1964 coup) back into power and breaking the very close link which had existed during the Medici government between the Presidency and the repressive, hardline faction of the armed forces. The peace was, however, broken by two unrelated events: the trebling of the world price of oil, which ended the supply of cheap imported oil upon which the whole 'economic model' depended; and the unexpectedly good showing of the opposition candidates in the congressional elections that year. There were other signs too that, after years of apathy, public opinion was moving strongly against the government. In 1973 the *Movimento Custo da Vida* (Cost of Living Movement) had been formed, largely at the initiative of church groups active in the poor quarters on the outskirts of the big cities. After 1978 this movement, which made basic demands, such as decent wage rises and the freezing of the retail price of basic foodstuffs, grew very rapidly, particularly among the poor sectors of the urban population. That year it sent to the President a petition about price increases signed by 1.4 million people. The student movement was also becoming active again and, despite considerable repression, it set up a national executive committee.

It was partly in response to these first signs of serious popular discontent and middle-class disenchantment that President Geisel cautiously embarked on his policy of political liberalization, later to be called *abertura*. Some interpret this shift as an attempt to pre-empt the protest movements before they could build up massive support. His very selection as President meant that the more moderate *castelistas* were in the ascendancy, and he was therefore in a position to move slowly against the hardliners, who had been largely responsible for the routine torturing of political prisoners. Towards the end of 1975, however, before his policy had made much progress, the hardliners reacted angrily and, as a manifestation of their autonomy, carried out a wave of arrests of alleged members of the Communist Party. Vladimir Herzog, a well-known television journalist, was picked up during one of the raids and died under torture at an army centre. His death caused a national scandal and large protest demonstrations were organized. Then, just a few months later, a worker, Manoel Fiel Filho, died in similar circumstances. This time Geisel acted rapidly, sacking General Eduardo d'Avila Melo, a well-known hardliner and commander of the second army, in whose area the deaths had occurred. His sacking was a serious blow for the hardliners. Geisel pushed ahead slowly with his reforms. He gradually lifted censorship of the press (although he retained it over television), and made some tentative moves towards easing the wage squeeze. But Geisel always lagged behind popular movements, which have grown very rapidly in recent years. His successor, President Figueiredo, has also failed to anticipate events and increasingly reacted to *faits accomplis*.

The amnesty movement which demanded the release of political prisoners, information on the whereabouts of those who had 'disappeared', the reinstatement of those who had lost their jobs for political reasons, and the right of those who had been exiled to return to the country, grew very rapidly during 1978. In the following year, the new President, Figueiredo, granted a partial amnesty. The biggest boost for political liberalization undoubtedly came, however, from the urban working class, which in 1978 organized the first strikes for ten years. Though strike action was illegal in all but highly exceptional circumstances, the government was obliged to give in to the workers, in practice if not in law. In 1979 the strikes were much more widespread and much better organized, but the government took a tougher line. It temporarily took over the metalworkers' union in São Bernardo, on the outskirts of São Paulo, which was headed by a dynamic young metalworker, Luis Ignacio da Silva, popularly known as 'Lula', who was rapidly becoming a national figure. But, despite its tough action, the government could not contain the buoyant new labour movement. All over the country, workers were laying down their tools to demand better wage increases to make up for the loss in earning power most of them had experienced over the last decade. The government used violence to repress some of these strikes. In October 1979 a military policeman in cold blood gunned down a young worker, Santo Dias da Silva, who was very active in the Church's workers' pastoral commission. About 10,000 people crammed into the city's cathedral to attend his funeral, presided over by the archbishop, Cardinal Paulo Evaristo Arns.

In an attempt to end this wave of industrial action, the government passed a new wage law in November 1979. It permitted six-monthly wage rises, instead of the old yearly increases, and gave poorer workers an additional ten per cent wage rise. However, the new law did not defuse the situation as rapidly as the government had hoped, and a new wave of strikes took place in 1980. The metalworkers in São Bernardo organized their biggest strike ever but the government moved even more firmly this time and, after the workers had turned down the offer of a modest wage rise from the labour courts, the strike was declared illegal by the labour tribunal. This was the green light for the government to use violence. On 19th April the army 'occupied' São Bernardo, where Lula and fifteen other labour leaders were dismissed from their jobs and arrested. Lula and eleven others were subsequently tried under the national security law for alleged acts of subversion in organizing the strike movement. However, despite the tough repression, the strike lasted another three weeks and, although it failed in its specific objectives, it turned into a huge political mobilization. On 1st May Bishop Claudio Hummes celebrated Mass in a packed church in São Bernardo, after which about 120,000 people marched to the local football stadium to express their clear repudiation of the government's repression of the strike. By removing Lula and other labour leaders from the official union movement, the government indirectly gave a tremendous boost to a small new party, called the *Partido dos Trabalhadores* (PT), which had been set up by Lula and other labour leaders in the previous year. The expelled leaders now had much more time to build up the new party, which became the first-ever grassroots party, genuinely organized from the base upwards. The Catholic Church indirectly played an important role in setting up this party, for it was the decision of thousands of the grassroots ecclesial communities (CEBs) to offer their support which gave the PT its first decisive boost. Indeed, the link seemed so close in the early days that prominent members of the Church felt it necessary to make public statements professing the non-party nature of the Church. The PT has grown very rapidly, and in mid-1981 it had about 200,000 members, over a tenth of whom were fully involved in the party's activities.

By 1982 the nature of *abertura* had changed somewhat. It depended no longer on measures in this direction undertaken by the government, for political parties, popular movements and the labour movement had taken over the initiative. Instead it relied on the government's capacity to control the hardliners within the armed forces, so that *abertura* could take its own course. So far the government has tolerated the emergence of left-wing organizations on the sidelines of the political process, but has made it abundantly clear that it will not allow any opposition party, not even the moderate Brazilian Democratic Movement (PMDB), to take over the reins of government. In November 1982 elections were held for state governors, one third of the Senate, the Chamber of Deputies and the municipalities, though there was no possibility of the elections changing the structure of power in Brazil. Anticipating defeat, the government had changed the constitution to ensure that the choice of the next President would remain in its own hands, as well as continuing control over key policy areas. None the less, the vote was a clear expression of the country's repudiation of military rule. The four opposition parties won 62 per cent of the votes, gained 51 per cent of the seats in Congress and the governorships of some key states, including São Paulo and Rio. Most votes went to the PMDB, which won nine state governorships and 200 of the 479 congressional seats. The elections signified a real advance in political freedom, but Brazil will not be a democracy, even of a limited nature, until the armed forces can accept alternation in power. This will be the most difficult step of all.

The Roman Catholic Church has been present in Brazil from the earliest days of colonization. Today it has about 110 million members and adherents, representing nearly 90 per cent of the total population, 160 dioceses, 268 bishops, 11,000 priests, 35,000 members of religious orders (mainly women), 72 monasteries, 54 seminaries, and 250 local radio stations, besides several centres for the research and social action. Over 10,000 Catholic missionaries from other parts of the world are at work in the country. The Holy See is represented by a nuncio in Brasilia.

The first churches and seminaries were founded in places which later grew into major cities, such as São Paulo, while the first Catholic priests furthered Portuguese colonization by converting the Indians to Christianity, facilitating indirectly their later enslavement and the seizure of their lands. Many priests protested at slavery but only the Jesuits actively resisted, sheltering thousands of Guarani Indians in fortified settlements known as 'reductions', where they taught them arts, trades and literacy. These Jesuit enclaves, which covered large areas of neighbouring Paraguay and Argentina, lasted until 1759, when the Portuguese and Spanish monarchies expelled the Society of Jesus from their lands. The close links between the Catholic Church as a whole and the monarchy continued after Brazil became an independent nation in 1822, but when a republic was declared in 1889, chiefly as a result of masonic and secular ideas, the Church lost not only its privileges but also its monopoly of religious practice, since freedom of worship opened the doors to the Protestant churches.

In the 1930s, the Catholic Church, at that time never very happy outside an alliance with those in power, regained some of its privileges, and today bishops and priests still attend state events. But in the 1950s there were two developments which led to a different alliance – with the people. On the initiative of the then-auxiliary bishop of Rio, Dom Helder Camara, the national bishops' conference, the CNBB, was founded in 1952. At the same time a number of militant Catholic lay organizations were also founded, bringing together students, young workers and others, committed to a programme to see, judge and act according to the Gospel. A basic literacy-by-radio scheme was launched, with the slogan 'educate to transform'. These organizations appeared in answer to a deeply-felt revulsion at the unjust structure of Brazilian society, with its tremendous gap between rich and poor and the pressing need for social change. But while the Catholic lay vanguard moved steadily to the left in its thinking, accepting Marxism as a valid method of analysis, the episcopate lagged behind, accepting moderate reforms, but not revolution. The gap between the two trends became abundantly clear in 1964, when many lay organizations strongly opposed the coup, but the CNBB produced a document which said: 'The armed forces have prevented the implantation of a Bolshevik regime, which would have led to the suppression of the most sacred freedoms and especially religious and civil freedom.' Yet even the bishops were divided and the document was issued only after bitter discussion.

Following the coup the Church gradually discovered that it was impossible to remain in alliance with a regime whose ideology gave priority to a narrowly-defined concept of national security rather than the goals of democracy, social justice and freedom. In May 1967 Catholic Action issued a manifesto about the effects on the local population of industrial expansion in the North-East; this had as its title 'Development without Justice'. Gaining support from the Second Vatican Council and the Latin American Bishops' Conference in Medellin in 1968, the Church began to seek a new relationship with those who had been excluded from power. But identifying with the people meant sharing in the suffering and persecution which the poor of Brazil had always borne. There was an immediate reaction from the government – churches were invaded, Catholic radio stations and newspapers were censored, bishops, nuns, priests, as well as laymen and laywomen, were arrested, tortured and even killed. The Church was accused of subversion and of interfering in politics, instead of concerning itself exclusively with souls. The Church had, however, come to promote and defend a new concept of politics, summed up by Dom Helder Camara: 'Politics, in the grand and beautiful sense of concern with the great and serious human problems, is the human and Christian right and duty of all the members of the Church, including the bishops.'

In Dom Helder Camara, since 1964 Archbishop of Olinda and Recife, in North-East Brazil, the Catholic Church has one of the twentieth century's greatest Christian leaders. Born in 1908, and only just over five feet tall, Dom Helder embodies the Church's identification with the poor and the struggle for justice. He refuses to live in the official episcopal palace and instead occupies three rooms in the outbuildings of a nearby church. His dress is a simple black cassock, adorned only with a pectoral cross of black wood. He has no car and travels either on foot or begs lifts from friends and passing motorists. Wherever he goes his warmth and love evoke a tremendous response. But this archbishop, who spends long hours in prayer, is more than a saintly pastor. He has an acute political mind too, and at different times has been nominated for Mayor of Rio de Janeiro, for Federal Minister of Education, and for Vice-President of the Republic. Yet, although he is essentially a churchman, and is deeply committed to non-violence, he is greatly feared by many politicians who are aware of his remarkable influence, not only in Brazil but throughout Latin America. So his life has been threatened, his books have been banned, and journalists have been forbidden even to mention his name in the press. To all of which he replies: 'Those who think we are acting too precipitately in seeking a change in the structures of Latin America should remember that the continent has been waiting for nearly five centuries.'

When the National Congress, trade unions and student organizations were closed, banned or placed under restriction, and the press censored, the Church found that it alone had the power to denounce violations of human rights, including police violence, torture, land evictions, neglect of urban housing and all the abuses carried out in the name of national security. Thus, and at times reluctantly, the Church became the mouthpiece of oppressed groups. Its statements had a national impact, putting the regime on the defensive. The national episcopal conference in 1973 published a statement on human rights, and this was followed in the same year by a document from thirteen bishops and some superiors of religious orders about human and social conditions in the North-East. It was headed, 'I have heard the cry of my people'. At the local level, the Church began to build up a parallel communications network, disseminating information in parish, diocesan and community bulletins in regions where newspapers were unknown and the heavily-censored radio and television told the people little of what was happening.

The military regime had persecuted and broken up the lay movements of the 1950s, and during the first decade of the military regime more than 500 priests, as well as some thousands of laypeople, were imprisoned, tortured or expelled. But a new and much more resilient form of lay organization emerged in the 1970s. The new groups, known as grassroots ecclesial communities (CEBs), were formed not by the middle classes, but by the working classes in the cities and rural areas. Most of them began as lay-led Bible study groups, compensating in some way for the chronic shortage of priests, and they went on to discuss their own day-to-day problems in the light of the Gospel. From talking about the need for water, lighting, crèches and schools, they moved to question the power structure and the distribution of income. They asked questions such as, 'Are we poor and in need because God wills it or because there are people who are taking our share of the country's wealth?'

No one really knows how many CEBs there are in Brazil today. Most estimates suggest that there are between 50–80,000 in rural and urban areas, involving half a million people or more. They constitute the largest organized contingent of people in Brazil and so have attracted the attention of all the political parties. Many people have gone on from CEBs to become trade union militants, community leaders or political party activists. The CEBs have provided, perhaps more than any other movement in Brazil, a chance for the people, especially the poor, to participate in a domestic organization and to make their voices heard, not only by the government authorities, but by the Church hierarchy, too. With their extremely simple, flexible structure, they are ideally suited to a country with a constantly shifting population where new frontier towns and shanty towns spring up overnight. A British visitor in 1982 reported:

The life of the grassroots communities moves between the twin poles of celebration and community action. Celebration was typified in a shanty town of squatters called Sossego (= Solace!) on the outskirts of Vitoria. In a wooden hall no bigger than 8m × 6m, a congregation that overflowed into the street – old people, women with babies at the breast, teenagers and children – sang hymns with gusto, conducted a dialogue sermon with the priest, and shared the bread and wine. In Vila Velha, another group of 30 people sat around discussing the kind of church they wanted to be. I was impressed by the level of participation – very few remained silent. As one woman put it: 'Before, we had to keep quiet and listen. Now we have the right to speak. Everyone is equal.' This sense of human worth, even of the least privileged members of the community, gives them courage to mobilize and to speak out beyond the confines of the Christian fellowship. It creates boldness to confront the inefficient and often corrupt local authorities, in demands for water supplies, rubbish collection services, the provision of electric power. Petitions are signed, public demonstrations organized. In one remote location, the people demanded a bus service to get them to work, but the transport company alleged that the road was too narrow. The people measured the width of the road and proved them wrong, and obliged the company to act. Another community built a health centre. In each case scheming politicians moved in trying to claim the credit when the work had been done – to the derision of the people.

One Sunday morning I sat in on a three-hour meeting of representatives of twenty local communities, gathered to exchange experiences and study ways of more effective action. Collecting signatures for petitions was considered useful only if the people who signed had been made aware of the issues – i.e. a petition had to be backed by a community who had been mobilized and knew what the score was. Every project ought to be properly documented so that the results achieved and the means used could be shared with other communities. There was also an insistence on a *permanent* popular movement, to monitor the continuance and development of gains already achieved – no flash-in-the-pan approach would do. Exchange of experience was given high priority. Problem-centred group discussion followed the plenary, and at least one of the five groups reporting back did so in the form of a sketch satirizing the local authorities – to the merriment of the others. I sensed a high degree of political awareness, which not only got things moving in a given locality, but which was creating a valuable human resource for the future of Brazil – people who were capable of self-motivation, accustomed to taking initiatives, and who are acquiring a nose for distinguishing between the politically valid and what is specious and corrupt.

Support for these communities is provided by the diocesan pastoral centre, both in resources for printing and publishing, and in human terms – priests, sisters, and lay people who serve as pastoral agents or 'animators' of the communities. I shall not quickly forget Bernardo, the French priest working as pastoral co-ordinator, Rita and Heloisa, two Brazilian sisters, a marvellous group of nuns of the Order of the Sacred Heart of Mary, including an Irish woman, a Scot, and a gutsy little Brazilian nun called Teresa, whose cousin had been killed by a para-military group as recently as two years ago, for his denunciation of human rights violations in Brazil.

A recent statement of the Brazilian bishops (February 1982) reflects the strength of their influence:

In the basic Christian communities the people find a renewed Christian life, which leads them to believe in their dignity and calling. It moves them, inspired by the light of God's word, to participate freely, responsibly and communally in the construction of a new and more fraternal human community. The Church grows more and more aware of the ability of the poor to resolve their own problems. It urges them to participate in all the decisions that affect their lives, and supports various forms of organized and popular movements, including neighbourhood organizations.

Several leaders of the Brazilian Episcopate have declared in more concrete ways their commitment to the movement. One example of many is in the diocese of São Paulo where a *pastoral operaria* has been set up as a pastoral outreach to bring neighbourhood workers together and, through links with the grassroots communities, to involve other parts of the Church in the workers' problems. The strength of the partnership between the hierarchy and the communities was demonstrated at the time of the metalworkers' strikes in 1979 and 1980 when, with the support and encouragement of Cardinal Arns, the Christian communities set up local networks with other opposition groups to collect and distribute material support for the strikers. Churches all over São Paulo were opened for meetings of the workers, and the Cathedral of São Bernardo became the headquarters of the Strike Fund. In a famous statement Cardinal Arns declared, 'If the workers cannot have their unions, if they are beaten in the streets, if they cannot meet in the football stadium and are persecuted, then they can meet in the churches of São Paulo. The churches belong to the children of God. We shall stay by their side.'

For many foreign priests who came to Brazil as missionaries direct contact with the harsh reality of suffering and repression has been their road to Damascus, converting them from conservatives to progressives. Dom Pedro Casaldáliga, for example, belonged to an extremely conservative Spanish order, the Claretians, and was in charge of organizing *cursilhos* (spiritual retreat groups) before he came to the Prelacy of São Felix in the state of Mato Grosso. Now, because of his outspoken denunciation of the harassment of peasant families by large landowners, there have been repeated attempts to have him deported for subversion. So far these endeavours have all failed, probably because of Casaldáliga's national – and international – reputation. Lesser-known priests have been deported in recent years for doing no more. Commenting on these deportations, former CNBB general secretary Dom Ivo Lorscheider pointed out that they were really an attempt to expel the Church from the side of the poor and oppressed. When the regime could not expel a troublesome priest because he was Brazilian they 'exiled' him within his country, as they did with Archbishop Helder Camara, whose name and words were banned from the press for several years.

Church-State relations reached a particularly low ebb in the early 1980s, probably because, out of its concern for human rights, the Church has widened the range of its criticisms to include the structure of Brazil's capitalist society. The Church has moved from criticizing the effects of the system to attacking its basis, and has not minced its words. In August 1981 the bishops stated: 'Over the last few years there has been an accentuated orientation of the economy towards priorities that favour high-income classes, including refined methods of bribery and corruption, in direct opposition to the people's interests. An economic model that concentrates income and stimulates sophisticated consumerism, in contrast with the basic needs of the population, has led us to become one of the countries with the greatest disparity between the highest and lowest income groups.' The bishops then declared that the model must be changed, not because the Church had party political aims or ambitions, but because it had the responsibility of recalling the ethical dimension of political decisions and the future of man. This meant, the bishops concluded, that the Church did not accept 'the opinion of those who want to reduce its mission to the formulation of non-temporal principles'.

There are about eleven million Protestants in Brazil, constituting just under nine per cent of the total population. This represents a considerable growth, for there were only 25,000 Protestants in 1860 and about 200,000 at the turn of the century. Of the present eleven million, by far the largest and the most lively are the Pentecostalists, gathered mainly in the Assemblies of God, with its highly developed lay ministry. The first Pentecostal groups came from the United States in 1910. The mainline Protestant denominations were also established chiefly from North America, this time in the second half of the nineteenth century, though German Lutherans arrived in 1823, and a famous Scottish Congregationalist, Robert Reid Kalley, arrived under the auspices of the London Missionary Society in 1855. The contribution of the Lutherans to education and to the advancement of literacy has been quite out of proportion to their size – there are just over one million of them – and one of their number, General Ernesto Geisel, became the first Protestant President of Brazil in 1974. A third strand of Protestantism is provided by the conservative evangelical bodies, of American origin, which have been very active since the end of the Second World War and still receive substantial support from the United States. There are about 30,000 professed

Anglicans, and another 30,000 adherents who attend Anglican churches in the four dioceses that constitute the Episcopal Church of Brazil.

The Pentecostalists offer an other-worldly faith which is especially attractive to poorer Brazilians living in the countryside or on the outskirts of the large cities. New churches are being built and huge warehouses, or even factories, are often converted into Pentecostal meeting places. Although the members are generally poor, they practise tithing and this yields a substantial income, which enables their leaders to buy television and radio time for the broadcasting of acts of worship and messages of salvation. Since these are without explicit political content, the authorities are happy for them to prosper.

The mainline Protestant churches are experiencing only moderate growth. Their restrained, conservative character offers none of the attractions of involvement in socio-political questions provided by the Catholic Church, or the charismatic fervour of Pentecostalism. Yet their influence in Brazil is not insignificant. They are well organized, especially among the prosperous middle classes, they hold nationwide evangelistic campaigns, and they propagate their faith through radio and television. They maintain an extensive programme of ministerial training, both at seminary level and in Bible Schools and networks of Theological Education by Extension. They also raise considerable sums of money for social relief work, though their work in this field is often of a paternalistic character, and little is done to question the root causes of the desperate social need. To do so would imply taking a political stance, and the Baptists in particular have a long-standing tradition of separation of Church and State, stemming from the apolitical position of the Baptists from the southern states of the USA who came to Brazil a century ago.

None the less, a political awareness among a minority of Protestants, notably Methodists and Presbyterians, is emerging. Its origins go back to the intellectual ferment in the churches prior to the 1964 coup, and although the consequences of this ferment were repressed during the period of military rule they are now surfacing again – finding expression in a critique of the social and political function of the Protestant churches. Chief among those involved in this is Dr Rubem Alves, who is one of the most able theologians in

97

the whole of Latin America. His early years were spent in a small town in the interior of Brazil, but he moved to the city when he was in his teens and, having embraced a fundamentalist faith, entered the Presbyterian seminary at Campinas with a view to becoming a Brazilian Billy Graham. During his time at the seminary, however, he ceased to be a fundamentalist and came under the influence of Richard Shaull, a member of the teaching staff who had recently been expelled from Colombia and who introduced him to the thought of Dietrich Bonhoeffer. At the end of the course Alves was ordained and became the pastor of a Presbyterian church in the state of Minas Gerais. Here he came up against the entrenched conservatism of his church which took strong action against the young pastors and lay people who in the 1950s were asking searching questions about the role of the Church in society. After taking his doctorate at Princeton, Alves returned to Brazil but left the organized Church and now teaches sociology at the University of Campinas. His first major book *A Theology of Human Hope* is concerned not only with the poverty, hunger and repression of Latin America, but also with the problems of a consumer-orientated society, which he sees as one of the inevitable results of Western capitalism. And although the future may be distinctly unpromising, yet 'Even when our human eyes cannot see the way out of the maze, we are sure there is a way out, and that the moment will come when we leave our exile and set out for the promised land.' By the time he came to write his second book *Tomorrow's Child*, he was even less optimistic about the prospect of an early liberation for the Latin American people, but wrote, 'We must live by the love of what we will never see.' And he now regards the Catholic grassroots communities as the main sign of hope for the future.

The renewal of the Catholic Church through the activities of these grassroots communities is raising in the minds of some thoughtful Protestants a question about the future role of their churches in Brazil and other parts of Latin America. When the Catholic Church was the compliant spiritual expression of the established political and social order, the task of the Protestant churches was to engage in missionary work among the millions of people who, though Catholic in name, had in fact lapsed into atheism, or more probably returned to the pre-Christian beliefs of their forefathers. But now that the Catholic Church itself is very active among these people, and is proving to be extremely successful in recovering their support in and through the grassroots communities, it is – for some Protestants at least – less evident that the Protestant churches have a distinctive role in the Church's mission. Thus for men like Rubem Alves the future of Protestantism is seen in terms of a movement supporting the Catholic Church, helping it to embrace the best Protestant insights, and to become more open. The leaders of the Protestant churches are still some way from sharing this vision, and the official ecumenical movement remains weak.

Meanwhile the religious cults which combine Indian and African beliefs and practices (mainly animist and spiritist) with traditional Catholicism continue to flourish. Thousands of centres of this syncretist religion, and millions of followers of it, are to be found all over Brazil. In some instances those involved retain their allegiance to the Catholic Church, and may correctly be regarded as still within the Catholic fold. But in many cases Catholicism is little more than a veneer on something that is incompatible with Christian faith. Yet it cannot be denied that Brazil remains a deeply religious nation, and there is abundant evidence to suggest that religious belief has a significant part to play in determining this remarkable nation's future.

Chapter 5

Argentina

Argentina does not readily fit any of the popular images of a Latin American nation. It is often described as the most European country in Latin America. This is due both to the massive waves of immigrants – mostly Spanish and Italian – who flocked to its shores in the latter part of the nineteenth century, and to the borrowed cosmopolitan looks and mores which its capital city, Buenos Aires, has sported since their arrival. It has for a long time been described as a 'middle-class' nation, owing to the demographic and political weight of its white-collar urban population and to its income levels, which for many decades have been far ahead of those of its sister republics. Statistical averages seem to confirm the picture: 93 per cent adult literacy, a teacher for every 27 children, a doctor for every 530 inhabitants, a life expectancy of 71 years.

Some Argentines and many foreign observers have used these traits to argue that Argentina is not really part of the Third World or even in the same category as the rest of Latin America. Hence the wealth of literature, native as well as foreign, bewailing Argentina's failure to enter the club of developed nations. Why is it that this country, which ranked ahead of Canada and Australia at the turn of the century, has failed to 'take off' economically? Why does this highly educated citizenry fall prey to a seemingly endless succession of military coups and ineffectual, short-lived, civilian administrations? Many explanations have been offered, ranging from the theory that Anglo-Saxon immigrants would have achieved more than the Spaniards and the Italians, to an array of supposedly inherent traits of 'the Argentine psychology'. Commentators on the right of the political spectrum see *Peronismo,* with its introduction of mass politics and its consolidation of the mixed economy, as the culprit; the left blames the oligarchy and its imperialist allies.

In fact, Argentina is very much a part of Latin America. It shares with its sister republics the same three centuries of colonial past, the same struggle for independence, the same painful process of nation building, the same pattern of insertion into the world economy, and the same crisis when the world changed around it. It has of course tackled each of these phases in its own particular way, and there is no way of denying that Argentina is rather more 'atypical' than others. But it is precisely because it is atypical that Argentina's experience can illustrate so vividly much of what Latin America has in common.

Territorially, Argentina is huge and covers an area of over one million square miles. The distance across its subtropical north is equivalent to halfway from London to Moscow; along its western border the spinal cord of the Andes runs for about the same distance as that between London and Cairo. It could comfortably accommodate the United Kingdom, France, West Germany and Italy and still have more than half of its land surface unoccupied. Virtually every climate and every form of terrain can be found, including the vast, flat expanse of the Pampas, with their legendary six feet of topsoil. This large chunk of South America is inhabited by only 27 million people, and just under half of them are clustered around the capital, Buenos Aires, a sprawling conurbation which has spilled out of the federal districts, absorbing one suburb after another so that it now stretches for tens of miles in every direction from its riverside centre, and is one of the world's largest cities.

This was not always so. Spanish colonization of Argentina in the sixteenth century did not begin in Buenos Aires but in the faraway North-West. Buenos Aires remained for many years a mean riverside settlement, its people living off the few snatches of trade permitted by the Spanish monopolistic system, and hunting the wild cattle of the Pampas for their hides. For almost two centuries the entire territory was ruled from Lima, as part of the Vice-Royalty of Peru. This changed in 1776 when, as the result of intense lobbying, the court at Madrid was persuaded to establish the new Vice-Royalty of the River Plate, with its capital in Buenos Aires. The country was turned inside out: a peripheral port became the centre, while the more populated areas of the North became the distant 'interior'. The struggle between capital and interior was to stretch well beyond Argentina's break with Spain in 1810 and its formal declaration of independence in 1816.

As elsewhere in Latin America, Britain was closely involved in the emergence of independent Argentina. By means of contraband, the British helped the merchants of Buenos Aires to break Spain's monopolistic stranglehold on trade. Twice during the country's late colonial years, in 1806 and 1807, the British mounted full-scale invasions of the River Plate. On both occasions Buenos Aires was reconquered in actions that did much to bolster the local creole population's assertiveness. Indeed, most historians see *las invasiones inglesas* as the cradle both of Argentina's own army and of its desire for independence. British commercial penetration followed the unsuccessful incursions in a process that ran parallel to Buenos Aires' growing dominance over its sister provinces. The largely British-built and British-owned railways which fanned out like a spider's web from Buenos Aires in the nineteenth century were designed to move the country's natural produce swiftly and cheaply to the port. They also served the purpose of swamping the interior with cheap British manufactures, effectively killing off the budding economies of the hinterland.

Argentina's peasantry disappeared early. In the more populated north, plantation cropping turned them into cane-cutters, cotton-pickers, lumberjacks – migrating to the tune of the seasons if they were lucky, locked into semi-feudal conditions as virtually indentured workers if they were not. The wide expanses of the Pampas evolved slowly from cattle-hunting to cattle-ranching, and this called for few, nomadic hands. Indeed it was not until the second half of the nineteenth century that the entirety of the prairie was wrested from the Pampas Indians, in a massive military operation that slaughtered many and pushed many more southwards and over the Andes into Chile. This coincided more or less with the end of long decades of violent internal strife, a period described with hindsight by historians as one of 'national organization'. Formally, full national unity was achieved when the provinces of the interior forced the province of Buenos Aires to relinquish its claims to primacy, carving out of its territory a federal district around Buenos Aires city. In real power terms, it was more of a deal between the Buenos Aires landowners and those of the larger neighbouring provinces, slightly expanding the top of the power pyramid but changing little else.

The 1880s, with a finally unified and relatively stable country, witnessed the emergence of the 'grand scheme' for Argentina's future. The country's ruling élite, the landowners and the merchants of Buenos Aires, saw Argentina as a huge farm, which only required latching on to European 'progress' to become a perpetual prosperity machine. The chosen formula was a simple one. Argentina would concentrate on producing farm goods — mainly beef and grains — and would import from Europe 'the fruits of progress': manufactured goods and machinery. Just one thing was lacking to complete the picture: people. Mass immigration from Europe was encouraged, in the hope that hosts of small farmers would settle in Argentina's empty spaces, transforming the countryside with European agricultural techniques. This was never to be: access to the land remained closed, and only a few managed to find a place in the country's grain belt; the rest flocked to the cities. But immigration did make a difference: by 1910 one in every three inhabitants was foreign-born. Foreigners also moved into industry, especially into the more 'modern' sectors, soon leaving Argentine owners in a minority, save in the sectors most closely linked to agriculture.

The end of the nineteenth century and beginning of the twentieth saw the emergence of the middle classes as a potent political force. Their challenge to the rule of the land-based oligarchy initially took the form of a series of armed revolts. Eventually they attained power, under the leadership of Hipólito Yrigoyen, thanks to the modification of the country's electoral laws. Yrigoyen's *Unión Cívica Radical,* mildly nationalistic, kept Argentina neutral during the First World War. This war had an important effect on the country's economy: it underlined the vulnerability of a system that depended almost entirely on foreign supplies of manufactured goods and industrial inputs. When the conflagration in the modern hemisphere choked this supply line, Argentina was forced into a first, very elementary bout of industrialization. Though much of this did not survive the end of the war, it planted in many minds the seeds of a different conception of how Argentina would have to fend for itself in a more complex world economy.

The global crisis of the late 1920s did not pass Argentina by. Recession and unemployment deeply affected the entire country, uprooting masses of people from the interior and driving them to the large cities, and particularly to Buenos Aires, where their arrival gave birth to the first *villas miserias,* or shanty towns. This crisis was a major factor in the events leading to the military coup of 1930 – the first in what has become known as 'the era of the military coups'. Ultranationalistic in outlook, it led to the restoration of conservative rule, only halfheartedly legitimized by recourse to wholesale electoral fraud. Since the turn of the century immigrant workers had been building up Argentina's labour movement. Largely confined to the European immigrants – craftsmen and skilled workers – trade unionism was often violently repressed, while internally it was riven by a feud between anarchists and socialists. The mass internal migrations from the provinces during the 1930s later created a new, mostly unskilled working class which remained mainly non-unionized and on the whole alienated from their more educated and politicized immigrant counterparts.

Against this background, the Second World War brought a repetition, albeit on a larger scale, of the 1914–18 experience. Once again Argentina found its supplies of manufactured goods interrupted, and once again it was forced to turn to its own resources. This time, however, the ensuing bout of industrialization was less haphazard. A coherent viewpoint developed, especially in the Army, which identified the establishment of local industries with 'national security'. A military coup in 1943 embodied this approach, and added an unexpected new dimension to the equation. One of the masterminds of the military administration, Colonel Juan Domingo Perón, got himself appointed to the secretariat of Labour and Social Welfare, from which he began to put into practice the mass of unapplied social and labour legislation which the country had accumulated over decades. Using this as his key weapon, he fostered the unionization of Argentina's disenfranchised workers and engineered the takeover of the existing trade unions from their mainly socialist leaders. Between 1943 and 1948 real wages rose by 37 per cent and the working class experienced significant improvements in their living standards. This was the foundation of the loyalty to *Perónismo* which would be such a crucial feature of Argentina's political life in the ensuing decades.

Most of Argentina's political establishment, right across the political spectrum, saw the military regime, and Perón in particular, as representative of a native brand of fascism. He had himself announced, 'We shall create a fascism that is careful to avoid all the errors of Mussolini.' In the name of democracy, and with the overt support of the United States, everyone from conservative to Communist ganged up against nascent *Perónismo*. An attempt was made to eject Perón from all positions of power, but mass mobilization of the Peronista workers, in a bloodless rebellion, forced his reinstatement. Perón then plunged wholeheartedly into the political arena, running for the Presidency in elections called for 1946. In the most free polls Argentina had experienced for many years, Perón won a landslide victory.

The rise of Perón must be seen against the background of the economic and social changes which had taken place in Argentina in the 1930s and 1940s. The social scene found by Perón differed greatly from that of the early years of the century, at the height of the immigration wave. At that time, genteel Congressmen were shocked to hear of the appalling conditions in the slum tenements that housed the new arrivals, the long working hours, the undernourishment, the promiscuity. But these urban workers of European origin had already received at least some degree of unionization, and on paper if not in practice had obtained social sanction for a number of basic principles of social justice. The crisis of the 1930s had brought a new wave of migrants to the cities, and particularly to the shanty towns of Buenos Aires. Unskilled, they flocked to the slaughterhouses, the meat-packing plants, the construction industry. Disconnected from the socialist and anarchist backgrounds of the European immigrants, they remained pariahs of Argentina's budding labour movement. Darker-skinned than their predecessors, they were disrespectfully dismissed as *cabecitas negras* and *peloduras* (literally, *blackheads* and *stiff-hairs*) by the large Europeanized middle classes, and as *lumpenproletariat* by the politicized trade unionists.

The crisis years and the ensuing world war gave birth to another new social factor: the small and medium-sized industrialist. By the early 1940s, Argentina had a considerable industrial base; in 1944 industrial production made up a larger proportion of total production than ranching, the production of cereals and agricultural raw materials. Nevertheless these traditional export activities continued to hold a key position in the economy, and the large landowners still had considerable political power. But this was diminishing as the new industrial class emerged with distinct aspirations and as their foremost ally, British capital, entered a period of definitive decline. Perón appeared on the stage of Argentine politics as old alliances were ending and new classes were rising. His appeal was directed at the new outsiders – the less-qualified urban workers who had migrated from the provinces, and the embryonic class of industrial entrepreneurs. During his first presidency (1946–51) he was able to use the State and the country's high level of foreign reserves at the time to favour both sectors.

Perón enlarged the scope of Argentina's social legislation, pursued industrialization more systematically, and placed the country's export trade under state control, thus checking, for the first time, the landowning oligarchy's power. Nationalization of foreign assets was also a key feature of Perón's policies, and the cornerstone of the highly protective mixed-economy model that has since been identified with *Perónismo*. It was an unusual process of nationalization. Over the years, British investors had come to control a huge share of Argentina's economy. Meat-packing houses, trading companies, railways, urban enterprises, telephone companies, gas, even ports, were British-owned, but during the war years Argentina had, through its sale of beef and grains, built up enormous foreign exchange reserves in Britain. When the war ended, these reserves remained blocked by the British, and the only readily available way to secure their release was to apply them to the purchase of British assets. This Perón did.

Perón's programme of reforms, though far-reaching, stopped short of overturning the country's traditional power structure. Land ownership remained concentrated in the hands of a few, in an agricultural system that relied very heavily on the country's natural endowments and very little on human effort. The government's emphasis on industrialization led to the neglect of agricultural output. But while many of the consumer goods previously imported could now be manufactured locally, larger amounts of foreign exchange earnings were spent on imports of fuel, machinery and raw materials for industry than were saved through import substitution. By the 1950s the favourable economic circumstances of the post-war period were coming to an end. Prices for Argentina's exports began to fall and Perón's programme of growth and redistribution could no longer be sustained without profound structural changes in the economy.

Perón was re-elected in 1951, but increasingly he moved to the right. The regime's distrust of democratic parties, which had opposed *Perónismo* since its inception, led to more authoritarian government. The press was muzzled or, more often, taken over by a huge holding company owned by leading government personalities. Dissident trade unionists and opposition leaders spent more and more time behind bars. The death in 1951 of Perón's wife, Evita, removed one of the government's most charismatic figures, who had mobilized much of its support. As the economic crisis deepened, dissent spread through the trade union movement, shattering the worker-entrepreneur entente on which Perón had built his power base. Then Perón clashed with another, albeit passive, pillar of his regime, the Church. When dissatisfaction began to permeate the Army, the demise of Perónista power became a certainty and Perón was overthrown by a military coup in 1955, after a presidency of nine years.

The years that followed were dominated by an attempt to 'de-Perónise' Argentina. Harsh repressive measures were adopted to ban all specifically political expressions of the Perónista movement and to destroy its grip on the trade unions. A parallel bid was made to dismantle the apparatus of state intervention in the economy, opening the country to foreign investment and easing government controls on trade and finance. The declared aim of the new military rulers was to restore democracy after the country had been completely de-Perónized; the methods they employed were far harsher than anything the country had known during the years of Perónista rule. Elections were, however, called after only three years and it was an open secret that the victorious candidate, Arturo Frondizi, had obtained his majority through an electoral pact with the Perónistas, promising them a return to legality.

Frondizi, presenting himself as a nationalist while campaigning, did a complete volte-face in office, launching the country along the path of *desarrollismo* ('developmentalism') – a formula for more rapid industrialization based on a massive inflow of foreign investment, particularly directed towards 'basic' industries such as steel, oil and petrochemicals. But industrial production was geared mainly to the home market and generated no foreign exchange earnings. Agriculture was still the country's main source of exports

107

but remained in the hands of a conservative landowing élite. By 1962 Argentina was in a severe balance of payments crisis. The chosen remedy – the IMF's classic 'stabilization' package – contributed to recession, unemployment and even higher inflation than it was designed to control. These economic problems were accompanied by growing social unrest, particularly as sectors of the left came under the influence of the Cuban revolution of 1959. The government's response was harsh. The press was censored, detention for political reasons became frequent, and cases of torture at the hands of the security forces made headlines several times.

Frondizi's rule was, throughout, a delicate balancing act between this climate of dissent and the pressure exerted by the military, fearful of what it saw as a Communist threat. In 1962 he ran foul of the military, first when he refused to join the US-inspired move to expel Cuba from the Organization of American States, and secondly when he failed to prevent a Perónista victory in provincial elections. Frondizi was ousted in a military coup and replaced by a figurehead civilian administration. By that time the main features of present-day Argentina were in place. Land, to be sure, continued to be the main source of social prestige and a formidable seat of power, but among the richest ten per cent of the population agriculture had shrunk as a source of wealth. Banking and industrial investment had taken its place – already some of the 'new' industrialists of the Perón era had made their way to the top of the economic pyramid. The labour movement had become a key protagonist of the country's political life, and its 'social conquests' seemed to be there for good. The middle classes had mushroomed; a car every three families was the norm; television had made its way even to the shanty towns (whose population had changed somewhat with the 'graduation' of earlier arrivals and the influx of new 'marginals', mainly immigrants from neighbouring Bolivia and Paraguay).

Argentina proudly sported the highest income per capita in Latin America, ate more beef than anyone in the world, and tried to cope with a university explosion that produced graduates by the hundreds without any clear market for their particular expertise. Though less skewed than elsewhere in Latin America, income distribution still favoured the few at the top of the pyramid; wage-earners were actually beginning to feel the erosion of the 50 per cent share they had achieved during the Perón years. Behind the official pride in statistical averages, awareness began to grow of 'marginalization' in many aspects of the country's life: on the fringes of the urban centres, of industry, of the educational and health systems. Illiteracy had been virtually eradicated, but school desertion and semi-literacy were high. Outright unemployment remained low by hemispheric or even world standards, but under-employment was rife. And the political system, under permanent threat of military intervention, made marginals out of large segments of the population.

By the time of Frondizi's removal, the military had split into two factions: the *colorados,* hardliners who wished to complete the unfinished task of de-Perónization even if this meant an indefinite postponement of the return to democracy, and the *azules,* who appealed to 'constitutionalism'. They proposed some form of re-integration of *Perónismo* into the country's political life, and after a series of clashes, some of which were very violent, the *azules,* led by General Juan Carlos Onganía, emerged victorious. The Peronistas were still banned when new elections were called in 1963, and the Presidency went to Arturo Illía, candidate of the *Unión Civica Radical del Pueblo.* Mildly interventionist and doggedly legalist, the Illía administration managed to run the economy relatively smoothly while restoring legality to the Perónistas. The Perónista unions, however, pushed their cause relentlessly through a *Plano de Lucha* ('Struggle Plan') which included the forcible occupation of factories and work places, and even the taking of hostages. Illia's government was accused of being slow – its achievements did not match the expectations created by previous rhetoric – and indecisive in dealing with the unions. Yet another military coup in 1966 was applauded by many, including an important faction of the Perónista trade union movement, and General Juan Carlos Onganía was called back from retirement to head the new military government.

It is sometimes suggested that the Onganía government repre-sented the first bid by Argentina's big business, in an entente with foreign capital, to establish itself as a power centre in its own right, independent of the landowning oligarchy and the unions. Foreign capital, particularly US capital, certainly increased its stake in the country in these years. US investment had risen from US $ 800 million in 1962 to US $ 1.5 billion in 1968, reaching US $ 2.6 billion by the end of 1976. Between 1963 and 1977, 53 Argentine companies were bought out by foreign firms. A total of 19 local banks were sold to foreign interests between 1967 and 1969. By 1970 foreign banks held 40.5 per cent of the total commercial deposits in Argentine private banks. By 1976 this had risen to 58 per cent. Public and private investment received a boost, massive public works programmes were started, and industry embarked upon a much needed process of refurbishment. For a time it seemed that Argentina was at last on the verge of its much announced 'take-off'. But three sectors of the economy began to resist government policies. The cattle ranchers, claiming that the government's support for industry was being carried out at their expense, allowed farm production to slump. The unions, suffering the impact of a strict wage freeze, began to fight back. Small business, alarmed at the spate of takeovers by foreign companies, began to demand protection. Party political activity was banned, so it was just a matter of time before bottled-up discontent found release in a violent explosion. A rapid succession of street riots and protest demonstrations in 1969 shook the regime to its core, and these outbursts heralded the appearance on the political scene of newcomers: the urban guerrillas of the *Ejército Revolucionario del Pueblo* (ERP), of Trotskyite inspiration, and the Montoneros. The latter were born of the nationalist right but soon became heirs of the 'national left', and eventually the most important armed wing of the Perónista left.

The guerrilla movements, after an initial 'Robin Hood' phase of daring but largely 'victimless' exploits, fell into a pattern of political kidnappings for ransom, assassinations and hold-ups. This in turn fed a hardening campaign of government repression which tended to spill over from containment of the guerrillas to wider persecution of political dissidents. General Onganía was ousted by his Army peers in 1970, and replaced by another general, Roberto Marcelo Levingston, who was himself removed from office shortly afterwards. The Army commander-in-chief, General Alejandro Agustín Lanusse, then took over the presidency with the aim of returning the country to elected government, and made a serious bid to compete with Perón as a political leader in his own right. His economic policies did not differ greatly from those being proposed by the Perónistas but opposition, spearheaded by the Perónistas and their demand for an end to Perón's long exile, had snowballed to an extent that was by now unstoppable. A number of attempts were made to ensure the proscription of *Perónismo*, in one form or another, but this proved politically unfeasible, as did the government's bid to secure some sort of agreement from the politicians on the nature of the post-electoral administration.

Argentina returned to the polls in March 1973, when victory went to a coalition headed by the Perónistas, whose candidate was Héctor Cámpora, a man handpicked for the job by Perón himself. This was not, however, merely a new edition of the formula which had taken *Perónismo* to power in 1948. For one thing, the Army was decidedly outside the victorious coalition. And although the 'national' entrepreneurs were visibly present (one of their representatives became the Minister of Economy), big business linked to foreign companies had also openly gambled on Perón as an answer to Argentina's political and economic instability. The unions were present, too, but their influence was challenged by the youthful Perónista left, openly committed to a war against 'union bureaucracy'. The *Montoneros* guerrillas had formally laid down their arms upon the restoration of elected government, but the ERP remained outside the ruling coalition and was still committed to armed struggle.

The Perónista left which had obtained substantial representation in Congress, was quite close to President Cámpora and had considerable influence in the state apparatus. They also had influence in the universities and in many sectors of the civil service. Adopting the slogan *la Patria socialista* ('the Socialist Fatherland'), they began to act as if Argentina had undergone, not merely the re-establishment of elected rule, but the first phase of a fully fledged revolution. *Perónismo*'s right wing, led by the trade union hierarchy, responded by rallying behind José López Rega, the Minister of Social Welfare, under the banner of *la Patria perónista* ('the Perónista Fatherland'). Antagonism between the two factions erupted into violent confrontation on 20th June 1973, the very day on which Perón returned to Argentina from his eighteen-year exile. At a mass rally organized to greet him, right and left engaged in a pitched battle, leaving scores of dead and hundreds wounded. Perón soon demanded Cámpora's resignation and called new elections which placed the ageing leader himself in the presidency.

Perón's third wife, Maria Estela Martinez – better known as 'Isabelita' – was elected as Vice-President.

The country to which Perón returned after an absence of almost two decades had changed considerably. Its population had risen from just over 15 million in 1946 to about 25 million. More than 50 per cent of industrial production was now made up of metallurgical products, motor vehicles, chemicals and electrical goods. Industry accounted for about one third of the country's export earnings. The political scene had also undergone considerable transformation during Perón's exile. Conservatism had all but vanished as an electoral force. Instead it was now represented in various pressure groups and also in a number of individuals with administrative talent and good international connections who placed themselves at the service of military regimes or elected governments facing financial crises. The traditional left had suffered a process of atomization, constantly splintering and regrouping on the fringes of the country's political life, or attempting to find niches next to or within the wide Perónista mass. The old *Unión Civica Radical* had split down the middle just before Frondizi's presidency in 1958. Frondizi's own faction had again subdivided since then, leaving the old rump, the *Unión Civica Radical del Pueblo*, as Argentina's second largest party – indeed, as the only grouping with a recognizable party structure of any sort. The interruption of normal political processes by successive military governments had led to widespread cynicism about the country's political institutions, to disillusionment with party political life (seeking appointment seemed a surer route to a political future than the hard slog of rising through a party pyramid), and to readier acceptance of untempered radical proposals. The result has been vividly described as 'black parliamentarianism': a system parallel to the established institutions in which the union bosses and the business associations acted as the real interlocutors of government. Within *Perónismo* itself, Perón retained ultimate leadership by playing the 'pendulum' – encouraging diverse groups and offering support and approval to each in turn, according to the circumstances. This allowed *Perónismo* to continue to embrace a wide ideological spectrum, but it also led to the growing autonomy of different internal power groups, whose invocation of loyalty to Perón became ever more formal and ritualistic.

In this context underground war began to brew between the right and left wings of *Perónismo*. Left-wing guerrilla attacks were coun-tered by right-wing murder squads. Initially, the former were more selective in their exercise of terror, choosing their targets mainly among 'trade union bureaucrats' and representatives of big business, while the latter acted more indiscriminately against all exponents of left-wing thought. By the time Perón died – nine months after becoming President – political assassinations were averaging more than two a day, and the economy was in serious difficulties, exacerbated by an ill-conceived price control system and uncontrolled, misdirected spending. The ensuing higher inflation was further boosted by the repercussions of the worldwide economic crisis, itself compounded by the 'oil shock' of 1973–4. The confrontation between right and left became more acute after María Estela Martínez de Perón succeeded Perón in the presidency in July 1974. The Army was formally charged with suppressing subversion, while right-wing murder squads, mostly acting under the umbrella denomination of AAA (Argentine Anti-communist Alliance), stepped up their own activity. 'Disappearance', abduc-tions carried out by armed groups claiming to represent the govern-ment, became an ever more frequent feature of political life, and it soon became difficult to discern between the actions of the security forces and those of the so-called AAA. The *Montoneros* guerrillas openly declared war on the new government, while the ERP attempted to set up a 'liberated zone' in the northern province of Tucumán.

Against the background of a deepening economic crisis, 'Isabelita' Perón's government fell out with Congress over allega-tions of corruption in high places, and later also with the unions over the adoption of a harsh package of corrective economic measures. With the country facing virtual civil war, runaway inflation and a breakdown in relations between the institutions of the State, and between government and unions, the military once more stepped in to overthrow the government in March 1976. Power was entrusted to a Junta composed of the commanders-in-chief of the armed forces, who in turn delegated the presidency to General Jorge Rafael Videla. Union and party political activity was banned, and stiff repressive legislation was enacted to further the war against 'subversion'. The death penalty was introduced and harsh penalties were imposed for a number of activities considered 'subversive'. The government's interpretation of subversion was wide, and included such concepts as 'economic subversion' and 'ideological subversion', but in actual practice the campaign against 'subversives' did not follow the pattern suggested by the legislation: 'disappearance' continued to be the preferred mode of repression. On the economic front, the avowed purposes of halting inflation, curtailing speculative activities and eradicating corruption were also widely interpreted, and amounted to an attempt to dismantle the entire apparatus of the mixed-economy system which had existed since the 1940s, cutting back state intervention, slashing protective tariffs and freeing prices and interest rates, while wages were kept down by decree.

The nature of political repression in Argentina since 1976 has been well documented, particularly by Amnesty International and other human rights organizations. Clandestine arrests and executions, the systematic use of torture as an instrument of terror, the establishment of secret detention centres and 're-education camps'; all are part of a well-known picture. No longer was it merely a matter of neutralizing an adversary for the sake of preserving a certain order; the aim was directly the annihilation of the adversary as part of a crusade, or what was sometimes described as the beginning of the Third World War. The grim statistics of this period include, apart from the known dead, an estimated 15,000 'disappeared' persons.

The violence reached its peak before 1978, and had already declined sharply when the military rulers of Argentina decided to institutionalize their regime, appointing General Videla for a three-year term, after which the Junta would designate a successor for a similar term, and so on. While insistently proclaiming the restoration of democracy as their ultimate aim, and constantly announcing the publication of a 'political plan', the military made no practical move in this direction other than slowly relaxing restrictions on the press, until after General Videla had been succeeded by General Viola in 1981. In the meantime, however, the regime's economic edifice had crumbled. Not only had earnings been drastically depressed, but production had actually fallen year after year, plunging the country into the longest recession since the 1930s. In 1980, as a direct result of the policies pursued by the military government, the country suffered a severe banking crisis, and several institutions collapsed. A rising rate of bankruptcies had been a feature of the economy since 1976, but in 1980 it engulfed a number of the larger companies, including some of the financial 'groups' which had been showpieces of the new approach.

In this atmosphere, the political parties and trade unions were not prepared to wait for formal re-enfranchisement, and began to voice a demand for return to elected rule, and for a reversal of economic policy. Government concessions in this direction were held back by a spectre that haunted the military: the possibility that once elected rule was re-established there would be 'another Nuremberg' – a public calling to account for the 'disappearances' and other abuses of human rights extensively documented by a number of human rights organizations. This fear was enhanced in 1980 by the award of the Nobel Peace Prize to Adolfo Pérez Esquivel, who headed the *Servicio Paz y Justicia* (Peace and Justice Service) – an ecumenical organization which campaigned for human rights. Then in December 1981, in an episode as yet not completely clarified, General Viola was replaced by General Leopoldo Fortunato Galtieri, who departed from tradition by retaining his post as commander-in-chief of the Army. Viola had attempted some modification of the military regime's early economic policies, but Galtieri's first act seemed to be a step backwards: the appointment as Minister of Economy of Roberto Alemann, a man committed to radical monetarist economics. Galtieri also appeared as the man who would mend fences with the United States. Relations with the US had become strained as a result of President Carter's human rights policies, so Galtieri began to align Buenos Aires with Washington on most international issues, and even began to provide military assistance to US allies, such as El Salvador, in Central America. The response from the political parties and the trade unions was an intensification of protest. For the first time since 1976, mass rallies and demonstrations were seen on the streets in 1981. Criticism of the government by the press became more direct, and political leaders began to call for elections no later than 1983. To many it seemed as if the military regime born in 1976 was re-enacting the cycle of its predecessor of 1966, and the return to democratic rule suddenly appeared to be only a matter of time. Yet the shadow of the human rights issue still hung over all prospects of normalization, and the country remained deeply divided.

On 2nd April 1982, Argentina launched a venture which was to have an enormous impact on the balance of forces within the country. The significance of the Argentine invasion of the Falkland Islands/Malvinas and the subsequent defeat at the hands of the British Task Force, will only be truly assessed with the passing of time, but by the end of 1982 it was clear that Argentina was on the verge of political changes which no one could have foreseen twelve months previously. This is not the place to assess the background to the Falklands/Malvinas war and the complex arguments over sovereignty and territoriality. But the depth of feeling in Argentina that the islands had been illegally seized by the British in 1833 cannot be underestimated. Generations of schoolchildren have grown up in Argentina in the conviction that the Malvinas are part of their country. It is perhaps the only issue on which Argentines of all political persuasions are united. Thus it was hardly surprising to find all political parties and movements, including those who had been demonstrating against the military government only days before the invasion, coming out openly in support of General Galtieri's actions. The trade unions also set aside, for the moment, their protests against the government's economic policies.

The invasion was a gamble. Had it succeeded, it would have considerably strengthened the Galtieri government at a time when the opposition to military government had reached unprecedented levels. But the gamble failed, and in June 1982 General Galtieri himself was forced out of the government in disgrace. The military regime was not only in a state of internal disarray over responsibility for their ignominious surrender to the British; but it also had to confront the undisguised contempt of the population. A retired Major-General, Reynaldo Bignone, took over the presidency in July 1982 and announced that the armed forces would return the country to civilian rule.

The humiliation of the Falklands/Malvinas adventure, the nation's economic problems and the campaign of human rights organizations, now a popular cause, forced the military into abject retreat. More and more information came to light about the fate of those who disappeared during the 'dirty war' against subversion. By the end of 1982 over 1,500 unidentified bodies had been found in cemeteries in various parts of the country. Most of these were assumed to be bodies of the 'disappeared', and hundreds more were found during 1983. The elections, held on 10th October 1983, made Raul Alfonsin – a lawyer – President of Argentina. He won 52 per cent of the popular vote and his Radical Party holds an absolute majority in the electoral college. So the 40-year-old legend of Perónism now appears to be receding, and the corrupt and bullying machine politics of the Perónists at the elections served only to emphasize the failings of their colourless candidate for the presidency.

The new government, taking advantage of the demoralization of the armed forces, has moved quickly to press charges against former military leaders held to be responsible for the killings and disappearances of the 'dirty war'. General Bignone has himself been indicted in connection with the disappearance of two military cadets in 1976. Nine former members of three military juntas will be tried by the Supreme Council of the Armed Forces, and 40 of the 60 generals in the high command have been forced to retire. On the Falklands/Malvinas issue, Alfonsin has politely but firmly restated Argentina's claim to sovereignty over the islands and indicated his readiness to negotiate with the British government. Britain, has, however, made it plain that there is no possibility of negotiations at which the question of sovereignty might arise.

The most intractable problem facing the new government is however on the economic front. Argentina's foreign debt is US $ 40 billion – the third largest in the Third World – with almost half of this due for repayment in 1984. During 1983 inflation was over 500 per cent, while the official rate of unemployment stood at 15 per cent. The country's only assets for the time being are a tide of international goodwill, and hope among the Argentines themselves that the Alfonsin government might possess the strength and the will to deal with problems which consistently defeated the military rulers during their $7\frac{1}{2}$ disastrous years in power.

The Roman Catholic Church in Argentina claims a membership of over 25 million, these constituting more than 90 per cent of the total population. And its place in the established order seems secure. After the military coup in 1966 the new regime dedicated the country 'to the Immaculate Heart of the Virgin Mary', and the Constitution still declares: 'The Federal Government supports the Roman Apostolic Catholic Church.' The Constitution also lays down that the President and Vice-President of the Republic must be Catholics, and although the right to nominate bishops is no longer vested in the State there are secret negotiations between the Church and the government before bishoprics are filled. The Catholic

Church receives substantial financial subsidies from the State. Yet the number of Catholics who attend Mass regularly is unusually small for Latin America. Estimates of 12 per cent are often made, these ranging from 7 per cent in Buenos Aires to 19 per cent in the smaller towns. Seventy per cent of Catholics attend only once a year or never at all.

Various explanations are offered for this low degree of commitment. Argentina has a larger than average middle class and, although this provides most of the Catholic clergy and the members of religious orders, its members have adopted some of the trappings of a secular life-style, with the result that a diversity of interests and commitments, long working hours, and a desire to be mobile at weekends often get in the way of church attendance. Some parishes have partly met this problem by offering Mass on Friday and Saturday evenings, but besides the competition for time many Argentines are for a number of contradictory reasons disillusioned with the way the Church operates in the moral and social spheres. Disagreement is manifested by the drawing of a distinction between the Church itself – with which in broad terms the laity still identify themselves – and the bishops and priests who often come under heavy criticism either for taking too rigid a line on certain issues, e.g. remarriage and birth control, or too radical a line on others, e.g. human rights, and social change. Anti-clericalism has a fairly long history in Argentina.

The first Catholic missionaries arrived in Argentina in 1539, shortly after the land had been sighted by a Spanish navigator. They were Franciscans and were followed about forty years later by Jesuit missionaries, whose main work was in the North-East before they were expelled from the country in 1767. After independence, in 1816, an attempt was made to establish a national church, but this came to nothing and the Catholic Church received massive reinforcements from among the four million immigrants who came to Argentina between 1857 and 1950. Of these, 46 per cent were Italian, 31 per cent Spanish, and the rest mainly Irish, Polish and German. By the end of the nineteenth century 99 per cent of the population were Catholics.

Over the years the Catholic hierarchy have often given the impression that they are willing to work with any form of government, and during the Perónista period most of the bishops were favourable to the government even though (unlike many of the priests) they were not actually Perónistas. Cardinal Aramburu, Archbishop of Buenos Aires, and most of his fellow bishops appeared to be quite at ease with the recent military regime, even though some of their colleagues and not a few of their priests fell foul of its repressive policies. In March 1982, on the sixth anniversary of the military regime, the senior military chaplain, Bishop Victorio Bonamín, celebrated Mass for a gathering of high-ranking officers and told them in his sermon that the coup had been 'an act of divine providence ... it was the work of God'. A few days later, immediately following the invasion of the Falkland Islands, Cardinal Aramburu embraced the President, General Galtieri, at a great public demonstration in support of the invasion. The shrine at Luján, thirty miles outside Buenos Aires, which has become the focal point for traditional Catholic devotion and is the Lourdes of Argentina, has sometimes been used by military regimes as a symbol of national unity. The tiny figure of the virgin, Our Lady of Luján, is regarded as captain-general of the Argentine armed forces and is credited with having helped to repel British forces on the two occasions in the nineteenth century when they attempted to capture Buenos Aires. State dignitaries take part in massive pilgrimages, and from time to time governments have found it convenient to emphasize the Catholic element in the Argentine character.

Since the Second Vatican Council, however, there has grown up within the Catholic Church a socially radical and militant wing, as well as a considerable ecclesiastical renewal based on biblical and liturgical studies. For a time, particularly in the 1970s, the politically active among the clergy identified themselves with a group known as 'The Third World Priests'. Theologically, this group was committed to the main emphasis of liberation theology, while politically it supported the left-wing elements of the Perónista movement, and was specially active in parishes in the poorest areas of the major cities. Members of the group and others of similar outlook are among those who have suffered most at the hands of the military since the 1976 coup. At least eight priests have been murdered by the security forces. One of them, Father Francisco Soáres, had just conducted the funeral of a woman catechist who had been seized, tortured and killed in February 1976, when he himself was shot by a group in civilian clothes who were later found to have police connections. Two other priests, Fathers Gabriel

Longueville (a Frenchman) and Carlos Diaz Murias, were killed by the police in La Rioja province. Soon afterwards, on 3rd August 1976, the Bishop of La Rioja, Monsignor Enrique Angelelli – one of the government's most outspoken critics – was travelling in a van from the town of Chamical, where he had been conducting the funeral for Fathers Longueville and Murias. The van was forced off the road by a powerful car and the Bishop was killed in the crash. No one in the area doubts the real circumstances of that 'accident'. In addition to those known to have been killed, another 20 priests have disappeared, 16 have been imprisoned, four have been deported and nine have left the country after being threatened with violence. The number of lay Catholics who have been killed or imprisoned is unknown, but is believed to be large.

The main theological spokesman for 'The Third World Priests' when they were at the height of their influence, between 1969 and 1976, was Lucio Gera. While in substantial sympathy with the general trend of liberation theology, he was particularly concerned to draw out the potentially revolutionary implications of popular Catholicism. His concern was – and is – to present the Catholic faith in such a way that it would promote radical renewal among working-class people alienated from the Church. Some people have considered him to be an exponent of a kind of populist theology. Today the more radical members of the Catholic Church have either withdrawn into relative obscurity or are working with grassroots communities, which are not very numerous in Argentina. Others are working in human rights organizations, but the Church as an institution has yet to put its weight behind those who are resisting repression. The Vatican has been more active on their behalf than has the national hierarchy. Father Juan Carlos Scannone, a Jesuit priest who is dean of the philosophy department at the Universidad del Salvador (Buenos Aires/San Miguel), is, however, a well-known exponent of liberation theology, as also are Lucio Gera and Severino Croatto.

The Protestant churches, with a total strength of about 750,000, or just under three per cent of the population, are clearly less influential than the huge Catholic community, and they can be divided into three main groups. Among the 'historic' churches, the Scottish Presbyterian (1826), the Anglican (1825), and the Methodist (1839) were first to arrive, and initially they were permitted to minister only to English-speaking immigrants. The

Presbyterians now have five congregations, worshipping in both English and Spanish, with some 2–3,000 members. The Anglican Church has about 15,000 members, in two dioceses, with special influence among the Indian tribes of the North. Here there are something like 50 churches, all pastored by Indians under the direction of an Indian bishop. The church continues to grow in this area, and there is strong emphasis on social projects, designed to give greater job security, and also on medical and literacy programmes. In April 1983 a new Anglican province – that of the Southern Cone of South America – was inaugurated. It comprises the dioceses of Argentina and Eastern South America; Northern Argentina; Paraguay; Chile, Peru and Bolivia; and its first Presiding Bishop, David Leake, is an Argentine. The Methodist Church, though small, has been influential in schools and publishing. Later in the nineteenth century, the Lutheran Church (now the second largest Protestant church with just over 100,000 members) sent pastors from Germany and Scandinavia to minister to the growing immigrant populations from Northern Europe, and Reformed Church pastors came from Holland. The small Waldensian Church was started by immigrants from northern Italy.

The second group of Protestant churches consists of the 'mission' churches, founded by the evangelistic zeal of missionaries from North America and Britain. The first of these missionaries, who founded no congregation, was the remarkable James Thomson, a Scottish Baptist who went on his own initiative to Buenos Aires in 1818 to establish schools and distribute Scriptures. At the end of the nineteenth century Plymouth Brethren from England arrived in Argentina in secular employment, mainly that of supervising the building of the railways. They were deeply committed to evangelism and were very successful in establishing churches. Their successors tend to display traditional patterns of belief, structure and activity, and form recognizable subculture. The Baptist churches, most of which belong to the Argentine Baptist Convention, are connected with the powerful Southern Baptist Convention of the USA, and are both lively and self-confident. They have their own theological seminary and run numerous other institutions. On the whole there is little contact between the Baptists and other churches, so they, too, create their own subculture in Argentine society.

Then, thirdly, there are the Pentecostal churches, which form the largest group among the non-Catholic churches, though they are not as numerous as in many other Latin American republics, nor are they growing so rapidly. They are divided into a number of different denominations, of which the largest is the Assemblies of God, and they attract to their membership people mainly from the lower and lower middle classes.

Of these three groups, only the historic churches are involved in ecumenical activities, as commonly understood. Together they run a Union Theological Seminary in Buenos Aires, an Evangelical Council for Social Action, an Evangelical Education Centre, and they have formed themselves into a Council of Churches. Some of the 'mission' churches have founded a separate Council of Evangelical (i.e. conservative) Churches, and there is some interchurch co-operation in the work of the Bible Society. The Catholic Church has a secretariat for unity, but so far it has not shown much enthusiasm for encouraging priests and people to co-operate with non-Catholic churches. In 1978 all religious bodies, except for the Roman Catholics, were required to register or re-register with the State. The Jewish community, over half a million strong, is the largest in Latin America.

Among the Protestant theologians, the Methodist José Míguez Bonino has an international reputation, and is well known in World Council of Churches circles, as well as in Britain, America and Rome where he has held visiting professorships. He is now Dean of Postgraduate Studies at the Evangelical Institute for Advanced Theololgical Studies in Buenos Aires, and his book *Revolutionary Theology Comes of Age* (1975) is both a survey of the history of Latin American Christianity and a statement of his own commitment to liberation theology. He is also committed to socialism as the political expression of Christian convictions in the present Latin American situation, though he is always at pains to emphasize that no political order can ever be sacralized, and, like Rubem Alves of Brazil, he believes that the liberation of the Latin American people will be a long haul – one requiring immense spiritual resources as well as great political skill. There is every reason for an Argentinian theologian to believe this.

Chapter 6

Chile

In 1973 a military coup rolled back fifty years of Chilean history, perhaps more. That fact is in itself tragic, for in retrospect they were quite good years, certainly less violent and more tolerant than those which followed. General Pinochet, who headed the Junta which took power in September 1973, immediately began the construction of a state which was to bear all the marks of a typical 'national security' regime: intense concern with geopolitics, and with Chile's role on a world military map where it stood aligned with 'Western Christendom', committed to a holy war against 'Communism'. It is a 'static' regime in the sense often described by the Chilean Roman Catholic Church, that is to say, it prefers to believe that the rights of the nation always take preference, especially when those rights are interpreted by the President of the Republic, and that all individual protest against them, like all individual rights which might be in conflict with them, must be suppressed.

The suppression of the opposition and the wave of terror against all those associated with the previous government shocked the world in the immediate post-coup period. No one knows exactly how many people died in the first months of the coup. Firm evidence of the scale of the massacre is difficult to obtain. Amnesty International estimates that between 1973 and 1976 over 5,000 died; some estimates suggest the figure was over 10,000. Many thousands more were arrested and tortured. It was planned brutality. In Santiago, the Junta turned the city's two football grounds – the National Stadium and the Chile Stadium – into concentration camps and interrogation centres. Workers captured in their factories were taken there, along with shanty town dwellers, students and intellectuals. The Chilean singer, Victor Jara, died in the National Stadium. The military aimed to extract information about the Chilean left and at the same time eliminate those who might lead a resistance.

123

After this first wave of arrests and killings, the Chilean Junta began to erect an apparatus of repression designed to create a climate of fear and deter further opposition. Arrests continued but they became more systematic; opposition leaders or those suspected of opposition began to 'disappear', particularly after 1976. Today an estimated 15,000 are still unaccounted for, although eye-witnesses often saw them being taken away by the security forces. An estimated half a million Chileans have been forced to leave the country. All party political and trade union activity was banned immediately after the coup, so association with organizations of this kind provides 'legal' pretext for arrest under the State of Emergency provisions which have been renewed every six months.

But the national security state implies more than repression. It is also an attempt to restructure political life and to provide an institutional basis for a new relationship between the State and the civilian population. In 1981 a new constitution was promulgated in Chile, and this aims to legitimize many of the powers previously exercised de facto by the State and invested principally in the person of the President. A report from the UN Economic and Social Council (1981) describes it as merely consolidating 'at an institutional level, the present situation, which is characterized by serious limitations on human rights'. Article 24 of the Constitution, for instance, empowers the Ministry of the Interior, on the authorization of the President, to deny entry to the country, to license both expulsion without trial and periods of up to 20 days' incommunicado detention without charge, or up to 90 days' internal exile. Under Article 8 political association is banned with a specific reference to those who are suspected of propagating doctrines 'based on the class struggle' or directed against the State or legal system.

Yet democracy has deep roots in Chile. A parliamentary tradition can be traced back to the legislative assemblies of the post-Independence period, established during the first half of the nineteenth century with one eye on British models and the other on French. In one fashion or another, Chile was ruled by parliaments from 1861 until 1924 (with a brief interlude of civil war in 1891) and then again between 1932 and 1973. Even the interlude from 1924 to 1932, when a military takeover was prompted by the collapse of world markets for nitrates (Chile's principal export at the time) and the economic confusion that followed, saw only three years of consistent military government as such. Thus the re-imposition of a military dictatorship in 1973, when the present government overthrew the socialist President Allende, was a great shock – not only to its victims, who had thought themselves safe with a military supposedly committed to constitutional norms, but in the end even to some of its instigators. Many of the civilians who campaigned hard in the period 1972–3 to ensure that the military would put an end to Allende's government expected that, after a short sharp period to eliminate the Marxist threat, civilian rule would return. Instead, Chile has suffered ten years of military dictatorship without the shadow of a parliament of any kind. It was an outcome which Allende himself predicted. In an interview he had at his own request with the President of the body representing Chile's manufacturers, the SOFOFA, one of the leading figures in the campaign against him, he said, 'You can get rid of me, but what hope will you have afterwards, in Latin America, of removing the military from power?'

Chile is a long, narrow belt of land running the length of the Pacific coast between the Andes and the sea: 4,270 kilometres long and 120 kilometres wide, a country described by one of its own historians as 'a geographical madness'. Dominated by the Andes, it spans most of the variations in climate and vegetation known to man, with the exception of tropical jungles. There are deserts in the North; a Mediterranean climate in the fertile Central Valley, which produces excellent wine; temperate forests in the South; and over its last 1,100 kilometres, glaciated fjords. For over a hundred years, commentators have predicted a bright future for this promising young nation which was part of Spain's vast empire from the sixteenth to nineteenth centuries. It is a country rich in natural resources. Gold, silver, iron, nitrates and copper have in turn provided the basis for Chile's ability to trade on international markets. In Latin American terms, Chile has also enjoyed decisive political advantages. It was relatively quick to coalesce around a strong central State, avoiding the debilitating battles between regional landowners typical of the rest of Latin America in the wake of Independence. Communications along the long sea-coast were sufficiently easy to allow for the early development of a strong national political culture, transmuting regional differences of interest into a countrywide debate on matters of political principle.

Recent Chilean history can, however, only be understood by examining in some detail a longstanding set of economic problems, not created by the advent of a Marxist government in 1970, but a source of headaches for all Chile's presidents. In the 1920s the answer seemed to be to switch from exporting nitrates to exporting copper, for which world demand was high at the time, and also to attempt to promote national industrial development through tariff barriers designed to protect the local market. The military rulers of that time were strong advocates of this model, which was also intended to give them the wherewithal to wage modern warfare. This commitment to industrialization remained under subsequent civilian governments, to whom it seemed the most viable response to the collapse of the world economy in the 1930s. In 1938 a coalition of Radicals, Socialists and Communists – the Chilean Popular Front – laid the basis for a combination of government-managed industrialization, together with a commitment to a rudimentary welfare state. A channel for investment, the Corporation for Encouraging National Production (CORFO) was established and was to dominate investment in many fields in the next thirty years. The government also set up a form of National Health Service, with a Dr Salvador Allende as minister in charge.

Thus by 1970 the Chilean State was very directly involved in the country's economy. It was not there primarily to hold the private sector to an expensive bargain with the public at large, but rather to maintain the tariff barriers needed to protect Chile's industries and to manage the flow of resources to them, providing loans and credits. Often it did more. CORFO provided the basis for a Chilean steel industry and did a great deal to develop Chile's hydro-electric potential, at the same time laying the basis for a timber industry in the South. A state-run oil development corporation was also created. Education, already well established as a national service by the 1920s, was revamped to provide better technical training for high school graduates, so that by the 1950s the technical schools were providing the nation with a flow of skilled personnel far beyond the capacity of its industries to absorb. The Chilean State also remained committed to a wide range of social services and had broad powers to ensure that private employers did the same. The

National Health Service made a basic provision for all. There was a basic state pension scheme for salaried workers, and a state board to oversee the operations of other schemes in the public and private sectors. Labour matters were subject to minute regulations, with legislation covering accidents at work and women's conditions of employment. An elaborate system of collective bargaining was supervised at every turn by representatives of the Ministry of Labour. Foreign observers have often criticized these schemes, which left so little funding for capital investment in a country where investment, at least by the private sector, seemed to have serious difficulty in getting off the ground. Nevertheless, there were considerable achievements. Governments between 1940 and 1970 were able to keep the rate of open unemployment well below 10 per cent – no mean achievement in a country with a rising birth rate and an evident surplus of labour. But the results as a whole were disappointing. By the end of the 1960s a number of basic structural problems with industrialization had begun to rear their heads.

Most of the machinery for industrial production had to be imported from abroad, as did the parts to service it. Chile paid for these imports with the proceeds from its exports of copper. But the world market for copper is a volatile one, and the prices the country could command for its metal on international markets varied sharply from one year to another, without any kind of predictable basis – a typical complaint of all Third World producers of primary products. Thus plans for investment in industry, made in one year when the price of copper was high and seemed likely to remain so, would the next year suffer from the consequences of a sudden sharp fall. The temptation for governments was always to maintain their investment programmes in spite of a sharp drop in their revenues. The consequence was a growing deficit on the balance of payments, and increasing levels of national debt. The volatility of copper prices, and their crucial role in government revenues, also affected the government's ability to spend money on social services. And since governments found it politically impossible to cut employment in this sector from one year to another, fluctuations in the price of copper transformed themselves into a massive pressure on governments to increase the State's resources by printing money.

So, for very obvious reasons, the period of conscious

industrialization from 1940 to 1973 was bedevilled by inflation, sometimes reaching dangerous levels. Worried governments were often forced to attempt to contain it by imposing a drastic wage freeze over the whole economy. Such measures tended to increase social conflict and were one of the prime reasons for a persistent history of general strikes. Conflict with organized labour – dominated by Socialists and Communists – also increased the tendency for governments to turn to 'national security' legislation to control the labour movement with a markedly anti-Communist bias. Some of the legal and psychological foundations of the future Pinochet regime were laid well before Pinochet came to power.

If Chile's dependence on copper to pay for industrial development created problems, so too did its small population and highly stratified class system. Economically, these factors made it inevitable that the country would suffer from a pattern of demand with two extremes. There was, on the one hand, a broad demand for very cheap basic goods, such as the poor could buy, and, on the other, pockets of relatively great wealth, clamouring for sophisticated modern equipment of a kind which could be imported – cars, refrigerators, washing machines and dishwashers (status symbols, as Chile's middle classes could well afford maids) as well as electronic equipment of all kinds. Such a pattern of demand made it difficult to use modern manufacturing methods economically. Owing to the small size of Chile's population, the only 'mass consumer' market was for basic consumer goods, and there was insufficient demand to make the production of more sophisticated goods cost effective. Yet Chilean planners and entrepreneurs alike were driven by the distribution of power and wealth towards those smaller pockets of prosperity craving for consumer durables – cars, refrigerators and electronics – and demanding 'the best and most modern', sometimes travelling to New York to check what was new. It is now apparent that Chilean industry worked best in its very early years when the basic consumer goods processes were being installed or updated – food and drink, textiles, shoes and clothing. These were the years when industrial employment expanded rapidly, peaking at about 17 per cent of the working population in the 1940s. The planners hoped that industrialization would provide enough employment at high enough wage rates to raise living standards for the majority of the population, but they failed to solve the bottlenecks of poverty, and in the end the labour-saving tendencies of modern equipment ensured that relatively few jobs were created in the industrial sector.

Chilean industry was therefore trapped in a vicious circle. New machines were installed but never used to their full capacity, and their relative idleness favoured a notorious disinclination on the part of the private sector to undertake any further investment. So, it was the State which pushed development forward, taking industry into new areas by *force majeure*: into raw materials, intermediate goods and consumer durables. Each time the State broke new ground it stimulated the demand that kept the economy going, frequently through the construction industry which provided new industrial plant, roads and, under progressive governments, housing for the poor. But whenever the State assumed the mantle of chief entrepreneur to the national economy it tended to stimulate demand from the poorer sectors of the population. This, too, had inflationary implications. Poor people with a little more money buy more food, but Chilean agriculture was never able to produce enough to satisfy the needs of the mass population with a little money in its hands. Inevitably the price of beef would rise, and basic foodstuffs would begin to disappear and have to be imported from abroad. As inflationary pressures worsened, the State turned to policies of deliberate deflation, with the inevitable conflicts with organized labour.

Chile had become primarily an urban country by about 1940. In 1970, after more than a century of drift towards the towns, agriculture accounted for a mere 20 per cent of the country's labour force. But the structure of land ownership was not very different from what it was when the migration began. Large estates or *latifundios* still dominated the fertile land of the Central Valley, operating with tied labour (*inquilinos*) who shared their time between the landlord's field and the vegetables they were able to grow on their own small plots. The *latifundios* were rural fiefs, buttressing their owner's claim to be part of the country's élite and, if he desired, giving him a virtually assured power base for election to Congress. The political upheavals of the 1920s and 1930s passed this world by. Successive governments, based securely on the urban population, found it safer to ignore this nineteenth-century redoubt.

They feared a struggle with its owners which would certainly have been bitter, and might have involved attempts at a military coup. Thus the rural areas were exempted from any pressure to introduce workers' unions, comparable to that which the State exerted in other areas of the economy, and their low levels of productivity went unchallenged and undisturbed. Stagnation in agriculture was no help at all to governments concerned with the problems of the urban economy. But the power of the rural landholders was great – for they would often be members of the urban élite and owners of manufacturing industry as well. Governments were therefore tempted to meet pressures on basic foodstuffs, with their inevitably inflationary consequences, by holding down agricultural prices artificially and importing the balance of goods needed to meet demand. Such a freeze on farmers' returns did little to stimulate further investment in the economy and did a lot of damage to Chile's balance of payments. But it avoided conflict with the urban masses over food prices.

By the 1960s the basic pattern of Chile's economy was clear. Inflation was a permanent headache; industrialization was bringing no significant improvement in the well-being of the population at large, and governments had to face periodic outbreaks of quite bitter conflict with the urban population – the sort of conflict in which, accidentally or not, police regularly killed one or two demonstrators. None of Chile's economic problems were unique. In some cases the country was in a better position than other Latin American republics, but sometimes its position was worse. Markets were much smaller than those of the giants of industrialization – Brazil, Argentina and Mexico – but it had the advantage of a population which was largely urban. The situation in Chilean agriculture might be bad, but it mirrored patterns in other countries where the agricultural work force represented 60 per cent, not 20 per cent, of the active population.

At this time other countries caught in similar dilemmas were beginning to experiment with a combination of authoritarian military government and drastic solutions. Brazil 'solved' its difficulties in 1964 by installing a military dictatorship which took steps to enlarge the real market for consumer durables by concentrating income in the hands of the rich. The infant mortality rate in the slums of its major industrial cities increased as a result. But the recipe 'worked' for a time: Brazil's growth rate soared, and international business publications began to discuss 'the Brazilian miracle'. Chile, however, had too small a middle class to try the Brazilian solution, even if it had been possible within the context of a popular democracy. Irritation with the status quo increased, and planners were unable to solve all the country's economic problems without trying to stretch some of the constraints under which they were being forced to operate. Manufacturers were notoriously unwilling to invest, even when the President came from their own ranks: the paper manufacturer who was elected President of the Republic on a free enterprise ticket in 1958 succeeded only in raising the level of state investment in manufacturing from 14 per cent to 40 per cent, in spite of offering tax incentives to the private sector. Government bureaucracies swelled, providing jobs that kept down open unemployment but creating a plethora of red tape. On the whole Chile was doing relatively well at providing employment for its people, but relatively poorly at using them productively. In other words, there was no 'development' in the sense that Europe and North America were enjoying development, and there was an undercurrent of dissatisfaction.

The next ten years were to produce two determined efforts to dynamize this sluggish economy, keeping its dual commitment to welfarism and industrialization. The answers had to be 'radical', i.e. they had to make some attempt to remove or weaken the structural constraints which hampered real economic growth. The first of these was President Frei's Revolution in Liberty from 1964 to 1970, and the second was President Allende's Chilean Road to Socialism from 1970 to 1973. Chile's Christian Democrats, led by Eduardo Frei, campaigned for power in 1964 on a programme of widespread and fundamental reform. They owed their victory partly to the traditional strength of the socialist vote in Chile, which had very nearly handed the Presidency to Salvador Allende in 1958. The right voted tactically to support the most popular anti-Marxist candidate. And the Christian Democrats also took advantage of a favourable climate for non-Marxist reforms in Latin America. President Kennedy had not long since created the 'Alliance for Progress' – an attempt to encourage 'reform from above' to prevent 'revolution from below'. In power, they were to receive a cool $251 million in US funds during the first two years.

Part of the price paid for such a dramatic increase in American involvement in Chile's internal affairs, making it the showcase of capitalist reform in Latin America, was the increasing integration of Chile's own officer-training programmes with US military training programmes in Panama and in the United States.

President Frei's economic strategy envisaged an attack on the structural constraints on the economy from several directions at the same time. The government attempted to buy control of the American-owned copper companies – the 'Chileanization' programme – in order to gain some power over this key sector of the country's economy. Initially, they also stimulated the construction sector in an attempt to buy popularity among the masses of the urban population, as well as increase the demand for locally-produced goods. But the major device for overcoming Chile's limitations was to take Chile into the Andean Pact – a common market based on five countries, all of them suffering from the same problems of rigid class systems and skewed patterns of demand. By pooling the markets of all five, they could massively increase the size of both popular consumer markets and, still more important, those of their élites.

With these new opportunities in mind, the Christian Democrats set about reviving the Chilean State's traditional role as chief investor, fostering the industries of the future, particularly petrochemicals and paper, where Chile would have advantages within the Andean Pact because of its own natural resources. Foreign investment in these and other fields was encouraged, not only because of its ability to contribute capital, but also because it would bring in up-to-date equipment. Besides, the 'Revolution in Liberty', closely dependent on American support, could hardly do anything less. Even so, the critical dimension of the 'Revolution in Liberty' was its determination to do something about the neglected rural sector. For the first time in their history, agricultural workers were encouraged to form unions. Faced with yearly wage demands, the *latifundistas* would have to be more productive. The government also outlined a programme of agricultural reform, to split up the old, unproductive estates, and turn them into small farms, owned by the original *latifundista* and his erstwhile workers.

But by 1967 the Revolution had ground to a halt. Its essential enemies were those which traditionally defeated Chilean Presidents: a drop in the world price for copper, growing foreign debts which would have to be repaid, and a tendency for the rate of inflation to get out of control. Predictably, the government responded by trying to freeze wages below the rate of increase in retail prices, concocting for this purpose a dubious forced savings scheme, and bringing collective bargaining throughout the economy to a standstill. Predictably, too, the result was an outbreak of social conflict. In November 1967 the Marxist-dominated union CUT called a general strike which, according to the government's own estimates, was supported by 150,000 workers. Clashes in the shanty towns around Santiago killed four workers and one child. It was the beginning of a pattern of open conflicts and deaths which was to dog the Christian Democrat administration ever after, and eventually lead their own supporters in the rural and urban unions to turn into an open alliance with the socialists against the government. At the same time, pressures to call a halt were growing from the employers' side. Tensions among the landowners were running very high, even though the Christian Democrats had hardly begun to implement the land reform programme when they left office. Urban businessmen (often landowners as well) were publicly concerned about the government's determination to force property owners to accept their social obligations, and also about the rising total of state investment in the economy. In 1970 the Christian Democrat candidate for President was opposed by a rival candidate from the right. This division in the political loyalties of the anti-Marxist camp allowed the election of Salvador Allende, the presidential candidate of a coalition of left-leaning parties known as the Popular Unity.

Allende was a socialist in the old Popular Front mould. He believed strongly in the importance of state activity in the Chilean economy – with apparently good reason, given the generally poor record of the private sector as an investor. He also believed that an economy should meet the basic needs of its people, as one might expect from the founder of Chile's national health service. He was a parliamentary politician with great experience in the wheeling and dealing which that entails. He also knew something about the dangers posed by military men to Latin American democracy – enough to be very unwilling to stage any confrontation with the armed forces. As a skilled political manipulator he took every chance to tell them that they should be proud of their record as 'constitutionalists'.

The Popular Unity coalition which Allende headed was not, however, a homogeneous force. Allende's own Socialist Party and the Chilean Communist Party were its driving forces, but it also included the Radical Party, MAPU – a left-wing offshoot of the Christian Democrats – and two very small social democratic groups. There were divergences, particularly between the Socialist Party and the Communist Party, on such issues as class alliances and the pace of the transition to socialism which later affected the implementation of a coherent strategy of government.

The Popular Unity programme was therefore essentially a compromise designed to satisfy the different sectors within the coalition. It was a programme which represented little more than an intensification of the old industrialization policy along lines similar to those proposed by Frei. He did not aim to nationalize the entire economy but simply to take over the big factories characteristic of Chile's industry, and use state power to reorganize their production so that it could meet basic consumer needs. If Chile had to have refrigerators, let it at least produce a 'people's fridge' which could be sold cheaply to the shanty towns. If it had to have cars and trucks, let the ten competing factories assembling imported parts for the automobile giants be reduced to one, so that the vehicles could be produced at the cheapest possible price. Allende also wanted to increase the supply of agricultural goods to the towns, as well as providing a better deal for Chile's rural population, where the worst pockets of poverty in the country were to be found. His government therefore determinedly set about carrying out the agrarian reform programme which the Christian Democrats had put on the statute books, but never really implemented.

A serious attempt was made, simultaneously, to develop agro-industry in the countryside, and to develop Chile's sorely neglected potential for a fishing industry. Allende began a well-publicized personal campaign to wean his people from the belief that any prosperous person eats beef five times a week, while the gifted songwriters of his Communist and Socialist parties wrote a 'Hymn to the Whiting' to go with their 'Waltz of the Armed Forces and Carabineros'.

All these steps were entirely reasonable elements in a strategy of reorganizing Chile's manufacturing economy to meet basic needs. But the government's decision to reflate demand in the early years of Popular Unity, as a means of transferring income to the poorer sectors of the population, was more problematic. Without the structural changes which the programme promised but which would take time to implement, and with an effective investment strike on the part of business, these measures inevitably resurrected Chile's old spectre of inflation. The essential problem was that any measures to take over the commanding heights of manufacturing industry inevitably meant expropriating the families who held real power in Chile. In many cases these families also controlled one of the major newspapers; they were also almost certainly going to be badly affected by the proposals for agrarian reform. They might be offered compensation, in the form of government bonds for land in the countryside, and payment for stocks in the case of industry, but they regarded such compensation as little better than worthless paper, given the country's record on inflation. And, indeed, a programme of compensation for nationalization on this scale was bound to be inflationary.

So the powerful of Chile began to fight back with all their considerable resources, which were not only financial but also included the means of communication. The government, they said, was attacking basic property rights: no businessman, however small, would be unaffected – not even the street-corner vendor. All this despite the fact that one of Allende's first moves was to remove all restrictions on the right of street-sellers to set up booths on any corner in central Santiago. Opposition to the government on both its right and its left was now growing, feeding off a variety of conflicts which the government could not hope to solve to everyone's satisfaction. And as inflation accelerated, and the potential for social conflict increased, it became increasingly difficult to paper over all the cracks in the fabric of society. Meanwhile, at the international level, Allende's government had been in deep trouble from the moment it took power. The very existence of a self-confessed Marxist government in Chile was a stimulus to American attempts to destabilize it. The fact that, far from being a one-party state, the new administration was a five-party coalition, trying very hard to reach a negotiated agreement with its 'democratic' but reform-minded Christian Democrat opposition, was a question of detail that hardly seemed to matter. CIA funds were sent to support opposition to the government as soon as the election was over, and plans were set in motion to cut off US credits for imported goods and the support for international loans.

Allende's own position on Chile's international economic links was also tougher than that of President Frei. This reflected in part the growing awareness among Third World governments as a whole that the balance of power in the existing world economy favoured the developed countries and the corporations that operated from them. Allende adopted stringent controls on foreign investment and nationalized the copper companies, in a move which had the unanimous support of Congress and was, at the time, immensely popular in the nation as a whole. As a consequence of this tougher line, Chile faced a near total collapse of foreign investment. More serious still, it faced a drying up of US credits for spare parts to its existing industrial machinery. The government had some success in replacing US credits with credits from Western Europe and the Socialist bloc, but these were not immediately useful for replacing the bits and pieces which had broken down on its American-made equipment.

By 1973 only the rate of unemployment – down to a historic low of 3.4 per cent – was favouring the government. There were persistent shortages even in basic consumer goods, and Chilean housewives were faced with long queues at the shops. Inflation was hovering around 300 per cent, and real wages were falling, in spite of the government's attempts to maintain popular buying power. There was an increasingly menacing pattern of politically motivated strikes, involving doctors, businessmen, and transport workers, among others, along with miners from Chile's second largest copper mine. Sectarian divisions were rife throughout the labour movement, although the left could still claim majority support. None the less, in the context of a collapsing economy, the country was polarizing into two bitterly opposed camps. A week before the coup of September 1973 a demonstration in Santiago involving nearly a million people called for 'No to Civil War'. It failed to stop the inevitable coup, or even to moderate its character as the bloodiest military intervention in Chile's history.

Against a background of repression, torture and bloodshed, and in the wake of the nine years of upheaval from 1964 to 1973, the

Chilean business community set about searching for ideas which would explain what had happened to them, and offer an alternative model of development which would ensure that it never happened again. The best set of ideas available seemed to be those developed at the University of Chicago, which, coincidentally, had been giving Chile's élite economists their postgraduate training since the early 1950s. Here Milton Friedman and, more importantly, Friedrich Hayek, had begun to develop a drastic critique of the whole idea of a welfare state and state involvement in the economy generally. It was argued that such involvement was bound to open the door to socialism and the totalitarian state. To the Chilean business community in early 1974 that proposition seemed evidently true. Hayek's solution was to return to complete dependence on the operations of the free market; it was no business of the State to manage industries or to try to protect employment in them when they were failing. Old industries were failing because the consumers no longer wanted to buy their products. It was better to let capitalist entrepreneurs operate as freely as possible, to establish *new* industries in line with consumer demand. Hayek also argued that trade unions were a positive hindrance to this kind of free development, establishing monopoly powers of the labour market in existing industries, which tended to drive employment down because employers would prefer to use machines to men. Unions were also one of the key forces behind the State's involvement in the economy, especially good at mobilizing political pressure on democratic governments. Hayek asserted that changes in the old model should be introduced quickly, and backed by a determined government commitment to see them through. The expectations of businessmen and workers alike would have to be changed through a short sharp shock, plunging them in the cold air of the real economic world. The immediate costs of adjustment would be high. But prolonging adjustment would only make the process a long drawn out agony, and would give its opponents a much better chance to bring it to a halt, on the grounds that its social costs outweighed its benefits.

So in 1975, supporters of the free market model within the government won President Pinochet's consent for a 'Shock'. They pointed out that oil prices had risen and that the government's revenues to cover this round of worldwide inflation were totally inadequate. They also argued that Chilean wages would have to be reduced by a third to bring them into line with world levels, and that the Chilean economy had to learn to live in the real world. State protection of entrepreneurs only fostered the development of Marxist totalitarianism. The argument appealed to a President committed to a 'total war' against Marxism. The 'Shock' in Chile sent unemployment figures soaring. From a low of under 4 per cent under the Allende government, they now reached levels of over 20 per cent. The real value of statutory minimum wages collapsed. Signs of infant malnutrition began to appear in the shanty towns, and the Chilean Catholic Church, in its Bishops' Conference, began to show signs of real concern: some forms of anti-Marxism, they said, were clearly worse than Marxism.

The government responded, not by abandoning the basic economic strategy, but by setting up programmes to provide food supplements to children in the shanty towns – supplements doctored to taste so strange that adults who were themselves often living on flour and water would not be willing to eat them. This strategy worked: Chile's problems with infant malnutrition, unlike those of Brazil, began to recede. Opposition from other quarters was dealt with more crudely. Those elements among the military, notably in the air force, who would have liked the State to maintain its traditional commitment to welfare, were edged out of power. An air force minister at the Department of Labour was rudely dismissed, and the way was prepared for the departure two years later of the then air force commander, who was a member of the Junta. General Leigh took seven of the most senior generals in the air force with him. Other forms of resistance were met, more simply, with an intensification of repression. 1976 was the worst year of repression since the period of 'open war' against Marxism declared at the time of the coup. The Amnesty International Report of 1977 concluded – 'During the period covered by this report, May 1976–June 1977, serious and systematic violations of human rights continued in Chile. In addition to the numerous "disappearances", torture is still a systematic practice: bodies showing signs of severe torture have been discovered in various parts of the country.'

In 1977 and 1978, however, the situation began slowly to improve, and in 1979, and even in 1980, business publications throughout the world began to talk of a Chilean miracle to match that of Brazil. Unemployment, though, was scarcely falling in line with Hayek's promises. At its lowest point, in 1981, when there was a boom in construction, it reached ten per cent; this was still higher than under any previous government and when account was taken of those employed under the government's minimum employment programme, which gave workers the equivalent of £26 ($45) a month and supplies of some basic foods such as flour, the real unemployment figure was even higher. Still, inflation was falling and Chile's national reserves were at unprecedented levels, helped by the confidence of a world banking system in the Chilean model, and its willingness to lend private entrepreneurs huge amounts of recycled Arab oil profits. The planners of the new model, like the planners of the old, were not unaware of the limitations of Chile's old economy. Strategically, they took the view that instead of maintaining an antiquated industry which none of Chile's consumers seemed to like, it should buy its products openly on the world market, securing the best and cheapest available. Imports would have to be paid for, of course, and the planners' intention was to develop those industries in which Chile had the natural resources to do well on world markets. Chile, they thought, should sell its fruits and wine to the rest of the world – hence the Chilean apples and onions so often seen in British shops. It should use its copper and its timber to make products which could also be sold abroad, and the encouragement of other non-traditional exports would reduce dependence on copper.

Such a strategy offered even less promise than the old one of providing the employment which would help the Chilean poor. The encouragement of modern farming methods reduced rather than expanded the jobs available in the agricultural sector. Again, timber manufacture and the production of copper goods did not require limitless supplies of manpower, and in any case they called for mainly unskilled labour on low wage rates. The logical implication of the planners' model was that vast parts of Chile's existing industry would have to go – textiles, electronics, automobiles, shoes, everywhere in fact where the world market could produce better and cheaper products using somebody else's hands. The collapse of industry in Chile which began with the 'Shock', in 1975–6, and slowed down over the boom years of 1979–81, accelerated rapidly once the world depression hit Chile with full force, in 1982. During that year world prices for primary products of all kinds stood at the same level as they had in 1929. Everywhere in the Third World, economies, and the governments that had to oversee them, found themselves in desperate trouble. Chile faced the uncomfortable reality that most of the wealth pouring into the country from international sources had been squandered on speculative construction of houses and offices for the rich or, worse, on the import of foreign-made goods. Real investment in the economy, without the intervention of the State, remained at one of its lowest levels ever. And unemployment spurted: by the close of 1982 it stood officially at 26 per cent, but government circles were admitting real levels of over 30 per cent.

As the government faced a growing crisis it began to take actions of a kind that Hayek would never have approved of. Banks were taken over, as they had been under the Allende government; this time, however, not as part of a planned drive to restructure the economy, but simply to keep them from collapsing. The government faced a drain on its reserves and found itself fighting desperately to maintain the value of the Chilean peso. In June 1982 the government announced a 15.2 per cent devaluation of the peso. This symbolized the beginning of the end of the government's economic strategy, for the fixed peso rate had come to represent the stability and credibility of this strategy. Its abandonment was a clear admission that the strategy could not be maintained in the face of the deepening recession. Bankruptcies in the first five months of 1982 stood at 243 compared with 180 for the same period in 1981; by September the figure had reached a record 600, and at the same time unemployment had also reached record levels. In a cabinet reshuffle on 30th August 1982 a new super-minister of finance and economy, Ralf Lüders, was appointed. Lüders was brought into the cabinet as a representative of the business sector who believed that the 'magic of the marketplace' would solve all the country's problems, but in office he was forced to recognize that state intervention in some form was inevitable. Lüders turned to the IMF for assistance with the country's balance of payments problems and to secure a 'stamp of approval' to renegotiate its large debt with the private banks. But by the beginning of 1983 the dimensions of the crisis, with industrial output having fallen officially 13 per cent during 1982, were inescapable. The business magazine *Estrategia* summed up its worst fears in its first edition of the new year: 'Now it is not just specific programmes and policies which are threatened, but the free enterprise system itself.' For the economic crisis was already having political repercussions. As faith in the monetarist economics of the Chilean Junta was being questioned by broad sectors of the population facing growing hardship, so opposition to the Junta itself was becoming more vocal.

The final outcome of the Chicago-style experiment in Chile in the 1980s is far from clear. The supporters of Hayek in the present government have introduced a set of major reforms: not only in the creation of 'non-traditional exports', but also in the creation of a new legal basis for labour relations (strongly anti-union), a new pensions system, and a new relationship between central government and the municipalities. In carrying out these sweeping changes, the present government has enjoyed a major political advantage, because whatever the nature of its experiments, they have been introduced at a moment when other, more traditional, models are widely seen to have failed. A great deal of popular effort and illusion went into the Christian Democrat strategy in the 1960s, and the socialist programme of the 1970s. Committees were created in every shanty town during the Popular Unity government in an effort to turn the government's proposed reforms into a living reality on every block. Chile's heritage of a political culture, which extends downwards from its élite into every urban pocket of population, offers governments enormous resources. But mobilizing those resources has a cost, and not just for governments which may fail to meet their supporters' expectations. Concretely, the hours which Chile's poor spent organizing for their parties in the 1960s and early 1970s were hours bought at the cost of their family life, and often at the cost of an increasing physical exhaustion.

Moreover, in 1973 a war without precedent was unleashed on Chile's people, in which thousands were killed. It was totally unexpected. Chile's military may well have believed that they were in the middle of the Third World War against 'communist subversion', and had entered an era of modern warfare which necessarily involved civilians and necessarily knew no limits, but the population of Chile's shanty towns, for all the Cuban-inspired rhetoric which had flowered within them, really had no experience which might have prepared them for such an event. Nothing like it had happened previously in Chilean history since 1900 – not even the massacres of the early years of the century, when soldiers had openly shot striking miners in the northern desert. Now it was a dirty, secret war, characterized by 'disappearances' and the use of torture.

In 1982 the Christian Democrats were speaking openly of a 'Centro-Americanization' of Chilean politics, a willingness to use violence and to continue using it, which would have been totally out of keeping with the old Chilean society. And there were all sorts of indications, small pointers here and there, that the ability of Chilean workers and shanty town dwellers to organize was far from dead. This was the message in the statement of the strikers in the textile factories surrounding Santiago: 'We know that by going on strike we can make absolutely no kind of economic gain, but in the face of the treatment we are getting, we feel that a gesture of protest has to be made. It is a question of dignity.' It can also be seen in the ability of other workers, in a ceramics factory in the old textile town of Penco outside Concepción, to organize in 1981 a local conference of the unemployed, to consider the question of unemployment, though half their own original work force had gone. There is the re-emergence of a movement of protest through folk clubs in the same period.

In 1983, from May to September, the opposition groupings organized 'protests' – popular demonstrations intended to show the depth of feeling against the regime, but without provoking military violence. Parents did not send their children to school, there was a widespread refusal to use public transport, and at 8 p.m. many people started to bang saucepans – an expression of discontent first used by the right against the Allende government. By the end of that year these protests had transformed the political scene. The pro-Pinochet forces were in disarray, divided between hard- and soft-liners, trying to negotiate with the more moderate political opposition, yet hampered by Pinochet's personal insistence on adhering to the fixed schedule for return to democracy, which is designed to keep him in power until at least the end of the decade.

Much of the opposition to the repressive policies and practices of the Pinochet regime has been located within the Roman Catholic Church, and more particularly in the archdiocese of Santiago, where, since the 1973 coup, Cardinal Raúl Silva Henriquez and many of his priests and people have been engaged in a heroic struggle on behalf of human rights. In the country as a whole there are about nine million Catholics, constituting some 82 per cent of the total population. These are served by just over 2,000 priests, of whom two thirds are members of religious orders, and they are organized in five archdioceses, 17 dioceses and two apostolic vicarates. Mass attendance is however low, averaging no more than 15 per cent attending weekly, and over 20 per cent who attend rarely or never. Weekly attendance at Mass has declined by over 40 per cent since the 1960s, and in Santiago and other urban areas it is down to 12 per cent.

During the late 1950s the leadership of the Catholic Church became aware of the serious decline in Mass attendance and initiated a number of measures which not only placed the Church in Chile in the forefront of the renewal of the Catholic Church as a whole, but also helped to equip it for the struggles of the 1970s and 1980s. A National Pastoral Council was convened in 1961, long before such councils had become commonplace in the wake of Vatican II, and in the following year a national plan was announced. This included study of the liturgy and the need for liturgical reform, pastoral reorganization to meet the needs of a rapidly changing society, especially the growth of urban areas, and the mobilizing of the laity as well as the clergy for the work of the apostolate. One of the fruits of this mobilization is now to be seen in the archdiocese of Santiago which has no fewer than 30,000 lay catechists. Steps were also taken to secure the greater involvement of the women's religious orders in the pastoral work of the dioceses. Previously the nuns, of whom there are about 5,000 today, had confined their work mainly to schools, clinics and homes for the elderly, but now they are specially concerned with the leadership of small groups and with evangelism.

In Cardinal Raúl Silva Henríquez, Chile has one of Latin America's most able and courageous Catholic leaders. Born in 1907, the sixteenth of nineteen children, his mother was Chilean and his father came from an old Portuguese family. After attending the Christian Brothers school, he qualified as a lawyer, but entered the Salesian noviciate in 1930 and, after further study in Turin, was ordained to the priesthood in 1938. Returning to Chile, he became director of a school, and then of a theological seminary in Santiago in 1951. During this time he also edited the theological journal *Rumbos* and founded the Santiago branch of Caritas International. In 1959 he became Bishop of Valparaiso, where he was concerned primarily with evangelism and social work, but after only two years he was translated to the archbishopric of Santiago, and in 1962 was appointed a cardinal by Pope John XXIII. Since then he has been in the thick of the battle to maintain the integrity of the Church's witness in a changing and often violent society. Cardinal Silva is essentially 'a man of the middle'. He has always been opposed to Marxism and was critical of what he believed to be the partisan politics of Christians for Socialism. Yet he has been even more critical of the Pinochet government and, soon after the coup, was singled out by the Junta for a smear campaign in which his concern for human rights was described as 'unpatriotic' and his general position that of a fellow traveller. After further criticism of him in a right-wing Catholic book, *The Church of Silence*, he responded, 'It's another feather in my cap. I consider it a sign that I am in line with the Gospel that they attack me.' His integrity and unwillingness to attach himself to either left or right has, however, enhanced his prestige in Chile, and indeed throughout Latin America. During the closing months of the Allende government he was the chief intermediary between the Christian Democrats and the ruling socialists, and though he failed to prevent the coup his reputation was, and remains, untarnished.

During 1966 synods were held in all the dioceses – the first in the world since Vatican II. In the archdiocese of Santiago over 500 gathered for the synod, having been elected mainly at grassroots level, and the result was a new emphasis on evangelism and church involvement in society as a whole. At this time special concern was being expressed about the serious decline in church attendance of young people, especially in urban areas, and the facts about this and other church matters were disclosed in a number of socio-religious surveys carried out at a professional level. Today work of this kind, and analysis of its results, continues at the Centro Bellarmino, run by the Jesuits, and at several other centres. Following the first synods, the new concern for social and economic problems, as well as evangelism, began to be expressed in the pastoral letters of the bishops. And the bishops also began to act in the economic sphere. The Bishop of Talca, Monsignor Larraín, the inspirer and first president of the Latin American Episcopal Conference (CELAM), distributed the church-owned land in his diocese to the peasants who lived and worked on it – an example soon followed by the other Chilean bishops, and in other parts of Latin America.

In 1971 eighty Catholic priests came together to organize a Christians for Socialism movement – yet another pioneering effort by Chile – and a year later the first Latin American meeting of this movement was held in Santiago. By this time the movement had become ecumenical and there were 40 Protestant pastors among the 400 clergy and laity who met together. Although it was always a minority movement, Christians for Socialism made a considerable impact in Chile, especially during the Popular Unity period. Greatly influenced by liberation theology, it brought together the Christian and political commitment of its members, many of whom joined left-wing parties. Seventy-eight per cent of the Catholic priests are said to have supported the election of Popular Unity. This political activity sometimes brought them into conflict with certain of the bishops and with Christian Democrats, but they always maintained that their aim was not to set up a rival or parallel church: rather was it to unify the churches in the struggle against a politico-economic system which had caused extreme poverty and underdevelopment. During the presidency of Salvador Allende surveys indicated that over half the priests in Chile believed that the attitude of Christians to Marxists should be one of 'friendly collaboration'. Relations between the bishops and the Allende government were cordial from 1970 until 1972, and Cardinal Silva was present at the installation of the government, as well as at the May Day celebrations in 1971 and 1972. But at the beginning of 1973 the bishops started to distance themselves from the government. Attitudes in the Church, reflecting Chilean society as a whole, became increasingly polarized, with some priests and nuns becoming involved in resistance to the aggression and sabotage of the extreme right, while others sought to turn people against the fragmenting and ever more desperate Popular Unity government. The military coup itself was supported by ten of the bishops, and only two or three bishops declared themselves against it. The Cardinal had attempted to mediate, and ten other bishops appeared to be neutral, explaining that the Church should not become

directly involved in political matters. The coup brought a swift end
to the activities of the Christians for Socialism movement, whose
members were persecuted by the new regime and driven to clandestine work with grassroots Christian communities, where many
of them remain.

Most Chileans believed that the emergency situation created by
the 1973 coup would be no more than a transitory phase and that
the military regime would not stay in power once stability was
restored. Indeed the Christian Democrats hoped to be the main
beneficiaries of the coup. They could not have been more wrong.
Pinochet and his colleagues consolidated their position by means of
savage measures of repression against all their opponents, not least
those in the churches. The sorry story of arrest, imprisonment,
torture, exile, execution and 'disappearance' is not yet ended. The
churches united in their response to the emergency and set up an
ecumenical Peace Committee. The Methodist, Lutheran, Orthodox
and Pentecostal churches, as well as the Jews, participated with the
Catholics, and a Lutheran bishop, Helmut Frenz, became the
director. This committee was the only place to which the victims of
repression could turn for help. Legal and humanitarian assistance
was provided, not only for the victims and families of those
arrested, imprisoned and killed, but also for the massive number
dismissed from their work for political, and subsequently economic,
reasons. By 1975 the committee had 24 offices functioning
throughout the country, 124 workshops and co-operatives for the
unemployed had been started in the shanty towns and rural areas,
35,000 poor children were being fed in dining rooms, and 40,000
people had been given legal and social aid. It was in this year that
General Pinochet more or less ordered the Cardinal to close the
committee, accusing it of harbouring 'Marxist subversives'. Personnel from the committee were harassed and arrested; Bishop
Frenz was refused re-entry to the country at the end of a visit
abroad.

The Catholic Church withdrew from the Peace Committee, but
the Cardinal moved quickly to set up the *Vicaría de Solidaridad*
(Vicarate of Solidarity) which took over much of the Peace Committee's work and is still in existence. The tone of its periodical
Solidarity, which is sent all over the world, has tended to vary
according to the degree of tension in Church-State relations, but in

general it has presented a consistently critical view of government policies, denouncing not only torture and arbitrary arrest but also the doctrinaire monetarist policies of the government, which even in 1977 and 1978, when the economic model was supposedly successful, pushed millions of Chileans below subsistence level and into the church-organized soup kitchens, financed by international aid agencies.

The Catholic Church also has its own mini-university in the form of a private institution called the Academy of Christian Humanism, headed by the Cardinal. The Catholic University itself, which had been a prestigious academic centre in Latin America, was taken over by the military after the coup and, although there is slightly greater freedom for teaching and research than in the other universities, the Chilean Church no longer has direct control over the running of the university. The new Academy has become an umbrella organization for more critical research and a limited amount of teaching, especially in the social sciences, which have been almost completely eliminated from the universities' curricula. It also publishes its own magazine, *Análisis*, which prints critical analyses of different aspects of the regime's policies and the state of the opposition. This magazine and the Jesuit magazine *Mensaje* are practically the only ones in Chile today which are critical of the regime and still allowed to circulate.

Here it is important to emphasize that the archdiocese of Santiago is not typical of the Chilean Catholic Church as a whole. The majority of the bishops are more conservative and have found it harder to champion human rights, especially when the victims of repression are Marxists. The imminent retirement of Cardinal Silva leaves a question mark over the future of the Church, and already attempts are being made to move the *Vicaría de Solidaridad* away from some of its more controversial activities to programmes of a more pastoral and ecclesiastical character. The work was drastically reduced in 1981, and the hierarchy is now attempting to heal the breach between Church and State by means of a new critical association with the regime. This has provoked a strong reaction from a few of the bishops, and from substantial numbers of priests and members of the Christian communities who believe that such an association would be tantamount to the legitimization o a regime whose actions are in direct contradiction to Christian beliefs and values. Thus the Catholic Church in Chile, whose first priest arrived from Spain in 1541 and whose first diocese (Santiago) was established in 1561, finds itself in a critical situation – part of a society with such disparate interests and concerns as cannot be reconciled. Officially, Church and State have been separated since 1925, but the Catholic Church remains an important moral and political force, and its actions are certain to have an important influence on the way Chile moves during the remaining years of the twentieth century.

The first Protestant missionary, an agent of the British and Foreign Bible Society, came to Chile in 1821 and established a number of schools. He was followed, in 1845, by a missionary from the Presbyterian Church in the USA, and a year later German immigrants brought Lutheranism with them. The Lutheran Church, which now has about 25,000 members, is still primarily German. Methodism came from America in 1877, and grew rapidly between 1893 and 1907; but then came a split, from which it has never really recovered. One of its ministers claimed to have been baptized in the Holy Spirit and adopted certain Pentecostal practices. He was thereupon expelled from the Methodist Church and in 1909 started the Methodist Pentecostal Church (IMP), which retained most of the Methodist disciplines, including infant baptism. A schism in 1933 led to the formation of the Evangelical Pentecostal Church (IEP), and in recent years the growth of the two churches has been phenomenal. Each now has upwards of 400,000 members and adherents, and the Jotabeche Pentecostal Church (IMP) in Santiago, with its 80,000 members, is the largest Evangelical congregation in the world. This growth has taken place without external support of any kind, and it is believed that the total strength of the various indigenous Pentecostal churches is in the region of 1.8 million, or 16.5 per cent of Chile's population. A large number of those who attend these churches are in fact described on government censuses as Catholics, having presumably lapsed from the church of their birth, or retaining only tenuous connections with it. About 250,000 people are believed to syncretize a folk Catholicism with various traditional religions, e.g. animism and ancestor worship.

The earlier emphasis on supernatural experience has tended to decrease in many of the Pentecostal groups, though there is still a widespread concern about prayer for the miraculous recovery of the sick (understandable when medical care is either not available or too costly for many), and a high proportion of those joining the Pentecostal churches owe their first interest to some case of healing in answer to prayer. Visions, dreams and revelations (not always distinguishable) also tend to occupy the minds of many who find serious Bible study and hard thinking less congenial. There are some signs of worship patterns becoming set and stylized, but generally there is still an atmosphere of hearty and enthusiastic participation, lively expectancy, warmth and fellow feeling among members, and a real concern to bring others to faith in Christ. ('Chile for Christ' has long been a watchword among them, and in some cases, the words 'in this generation' are added.) Most Pentecostal churches have services most nights of the week, to which the majority of members usually come; in many cases they are preceded by open-air preaching, with columns of guitar-accompanied hymn singers going from street corner to corner, gradually rounding up extra people, or at least creating a public awareness of their presence. This very full programme of activities is shared between all the members. Once converted, they are expected to be active, and will be set to work initially in simple tasks, perhaps that of the doorkeeper, then giving testimony at a street corner meeting, gradually progressing to leading worship, preaching, taking on leadership responsibilities, right up to the highest positions in the denomination. This means that anyone who proves to be a faithful, zealous Christian need not feel limited by previous lack of educational opportunities. The common background produces a leadership which understands the members; and members who feel understood and represented by their leaders. The Pentecostal phrase for this process of leadership preparation is 'training on the streets' and, although it has many advantages, the level of Bible and theological knowledge among leaders is not high – in fact, among members it is often very low. Everyone is sure that the Bible is the Word of God, and carries his Bible to show it – but studying it closely is not usually encouraged, while study of anything else is often positively discouraged.

The usual style of Pentecostal leadership is very authoritarian – in many churches, permission needs to be requested from the pastor even to visit another church. Pentecostal groups have remained fairly closed to outside attempts to help with Bible teaching and training, but some help has been given through projects using the approach of Theological Education by Extension (TEE), run by the Comunidad Teológica Evangélica de Chile, Seminario por Extensión Anglicano (SEAN) and possibly others. Along with big demands on members' time and money (tithing is widely required), there are very clear moral requirements for members in good standing. Apart from obvious changes like total avoidance of alcohol (very necessary in view of the widespread drink abuse in the circles from which converts come), tobacco and 'worldly amusements', there is often a very clear break with previous patterns of dishonesty, laziness, irresponsibility, etc., and growth in positive virtues like good neighbourliness and practical care for others. Most Pentecostals have followed a fairly rigid policy of keeping out of politics, and if challenged quote various examples of others who, starting from a Christian basis, became involved in politics (whether from selfish or good motives), and became totally lost to Christianity. The fact that the vast majority live in shanty towns might have been expected to make them lean to the left politically; in fact the largest single congregation (Jotabeche, the Methodist Pentecostal 'cathedral' in Santiago) has been glad to welcome President Pinochet for the annual Independence Day celebrations (something that previously only ever happened in the Roman Catholic Cathedral) – a liaison which both parties seem glad to use for the good impression it can make on the general public.

The non-Pentecostal Protestants number something under a quarter of a million, or about two per cent of the population. They include Baptists, whose origins can be traced to German immigrants in the latter part of the nineteenth century and to American Southern Baptists who came in 1917. There have been several Baptist schisms, but this church has not been much affected by Pentecostalism and is growing at the rate of about five per cent a year. The Seventh Day Adventists came in 1890 and, with 30,000 members, constitute the largest of the non-Pentecostal Protestant churches. There are just under 4,000 Anglicans.

In recent years the Protestant churches have formed social institutions, generally on ecumenical lines. Two of the most significant today are Social Assistance Foundation of the Christian

Churches (FASIC) and Evangelist Church Aid (ACE). FASIC was set up in 1976 and defines itself as an ecumenical institution committed to the defence of human rights in a Christian perspective of liberation. Its primary concern has been for the most underprivileged sectors of society and the victims of the repression. It has organized programmes of legal aid and social assistance for political prisoners and their families, and co-ordinated the special prisoner release scheme agreed by the government in decree law 504. This allows sentenced political prisoners to commute their sentence to exile, provided another country is willing to receive them. FASIC has also collaborated with the United Nations High Commission for Refugees (UNHCR) in arranging reunions for the families of refugees and, more recently, in assisting those refugees who have decided to return to Chile and are legally allowed to return but suffer considerable difficulties in re-adapting and finding employment. One of the most outstanding achievements of FASIC is its psychiatric and medical work, which has provided care for ex-prisoners, victims of torture, their families and those who have developed psychological problems as a result of extreme social and economic hardship and tension. This experience has been systematically recorded and is providing invaluable material for other Latin American countries faced with similar or worse needs.

ACE was founded by the Pentecostal and Conservative Evangelical churches in 1966, and was joined by the Methodists, Baptists and Anglicans, with the aim of promoting social commitment of Christians in the community. The evangelical churches in Chile are firmly located in the urban and rural poor communities. After the coup ACE was also involved in emergency assistance but soon shifted its emphasis back to supporting longer-term organizational activities carried out by autonomous groups such as youth, women, housing and health committees. They provide social and technical support to projects in different parts of the country, in rural and urban areas. Their services are defined in terms of solidarity and aim to promote self-help and consciousness-raising related to the causes of oppression. ACE has developed important technical and educational programmes with peasants, the Mapuche, trade unions and in the shanty towns. It still attempts to incorporate the communities of the member churches into its work at the grassroots level and to promote collective reflection and action on the problems of the community.

The Protestants are, however, as sharply divided as the Catholics in their attitude to the Pinochet regime. On 23rd August 1974, the Lutheran bishops and Methodist bishop joined Cardinal Silva Henriquez and the Chief Rabbi (there are about 10,000 Jews) in sending a letter to General Pinochet pleading for a policy that would bring reconciliation and peace. On 19th December of the same year representatives of 32 evangelical churches responded by taking a full page in the magazine *El Mercurio* in which they declared their support for the Junta. There is evidence that this statement was in fact compiled by a government official. In 1975 the new Jotabeche Pentecostal Church in Santiago was opened by none other than General Pinochet. The division within the Christian camp has greatly exercised one of Chile's leading theologians, Father Ronaldo Muñoz, and is discussed in his major book *Nueva Conciencia de la Iglesia en America Latina*. Father Muñoz, who is a member of the Picpus Order, has studied and taught in Europe, and is now working in the theological faculty of the Catholic University of Chile in Santiago. His book consists of an examination of about 300 documents, written by various groups and individuals in Latin America between 1965 and 1970. These documents reveal what Father Muñoz describes as a 'new awareness' among certain Christians, particularly concerning society and its structures. The basic polarization in Latin America, he concludes, is not between the Church on the one hand and society on the other, but between those Christians who have the 'new awareness' and those, mainly in the established church, who have not.

Faced by the prospect of the present military dictatorship continuing in power until the end of the twentieth century, Christians in Chile, whose 'new awareness' has driven them to make a clear choice to work with and for the poor and the exploited, are now being driven to decide whether violence may be the only possible way to bring about change. Further polarization around this particular point seems inevitable.

Chapter 7

Paraguay

Paraguay claims a particular distinction in Latin America. Its President, General Alfredo Stroessner, is the longest surviving military dictator in the continent. During the first two decades of his rule, Paraguay underwent little economic development and was characterized by stagnation, isolation and backwardness. In the 1970s the country entered a period of economic boom due primarily to the joint construction with Brazil of the largest hydro-electric project in the world, at Itaipú on the River Paraná. But the completion of the dam in 1982 coincided with the deepening of the world recession, and Paraguay now faces renewed economic crisis. Despite these shifts in Paraguay's development and the socio-economic changes they have brought with them, Stroessner has so far managed to hold on to the reins of power. His regime has rested on an alliance between the Colorado Party and the military, and is characterized by widespread corruption and systematic repression, swiftly invoked whenever the opposition shows any sign of confidence. Paraguay is one of the most politically stable countries in Latin America; it is also one of the most oppressive.

This land-locked country, wedged between Argentina and Brazil in the heart of South America, is nearly twice the size of Britain, but has a population of only three million. The country is divided into two distinct topographical regions: the North-West Chaco, a dry scrubland covering 60 per cent of the territory; and the fertile, semi-tropical lowlands of the South-East, where 95 per cent of the population live. Only 35 per cent of the population live in urban areas, and the capital, Asunción, has a population of 750,000. The people are one of the most homogeneous in Latin America; the bulk of the population being *mestizo* (a mixture of Indian and Spanish blood), and the pure Indian population, which numbers about 100,000, declining. Guaraní, the national language, predominates over Spanish in daily usage.

The geographical position of Paraguay has played a key role in the formation of Paraguayan society. Since independence from Spain in 1811, the territorial integrity of the country has been difficult to secure against the incursions and aspirations of Paraguay's neighbours, and the country has been embroiled in two national wars against invading armies. This has had the perverse effect of conferring a high status on the military caste because of their role – both real and mythologized – in the defence of Paraguay's national sovereignty. Military history is the most researched and written about subject in the country.

The distance between Paraguay and the maritime trade routes linking South America with Europe and the United States has also, until fairly recently, been a considerable constraint upon the development of an export economy and has tended to isolate Paraguay from international trade. The Spanish colonizers, up to 1811, did not develop agricultural plantations on a significant scale, as they had elsewhere in Latin America, because of the transport difficulties and the cost of moving Paraguayan exports to foreign markets. In fact Paraguay was of little strategic economic interest to the Spaniards because of the absence of precious metals and the country's isolation. Asunción was founded in 1573 as an entrepot depot, a watering hole on the Peru-Argentina overland trade route. Similarly, during the waves of migration from Europe to the Americas in the nineteenth century, few migrants reached Paraguay. The 1865–70 war against the combined armies of Brazil, Argentina and Uruguay destroyed Paraguay's attempts at independent, self-sufficient development. Subsequently, the Colorado governments of the 1880s began to sell the lands held by the State – about 90 per cent of the territory at the time – to foreign immigrants, who were to be the backbone of Paraguay's economic recovery. But, in order to compete with the land sales occurring at the same time in Brazil and Argentina, the government was obliged to sell land at rock bottom prices. Instead of encouraging the foundation of a class of immigrant farmers of export crops, the land was bought up in huge tracts by Anglo-Argentinian logging and cattle companies, and by rich families.

A great deal of the land was in fact to lie idle for decades, but the Anglo-Argentinian companies exported wood, wood extracts (in particular tannin) and meat products as part of Britain's expanding commercial empire in Latin America. Their labour forces, numbering up to 20,000, were treated like slaves and controlled by armed company militias in the remote areas of the interior. And, although the companies made vast fortunes, the profits were not invested in Paraguay, but sent home. Thus, as these companies integrated Paraguay more closely into the international economy, the country began to display a number of the classic symptoms of underdevelopment: an extremely unequal system of land tenure which compelled the poor peasant majority to scratch a living on tiny plots; the concentration of wealth in the hands of foreign companies and a small Paraguayan landed and business élite; and a repressive state and political system dedicated to maintaining the status quo.

This *laissez-faire* economy, dominated by foreign companies and established in the post-war period, experienced a process of erratic growth until the 1930s and the onset of the world recession. After this, however, the economy was always in a simmering crisis, boiling over every so often, until the 1960s. Between the end of the Second World War and 1960 the growth rate was a meagre one per cent a year, and the stagnation of the economy appears to be the factor behind the acute political instability of the period, which witnessed a considerable number of coups and counter-coups, and a civil war in 1947.

During the 1960s the military-Colorado Party government of General Stroessner promoted the export of beef at the cost of domestic consumption as a means of sustaining the economy. Yet the boom in meat exports did little more than compensate for the decline in Paraguay's other traditional exports: tannin, yerba maté – a bitter green tea – and wood. The modest economic growth recorded over the period is largely explained by the expansion of government infrastructural works financed by international aid agencies. The economy was completely open to foreign investors, but foreign investment was largely confined to a number of international banks which set up in Asunción to manage the aid flows and finance the growing smuggling trade. The smuggling was in fact controlled by the military and the Colorado Party leadership, and involved whisky, cigarettes, narcotics and all manner of consumer goods.

From 1973 until 1980, however, the economy experienced a

period of spectacular growth. The combination of a rise in the international prices of a range of agricultural products in 1973/4, leading to a boom in Paraguay's cotton and soya bean exports, and the starting of the joint Paraguay-Brazil hydro-electric dam project, Itaipú, had a dramatic effect upon Paraguay's economy. Exports doubled between 1973 and 1977, and during the period 1977 to 1980 the economy as a whole experienced the highest rates of growth in Latin America, averaging nine per cent a year in real terms. Foreign capital flooded into Paraguay's agricultural and civil engineering sectors, and between 1974 and 1979 represented over 40 per cent of total private investment in the economy. About 60 per cent of this investment was concentrated in the four departments which together constitute the country's expanding agricultural frontier in the Eastern Border Region: Alto Paraná, Amambay, Itapúa and Canendiyu. The Itaipu Binational Entity, the joint Paraguayan-Brazilian authority established to administer the dam's construction and its future electricity flows, invested billions of dollars in Paraguay, and at the same time many multinational banks increased their presence in Asunción, attracted by the opportunities for high profits from financing the increased trade and investment flows.

Although the government pays lip service to the idea of development planning, the actual economic policy it has pursued throughout these years is essentially *laissez-faire* in orientation, and has much in common with the 'monetarist' experiments pursued elsewhere in South America in the 1970s. Paraguay's Planning Secretariat, for instance, is restricted to producing 'indicative' plans which merely attempt to indicate the likely evolution of the economy. 'Development' is seen as synonymous with private sector economic growth based on the free play of domestic and international market forces. With the exception of a number of state-owned corporations, the role of the State within this development model is essentially a passive one, limited to providing infrastructure, such as roads and other services which the private sector cannot provide because of their large scale or the limited opportunities they provide for making profit. To the extent that the State has an active role in the economy, it is largely confined to directing resources to the agro-export sector and maintaining the conditions in which foreign capital can be attracted to Paraguay.

The pursuit of this economic model produced extremely impressive results during the last decade – at least at the level of broad macro-economic indicators such as growth of Gross Domestic Product, the ratio of investment to GDP, the increased magnitude of trade flows and so on – but the benefits of the economic growth have been meagre for the majority of the population.

The *laissez-faire* approach of the government in matters of economic policy has been accompanied by a *laissez-faire* approach to social and welfare services, relying upon private sector economic growth and private institutions to meet basic social needs. Despite the fact that Gross Domestic Product doubled between 1973 and 1980, at the end of that decade the government was spending only US $ 2 per head per year on health services, and US $ 11 per head on education – about the same level as in 1972. There is only one doctor for every 2,150 inhabitants and the proportion of the population with access to safe water has grown only marginally, currently standing at around 15 per cent. The level and distribution of private income has remained the key determinant of the benefits of the economic model for Paraguay's working class and peasantry, and looking ahead this leaves little room for optimism. Over the period 1969 to 1979, real wages paid in Paraguay's small industrial sector fell by some 15 per cent, while non-wage income – which includes profits, independent producers and government – rose by more than double, or 104 per cent. At national level the top 20 per cent of the population were receiving at the close of the last decade 62 per cent of national income, while the bottom 20 per cent received just four per cent.

Government control of the trade union movement ensured that urban workers did not benefit substantially during the period of growth in the 1970s. Wage increases were consistently kept behind the rate of inflation and in this way income was directed away from the working class and towards Paraguay's middle classes and economic élite. The peasantry also faced the structural obstacles which have always prevented them from reaping benefits from any rise in world market prices for Paraguay's agricultural exports, such as occurred in the 1970s. They had to accept disadvantageous terms of trade between the agricultural products they sell in the market and the goods they have to buy to maintain production, and for family consumption. This unequal trade between the rural and urban areas is the principal mechanism for extracting an economic surplus from rural producers and concentrating it in the hands of the urban élite.

This is clearly illustrated by the case of cotton. In Paraguay about 60 per cent of cotton output is accounted for by small peasant producers, and cotton is the principal crop for around 65,000 peasant families. The overwhelming bulk of Paraguay's cotton harvest is exported and its price is therefore subject to often wild fluctuations in the international cotton market. Each year the government fixes a reference price for the domestic buying and selling of raw cotton, a price which is based upon the recommendation of the National Cotton Council – on which the peasants are not represented. The effect of this Council's policies has been to require the cotton producer to cultivate increasing quantities of cotton simply to maintain a constant level of income. If the peasant were actually in a position to increase output and productivity then his income levels could be maintained and even increased. But over 90 per cent of those who grow cotton for their livelihood have to mortgage their future harvest to middlemen in return for advances of production materials (tools and seeds, etc.) and means of subsistence. At the end of the day, the income of the peasant producer of cotton is so small that it does not allow him to accumulate enough resources to finance the production of the next crop.

The rates of interest demanded by intermediaries are very high, and the whole system is reinforced by national and international firms which export cotton and provide interest-free loans to intermediaries to ensure sufficient deliveries of the raw cotton. Only four per cent of all cotton sales in the domestic market in any one season are conducted by rural co-operatives; and no less than three quarters of this four per cent is accounted for by two Mennonite colonies and one Japanese colony. The principal beneficiaries of this economic chain, which links the small Paraguayan peasant and the cotton houses of Liverpool and elsewhere, are the exporters, the cotton processors, the intermediaries and the transnational banks. Moreover, the complex system of peasant exploitation is not confined to peasant producers of cotton, but operates in a similar fashion for all crops grown by the Paraguayan peasantry for sale in national and international markets. So while it is true that peasant producers of cash crops for international markets received windfall gains from the dramatic rise in international prices in the early 1970s, these gains have been eroded in recent years as the value of their crops has declined in relation to the cost of production and subsistence.

The overwhelming bulk of Paraguay's population are peasants, but they are not all cash crop farmers. There still exist large pockets of subsistence and semi-subsistence peasants in the countryside and, together with peasant producers of cash crops, they are facing growing problems of access to land. Paraguay, in fact, has enormous potential for developing agricultural production, with one of the highest ratios of arable land *per capita* in the world. Yet about one million Paraguayans live outside their own country, largely as a result of the grossly inequitable system of land tenure. Official statistics published in 1956 indicated that 185 owners held 53 per cent of the country's total land area. The agricultural census of 1981 showed that 77.2 per cent of Paraguay's land area was concentrated in a mere 0.8 per cent of total landholdings.

In the early 1960s, and in response to the escalating land conflicts between the *minifundistas* and the cattle barons of the Central Zone, the Paraguayan government initiated a colonization programme which involved resettling peasants from the Central Zone in the Eastern Border Region (EBR). Until recently the land in this area was owned by half a dozen semi-feudal landowners. The Institute of Rural Welfare in charge of the operation carried out one of the most inexpensive colonization schemes in the history of Latin American land reform, which left thousands of peasant families clearing land in Paraguay's eastern forests with rudimentary tools, no credit facilities and no social services.

While the resettled peasants were struggling to survive, Brazilian immigrants, attracted by the availability of cheap virgin land, began to cross the Rio Paraná which separates the two countries. They brought their own capital, purchased land outright and thus had better access to credit. By 1980, there were an estimated 350,000 Brazilian settlers in the EBR region and these are now responsible for about 40 per cent of Paraguay's output of soya beans. Portuguese is the dominant language in the region, and the Brazilian cruzeiro the dominant currency. Large areas of the EBR are now in foreign hands, for besides the Brazilian settlers and agribusiness and land companies, transnational corporations have also availed themselves of huge estates in the region. Brooke Bond Liebig of Britain, Gulf and Western of the USA, Fiduciaria Transatlantica Alemana of Germany and Agropeco of Italy are among the foreign companies which now own up to 100,000 hectares in the zone.

One consequence of this onslaught of powerful commercial forces is that the colonization scheme initiated in the early 1960s has begun to break down. The Paraguayan colonists, holding only provisional titles to their lands, often fall into arrears with their payments and then become part of an embryonic rural proletariat in the employ of large foreign and national agricultural enterprises. A recent census of Alto Parana, for example, revealed that well over half the heads of families from seventeen Paraguayan agricultural colonies had to resort to wage labour to supplement the income from their own plots. The colonization programme has, therefore, served only to provide the expanding agricultural frontier with a mobile and cheap labour force at the service of multinational, national and Brazilian enterprises. Land sales in the region are often negotiated free of occupants who have been forcibly removed by the police and the armed forces. There is tragic irony in the fact that, while Paraguay's rural population is faced with an acute land shortage, there are thriving Brazilian, Japanese, German and Mennonite agricultural communities dotted around the interior of the country.

During the economic boom of the 1970s Paraguay's working class doubled in size, and thousands of peasant families entered the money economy as cash crop farmers. Whatever scant benefit these groups derived from the economic growth over the last decade, their economic welfare since 1980 has been severely eroded as the Paraguayan economy has slipped through recession into slump. Falling international prices for Paraguay's principal exports – soyabeans and cotton – coinciding with the ending of the construction of the Itaipú dam and the reduction of foreign investment to a trickle, has brought to a halt the dynamism of the economy's principal driving sectors: export agriculture, agribusiness, construction and civil engineering. The slump has also spread with ripple effect to other parts of the economy which depended upon the main driving sectors for their buoyancy. GDP fell from 11.4 per cent in 1980 to 8.5 per cent in 1981, and then to the catastrophic level of minus 2.5 per cent in 1982. This has led to increasing economic misery and hardship for large numbers of Paraguay's workers and peasants, whose meagre livelihoods have been destroyed by waves of redundancies and cutbacks in farm output. It has also shown that the growth model pursued during the 1970s, far from being the resounding success it looked in 1979, actually grew up in conditions that could not last and were incapable of laying the foundations for future growth. Moreover the slump has demonstrated the vulnerability of the economy to external factors over which Paraguay has no control, such as the evolution of international prices for primary commodities and the willingness of transnational corporations to invest in the country.

The golden economic future, once promised by the massive sale of hydro-electricity from Itaipú to Brazil and Argentina, has turned from a dream into a nightmare. Argentina is now suffering an acute economic crisis, and Brazil's 'economic miracle' has ended, with a consequent slump in the demand for electrical energy in the industrial heartlands around São Paulo. Paraguay, in the meantime, is faced with the huge debts it incurred in order to finance its share of the construction of Itaipú, and which were to be paid off from energy sales that have not in fact materialized. The financial state of the country is little short of disastrous, and the growing unease about the country's economic solvency and future has been reflected in a rapidly fluctuating exchange rate for the guaraní, and the rapidly declining inflows of foreign capital. Disquieting levels of inflation have been reached after a decade of relative stability, and investment as a proportion of GDP, the main determinant of future growth, has fallen dramatically. Work on the joint Paraguay-Argentina Yacyretá hydro-electric dam, which could provide new stimulus for the economy, has been suspended because the major financial partner in the scheme, Argentina, is itself in deep trouble.

The chronic situation since 1980 has clearly shifted the terms of debate between the different sectors of Paraguay's economic élite. During the boom it was a question of how best to exploit the unprecedented economic opportunities that lay before the country. Since 1980 it has been a question of how best to survive the ravages of slump, and the impact of the slump has been felt across nearly all sectors of Paraguayan society, thereby increasing disaffection with the government's management of the economic crisis. It is, however, undoubtedly Paraguay's peasant and working-class population who will bear the greatest burdens of the economic crisis. Since coming to power in a military coup in May 1954, Stroessner and his supporters have constructed a system of government designed to ensure that these groups have no independent means of defending their interests and that all opposition to the dictatorship is kept within the strictest limits. This system of government has involved the skilful fusion of the military (the iron fist) and the Colorado Party (the velvet glove). It has endured to this day with some minor cosmetic modifications such as the opening of a sham parliament in 1962. The Colorado Party has itself been transformed from a relatively small traditional party of the oligarchy into a fascist-style mass movement with a popular base among sectors of the peasantry, the working class and the economic élite. Party affiliation is compulsory for civil servants, military officials and teachers, and Paraguay's other parties allow their members in these professions to hold two party cards. The use of the Colorado Party to develop a large civilian following distinguishes the military regime in Paraguay from other Latin American military dictatorships and helps explain the political stability which has characterized Stroessner's rule.

The opposition political parties have so far displayed little capacity to challenge the military-Colorado alliance. *Acuerdo Nacional* (National Accord) is an alliance formed between the Febrerista Party, the Christian Democrats, the Authentic Radical Liberal Party and the Popular Colorado Movement (in exile in Argentina). It has been unable to mobilize a sufficient degree of public support behind its demands for the lifting of the state of siege and its vociferous opposition to growing Brazilian power and influence in Paraguay. The co-ordination of its activities has been hampered by strife within and between the four constituent parties. Moreover, only two of the parties are legally recognized by the government – the Febreristas and Authentic Radical Liberals – and they have both followed a policy of abstention from the electoral process. The Christian Democrat Party has lost support since its heyday in the early 1970s, when it was closely allied with the radical clergy and involved in the Christian Agrarian Leagues and a small sector of Christian trade unions. In June 1981 the party suffered a major setback when their charismatic leader,

Alfonso Resck, was exiled. He had made a public statement expressing his agreement with a resolution condemning the Paraguayan dictatorship adopted by the Venezuelan Senate.

Among the two legally recognized parties in the alliance, the more conservative wing of the Febrerista Party gained power within the party after the demise of the progressive interim President, Euclides Acevedo, during the November 1981 Party Convention. The Authentic Radical Liberal Party, under the leadership of the populist Domingo Laíno, is heavily persecuted; it is abstentionist and has yet to realize its full potential as a political force. The party is distinguished from the numerous other Liberal parties that have damaged their integrity and credibility by participating in the sham parliament set up in 1962. However, it remains to be seen how the party and the *Acuerdo Nacional* will cope with Laíno's expulsion from the country in December 1982; this followed the publication of his book *El General Comerciante,* which deals with ex-Nicaraguan president Somoza's life in Paraguay from the time he fled from the Sandinista victory until September 1980, when he was assassinated by an anti-tank bazooka in the streets of Paraguay's capital, Asunción.

If Paraguay's traditional opposition parties are suffering a prolonged crisis of identity, the Colorado Party is not without its own internal contradictions. Its polyclass nature and its massive expansion over the last twenty years is the source of its strength but also, potentially, of its weakness. It is the party of businessmen, landowners, the middle class, the peasants and the workers, all of whom have potentially rival interests. Pressures have been building up in the party for some time as a result of the social and economic changes of the last decade, and cracks have now begun to appear in the Colorado monolith. One example is to be seen in the refusal of the party branch in Fernando de la Mora, in Asunción, to accept the official slate of candidates for branch elections and the subsequent mobilization of local party members against the party leadership.

Similarly, in recent years the government-controlled Confederation of Paraguayan Workers has manifested a growing division between the pro-Colorado *continuista* current and the more independent-minded *aperturistas*. The former have maintained the upper hand due to their capacity to rig elections for union leadership and intimidate the rank and file. It was for these reasons that the Asunción branch of the Institute of Free Trade Unions, an international arm of the US trade union confederation, the AFL-CIO, announced in April 1981 that it was closing down after ten years of attempting to work for democracy in the Paraguayan labour movement. All international trade union bodies have condemned the interference of the Paraguayan government in union affairs, the undemocratic conduct of union elections and the fact that the Paraguayan workers are not free to elect their own representatives.

Government control of the labour movement was, however, severely threatened in August 1982 when a remarkable rank and file mobilization involving an alliance of 17 trade unions fought the local subsidiary of Coca-Cola over the right to organize. The unions organized a successful boycott of Coca-Cola products, and attracted a great deal of public sympathy after several union leaders attempting to organize a union branch were dismissed by the company. Such was the pressure brought to bear by this unprecedented display of union solidarity that the dismissed workers were eventually reinstated. The fact that the Confederation of Paraguayan Workers failed to represent the Coca-Cola workers further discredited it as the defender of workers' interests. The expansion and development of the labour movement as a consequence of the economic boom of the 1970s may lead to other serious challenges to the military-Colorado monopoly of political power as the recession begins to hit workers even harder.

The most recent developments in Paraguay suggest that the government is now feeling threatened by the increased social and political mobilization taking place outside the confines of the political structures it controls. The slump in the economy in 1983 has led to widespread disaffection from the country's rulers. Sectors of the national business class have become increasingly critical of the way the economy is being managed; Asunción's professional middle class have seen their standards of living eroded by inflation and the paralysis of economic activities; students in the universities have been establishing independent organizations to pressure for more freedom of study and for jobs when they leave university; the intellectual strata have also been more openly critical of abuses of power and lack of democratic freedoms, and the massive lay-offs and unemployment have increased worker militancy; finally, the peasants producing cash crops for market have been severely affected by the crisis of the agro-export model of growth and their living conditions are increasingly precarious.

The response of the government to increased mobilization and agitation has been in the time-honoured method of the Stroessner regime: preventative repression. Violation of the most elementary human rights has been an institutionalized feature of Paraguayan political life under General Stroessner. The personal freedoms and liberties embodied in the country's constitution are meaningless inasmuch as a State of Siege, which annuls the individual guarantees expressed in the Constitution, has been in force during the entire period of Stroessner's rule, although Paraguay has remained virtually immune from the kind of bitter political conflicts and armed struggles that have characterized life elsewhere in Latin America. The effect of the State of Siege on human rights in Paraguay was described in the 1980 report of the Third Commission of Inquiry of the International League for Human Rights:

Under Article 79 of the Constitution, every three months President Stroessner issues a decree announcing that a state of siege is in effect, the territorial limits where it is in effect and the reasons for his decision. The state of siege powers of the President are used in plenary fashion to arrest, imprison and to banish persons considered to be security risks, or politically undesirable, as determined by the President and the men on whose counsel he relies. The judgement of the President, whether to issue a decree, its supporting reasons and a decree's application to particular persons, are final and non-reviewable by any other branch of government. Under state of siege decrees people have been imprisoned without charges, indefinitely, and in some cases in excess of twenty years. Both the arrest and the duration of imprisonment are exclusively and entirely at the will of the President.

Having reviewed the state of siege decrees as they actually operate, questions must be asked: Why have so many deaths, disappearances, tortures and the breakup of families taken place, why have so many people been imprisoned for long periods without trial or evidence of wrongdoing, to be released as arbitrarily as they were arrested, neither convicted nor exonerated, suffering from a high incidence of physical and mental ill-health, their reputations damaged, and why after release do so many continue to suffer harassment and punishment? The government's official answer is two-fold: a denial that the most egregious abuses have occurred and a justification of the mass imprisonments as a matter of necessity, duly sanctioned by Article 79 of the Constitution.

Though intended by the Constitution to be an exceptional emergency measure, state of siege has, after 25 years, become an institutionalized and permanent part of the machinery of government. In expression and in conduct, almost all governmental leaders reflect a deep and abiding state of siege mentality. They cannot conceive of governing without a permanent condition of state of siege which, in effect, permits government to exercise absolute discretionary powers without regard to legal rights or constitutional guarantees.

The record of experience ... under state of siege Law 209 prosecutions and the negation of law in the administration of the legal system, demonstrates that subversion by the government of its own legal order is a condition which grievously affects both individual rights and rights to act in a concerted and organized fashion.

There is no justification, grounded in real danger from within or without, for the present State of Siege Decree. It should therefore be lifted.

Every year many Paraguayans pass through the sinister police Investigations Department, the institutional heart of Paraguay's political police. Most of these are short-term detainees who are brought in under suspicion of political dissidence and are subjected to mental and physical abuse, including torture, as a means of 'corrective punishment'. From 1960 to 1977 the long-term political prisoner population was rarely fewer than 600, many of whom had been detained for over ten years without trial in police stations in the suburbs of Asunción. Amnesty International documented ten deaths under torture in 1976, and the disappearance of 20 people

166

between 1976 and 1978. After 1978, the pressures brought to bear on the Paraguayan government by the Carter administration in the US and by international human rights organizations resulted in a sharp drop in the numbers of long-term political detainees. In the words of the Minister of the Interior, 393 'political delinquents' were released at that time. However, the expressed commitment of the present Reagan administration to increase military aid for Paraguay is a clear reminder that the Carter years, when the US made an effort to keep the excesses of Latin American regimes in check, are over. Stroessner's apparatus of repression remains intact, and the flow of short-term detainees has not abated. If anything, the activities of repression have become more professionalized, with the military – the most 'professional' of Paraguay's political institutions – taking a greater role in the co-ordination and deployment of the security forces.

Opposition politicians and parties, independent journalists and intellectuals, and social institutions that distance themselves from the excesses of the regime continue to be harassed and obstructed. The labour unions remain under the control of the political police and its paid network of informers. In the countryside the military, police and the Colorado Party still terrorize peasant families, forcing them either to sell up or simply to move away without compensation. The ultimate aim of the repression in Paraguay is to forestall the emergence and crystallization of political opposition. This strategy of 'preventative repression' involves nipping in the bud any signs of growing organizational strength among independent groups outside of government control. As a result, there exists in Paraguay today a culture of fear, a suspicion of outsiders and an acute degree of self-censorship in daily social discourse.

Over 60 per cent of the population were born after General Stroessner took power and have experienced no other system of government. Several typical features of Latin American political culture have been completely absent since 1960. Street marches and open-air public meetings by opposition political parties, workers and students are simply forbidden. Political graffiti are only rarely found on Asunción's walls, and the distribution of social and political literature is vigorously controlled by the govern-ment – restricted, even in the universities, to works that support the government's 'world view'. In 1981 a university student of philosophy, Perla Yoré, was held in prison for several months for the crime of having in her possession 'subversive literature', amongst which the police cited E. H. Carr's scholarly *History of the Russian Revolution,* and Eric Hobsbawm's *Primitive Rebels.*

At another level, the invocation of the State of Siege and the arbitrary violation of human rights is a result of the Paraguayan government's adoption of the doctrine of 'national security' which has spread to all the military regimes of Latin America over the last decade. According to this doctrine, all political conflict is seen as a struggle between Communism and democracy, between East and West. In Paraguay's case, the renewal of the State of Siege decree of 2nd May 1978 refers to the need for 'national security' and to the existence of 'international organizations whose principal objectives constitute the subversion of legitimate authority as well as the use of violent means for the purpose of destroying the fundamental bases on which our society rests'. The doctrine of national security also underpins the foreign policy and international relations of the Stroessner government. Stroessner himself was a close friend of the former dictator of Nicaragua, Anastasio Somoza – who was assassinated in exile in Asunción in 1980 – and is a leading figure in the World Anti-Communist League established by Chiang Kai-shek in Taiwan. Under the pretext of communist persecution, refuge in Paraguay has been granted to leaders of the Italian neo-fascist organization, *Ordine Nuovo,* and to Croatian terrorists wanted in Europe on murder charges. Many former Nazis have found protection in Paraguay, most notably the infamous Josef Mengele, the 'Doctor of Death' at Auschwitz concentration camp, and Eduard Roschmann, the 'Butcher of Riga'. The Stroessner government also maintains close links with the South African government. Stroessner became the first post-war Head of State to visit Pretoria in 1974, and the then South African Prime Minister, Vorster, subsequently paid a return visit to Paraguay. The South African government financed the construction of Paraguay's new Ministry of Justice and Ministry of Foreign Affairs and maintains a military mission in the country. In 1981, Paraguay was cited in the German press as a 'bridgehead' for illicit sales and shipments of arms to South Africa, while the Paraguayan Embassy in Pretoria is actively encouraging the emigration of white

South Africans to Paraguay. An information office with the same objective has been opened in Namibia. The Paraguayan security apparatus has also collaborated closely with its counterparts in Uruguay and Argentina in the kidnapping and torture of opponents to all three regimes.

In May 1983 the regime's political police began a new wave of repression aimed at individuals and institutions which had begun to criticize the government more openly during the previous year. There were some 50 arrests, involving students, intellectuals and union organizers. The government claimed that those arrested were plotting to form a 'workers' party' – something forbidden by the Paraguayan constitution, which expressly precludes the formation of political organizations on a class basis. But the increased disaffection both inside and outside the totalitarian structures of military-Colorado domination, combined with the grim economic prospects, makes the future of the regime, as presently constituted, look decidedly shaky. The key factor is probably Stroessner himself and how long he will remain at the apex of power before ill health, old age or death removes him from the presidency. His demise seems certain to bring about a realignment of political power.

The Paraguayan Catholic Church has, to all intents and purposes, been an arm of the State since the Spanish Conquest in the mid-sixteenth century – except during the Francia popular dictatorship of 1814 to 1842, when the Church was severely repressed and had its land and wealth confiscated. Today, Article No. 6 of Paraguay's National Constitution recognizes the Roman Catholic Apostolic Religion as the religion of the State, the President is required to be a Catholic and, since its inception by the Mussolini-inspired military dictator Morinigo (1940–7), the Paraguayan Council of State has always reserved a seat for the Catholic hierarchy. About 2.9 million (98 per cent) of the population are professing Catholics, though probably only half this number attend Mass. There are ten dioceses and Apostolic Vicarates, and just under 500 priests, of whom rather more than half are non-Paraguayan. The Catholic Church is in fact the only other social organization that approaches the size and spread of the Colorado Party in Paraguayan society and, unlike the opposition political parties, the Catholic Church has the potential power to mobilize large sectors of the population. And, unlike the opposition parties which are denied access to the mass media for campaigning purposes, the Catholic Church has its own radio station – the key means for reaching a wide audience in a predominantly agrarian society with only rudimentary communications networks. Thus in the context of a harsh, exploitative economy and a very oppressive system of government, the potential for conflict between the Church and the government is high.

Until the 1960s, however, this potential scarcely materialized and the Catholic Church in Paraguay was a conservative, devotional force serving to sanction the poverty and subservience of the poor. Church-government relations until this time continued to be based upon the legacy of the *Patronato* established during the period of Spanish colonial rule. The government of the day patronized the Church, and the Church restricted its activities to spiritual, 'other-worldly' matters. Bishops were nominated by the government and priests were regarded as chaplains in the State's religious establishment. Collaboration between the government and the Church was the practical outcome of this arrangement, and the mentality of the *Patronato* survived long after its legal dissolution. As late as 1963, the Archbishop of Asunción, Mgr Anibal Mena Porta, successfully lobbied the government for a new law which, for the first time, drew together the numerous concessions to the Church in the form of widespread tax exemptions and an entitlement to a share of the national budget.

None the less, the monolithic character of the Catholic Church had begun to show signs of disturbance in the 1950s. There was a growth in the activities of the Church, and in particular of the lay movement *Acción Católica* (Catholic Action) which since 1942 had been in the forefront of a debate about the role of the Church in society and had organized training seminars for priests, encouraging them to pursue a more active pastoral role. Between 1957 and 1968 the number of bishops in Paraguay rose from five to twelve, and the number of priests rose from 202 to 510 between 1945 and 1969. The expansion of the Church, mainly in the rural areas, weakened the traditional ties between Church and government and also exposed the bulk of the clergy to the suffering of Paraguay's poor. This, combined with an influx of young progressive Spanish Jesuits and the worldwide dissemination of the Social Encyclicals

170

of Pope John XXIII and later of Pope Paul VI, stimulated many priests and nuns to question the traditional response of the Church to exploitation and poverty. The continent-wide debate and inspiration which led to the Medellín conference in 1968 was reflected in Paraguay in 1963 when the Bishops' Conference published a pastoral letter entitled 'The Social Problem in Paraguay'. This contained a high level of social analysis and an affirmation that the role of the Church is not simply to preach personal and social morality, but also to judge prevailing social institutions in the light of the teachings of Christ. By 1967 this new role seemed to be gaining acceptance with the publication by the church hierarchy of a critique of the draft of the new Constitution which contained a clause permitting President Stroessner to stand for a third five-year term – something prohibited under the Constitution of 1940.

During the Medellín conference itself the church weekly *Comunidad*, which, since its foundation in 1963, had provided a public forum for criticism of the injustices of Paraguayan society, was confiscated for featuring the prevailing student opposition to the appointment of Mgr Juan Moleón – the then Rector of the Catholic University and a close friend of the President – to the post of Auxiliary Bishop of Asunción. For the first time, the government denounced what it identified as 'communist infiltration' into the Church, and the government newspaper, *Patria* (literally 'Fatherland'), said at the time: 'The Church is a sacred precinct, consecrated to meditation, ecstasy and the adoration of God ... any preaching on subjects such as colonialism, change in structures or the social functions of capital, is anti-liturgical, subversive and contrary to representative democracy.' During 1969 and until the mid-1970s, Church/Government relations were generally at a low ebb. In June 1969, at the time of a visit to Paraguay by US President Nixon's special envoy, Nelson Rockefeller, 35 student and opposition groups published a joint communiqué denouncing the lack of human rights in the country. A number of student leaders were arrested and subsequently went on hunger strike, whereupon three churches were occupied by students and novice priests in order to secure their release. The government blamed the Church for inciting the students, began imposing censorship on the weekly *Comunidad,* and in August announced a new bill 'For the Defence of Democracy', which proposed harsh prison sentences for minor infringements of public order. The Church responded by describing the bill as 'absolutist and totalitarian', and argued that 'no Christian legislator could approve it without relinquishing his most sacred moral and religious values'.

In October more students went on hunger strike in a bid to free the arrested students, and the government-imposed media blackout was broken only by a Jesuit, Father Oliva, who spoke out on the church radio and from the pulpit of the Cristo Rey Church in Asunción. Women relatives of political prisoners who held a prayer meeting for hunger strikers were assaulted by police as they left the cathedral, and on 22nd October Father Oliva was deported from Paraguay despite his being a Paraguayan national. In protest against his banishment 200 students, priests and nuns held a silent Via Crucis procession outside the Catholic University which was attacked by police and government hired thugs. In the ensuing fracas, during which tear gas was used and classrooms were destroyed, seventy-three-year-old Father Juan Gomez Rocafort was amongst a number of people physically assaulted by the police. The Church then decided to excommunicate the Minister of the Interior, Dr Sabino Augusto Montanaro, and the Chief of Police, General Francisco Britez, for their complicity in the violence. No church services were held in Paraguay on the following Sunday, and Stroessner himself responded publicly stating that the clergy should not 'hide behind their cassocks' and that excommunication was invalidated in cases where the law had been broken.

A Pastoral Letter of 1969, 'The Mission of Our Church Today', spoke directly of the closing down of *Comunidad*, the violation of church lands and property, the expulsion of priests and government violence, and concluded that it was legitimate for the Church to take a more active role in society. At this time, the church hierarchy contained a nucleus of three extremely popular and progressive bishops who commanded wide support within the Church and amongst peasant communities – Mgrs Ramon Bogarin Argaña, Anibal Maricevich and Felipe Santiago Benítez. They were the strength behind the radicalized and increasingly autonomous position of the Church *vis-à-vis* a government that was fearful of alienating a large sector of the populace. Throughout 1970 the government resorted to its usual strategy for moments of stress, and attempted to clamp down upon and control the activities of the Church. Its telephones were tapped, its mail opened and defamatory leaflets were distributed in the streets, purporting to demonstrate the immorality of church leaders. The message for the peasantry was simple: they were exhorted to make sure they knew the distinction between a good priest and a bad priest. Daily official radio broadcasts warned the peasantry of 'dangerous priests, many of whom are Communists in disguise'. This barrage of propaganda had, however, the opposite effect of radicalizing many conservative, traditional priests who now found themselves regarded with suspicion by local Colorado Party officials a d members. And in a number of rural townships peasants belonging to the Colorado Party were harassed and assaulted for attending church services in preference to party meetings timed to coincide with the hour of worship.

The government then began a campaign to link the Church with those advocating armed overthrow of the existing order. Father Uberfil Monzón disappeared in the centre of Asunción in January 1971 shortly after arriving in Paraguay from his native Uruguay. A week later the government announced that Father Monzón was being held on suspicion of being 'an envoy of the Tupamaro urban guerrillas in Uruguay'. On 10th March the government released a press statement consisting of a long 'confession' by Father Monzón that he was a 'subversive'. This consisted of little more than a potted history of the Tupamaros, and was in fact an exact replica of an article recently published by an Argentinian newspaper which interviewed the leader of the Tupamaros, Raul Sendic. The Paraguayan police had simply substituted the name of Father Monzón for that of Sendic. The savage torture to which Father Monzón was subjected before signing the confession was duly corroborated later, despite the fact that the Paraguayan authorities kept him in the police hospital for over a month in order to allow the worst signs of torture to recede. On 8th March that year Mgr Andrés Rubio, the Auxiliary Bishop of Montevideo, arrived from Uruguay to plead with the government on behalf of Father Monzón. At the airport he was attacked by a group of drunken and hysterical policewomen who broke his spectacles and pectoral cross, pelted him with eggs and tomatoes and clawed at his face – all in full view of four awaiting Paraguayan bishops and astonished

North American tourists. His companion, Father Lelio Rodríguez, was similarly abused. The response of the Paraguayan Church was swift and sharp: Mgr Ismael Rolón, after less than a year as Bishop of Asunción, once again excommunicated the Minister of the Interior and the Chief of Police for their complicity in the kidnapping and torture of Father Monzón and the physical assault on Mgr Andrés Rubio and Father Lelio Rodríguez. He also refused to participate in the sessions of the Council of State during the next year. In May 1972, Father Caravias, a Spanish Jesuit working with the peasantry in the zone of Piribebuy, south of Asunción, became the eighth priest to be expelled by the government in three years. At a press conference, the Minister of the Interior described the proceedings of the Medellín conference as an example of the 'subversive literature' found in the priest's possession.

The underlying reason for the deterioration of Church-Government relations after 1969 was the threat posed to the socio-political structure of Colorado power in the countryside by the upsurge of the *Ligas Agrarias Cristianas* (Christian Agrarian Leagues) – a form of rudimentary social organization for peasants which was the direct outcome of the new church theology that emerged in the 1960s. The initial impetus came from the urban-based Catholic Youth movement and the progressive sector of the fledgeling Christian Democrat movement, but many rural priests and nuns, particularly Jesuits and Franciscans, took up the watchwords of the theology of liberation and applied them to Paraguayan peasants: self-help in improving their material well-being and self-education for understanding their deprived position in society. The basic unit of the movement was the *comunidad de base* (base community), consisting of up to ten families meeting regularly in their village. Each *comunidad* elected a member to meet with delegates from other *comunidades* around the nearest small town, thus forming the *Liga Agraria* (Agrarian League). Members of the *Ligas* worked together on self-help projects, *onondivepá*. Income from communal farming ventures was used to buy in bulk and store basic necessities such as soap, flour and cooking oil in order to save the peasant from falling into heavy debt with local retailers and middlemen selling at inflated prices. Around the zones of Quindy and Misiones, where *comunidades* were well established, the *Ligas* organized their own primary schools in which children were taught in Guarani and education was specifically geared to the practical needs of the peasantry. The young teachers, *pytyvojhará*, were themselves the children of members of the *Ligas*.

By the early 1970s the *Ligas* had an estimated 20,000 active members and were beginning to undermine traditional rural social relationships. In particular the economic interests of those who lived by exploiting the peasantry suffered with the growth of peasant co-operatives and mutual aid associations. Persecution of peasant organizations and communities was therefore stepped up during the early 1970s, and the government mounted a virulent campaign denouncing the *Ligas* as the work of communist agents and warning other peasants not to affiliate to them. The effect was to make the *Ligas* more politicized and they began taking what amounted to a radical left-wing position. Divisions began to appear in the church hierarchy and the *Ligas* began to publish criticisms of the Catholic bishops for not defending the *Ligas* more vigorously. For its part, the government was manoeuvring frantically behind the scenes in a bid to encourage and capitalize upon the growing rift between the hierarchy and the grassroots church and the *Ligas Agrarias*. Gradually, the suppression of the *Ligas* began to take on a new form, and instead of being left to the local Colorado Party bosses it was co-ordinated by the police from their headquarters in Asunción.

In 1975 anti-guerrilla units of the armed forces were used for the first time for suppressing the *Ligas*. On 8th February seventy armed soldiers carried out a dawn raid on the *comunidad* of Jejuí, and although they met no resistance, they shot dead several peasants and wounded others, including the local priest, Father Braulio Maciel. Amongst those arrested were Mgr Roland Bordelon, South American Regional Director of the Catholic Relief Services, a US church-based charity, and Kevin Kalahan, CRS Programme Officer in Paraguay. The *comunidad* was disbanded and its members were forced to disperse. Suppression of the *Ligas* reached a climax in 1976 when the Minister of the Interior announced the discovery of an embryonic guerrilla movement, the *Organización Primero de Marzo* (1st of March Organization), whose foremost leader was Father Miguel San Martín, a Spanish Jesuit who had earlier been expelled from the country. Despite the

175

fact that the OPM had not carried out any military operations and was confined to a relatively small number of middle-class Paraguayan students and peasant leaders; and even though the government was able to round up the nucleus of the organization with ease, the OPM scare served as a pretext for the government's efforts to wipe out the *Ligas Agrarias* once and for all. Some thirty leading *Liga* activists were assassinated within days of each other in widely different areas of the countryside. Over 2,000 *Liga* members were arrested in raids on *comunidades* throughout the rural areas and, although most were released within a few weeks, about 500 suspects were taken to Asunción to face interrogation and torture. Many of these were subsequently imprisoned in the prison of Emboscada, fifteen miles from the capital. The Church came under considerable pressure from the relatives of detainees and of peasants and students who had simply disappeared. As a result, an ecumenical organization the *Comité de Iglesias* (the Inter-Church Committee) was founded by the Catholic, Disciples of Christ and Lutheran churches for the purpose of extending relief to political prisoners. Food, medical attention and legal aid were provided for prisoners, together with financial help for distressed families of prisoners and loans to released prisoners seeking employment. After the reduction of the political prison population in 1977–9 the emphasis of the work of the Inter-Church Committee shifted to the constant stream of short-term political detainees, meeting the long forgotten needs of common law prisoners and developing a programme of rural work for assisting the peasants with their land problems.

In many respects, 1976 marks a watershed in the relations between Church and Government, after which the Church gradually abandoned its radical position and assumed a more accommodating relationship with the government. The government had managed to discredit the Church and its radical tendencies through the 'exposure' of the OPM and the linking of members of the Church with plots to overthrow the government by violence. This sharpened the divisions within the Church and strengthened its conservative sector, a development reinforced by the death in 1976 of Mgr Ramón Bogarín Argaña, the leading force among Paraguay's progressive bishops. In spite of the directives of the Puebla Episcopal Conference in 1979, the Church has since

176

been largely confined to reactive interventions rather than the initiatives which characterized the late 1960s and early to mid-1970s. In 1980 the XI Assembly of the Paraguayan Episcopal Conference was dominated by what has been called a 'culturalist current' which defined itself as a 'third way' – somewhere between the traditional approach of the hierarchy and the most advanced elements of the theology of liberation. The Church's emphasis shifted from the *causes* of poverty and exploitation to their *symptoms* in the lives of the people. This does not mean that all traces of conflict in Church-Government relations have disappeared. Rather, open conflict has been reduced to friction, with the Church continuing to speak out on human rights abuses, government corruption and the violation of legal and constitutional guarantees by the government. The lasting legacy of Medellín and the Church's experiment in radical and progressive politics is evident in the following passage from the 1979 Pastoral Letter of the Bishops of Paraguay:

> We have also been witnesses of repeated acts of abuse of authority and superior power, above all in the interior of the country, which have not received their due attention or just punishment. It is necessary to mention here also the acts of abuse and despoliation against country people and farmers with the backing of local authorities and the indifference of their superiors. Often the institutions charged with promoting rural welfare are responsible for these situations: double property titles, defective surveying and property lines, favouritism and unjustifiable influence. ... These facts are always prejudicial to the public peace and sound community life, because those who cause the problem are precisely the men who exercise authority or public office whose responsibility it is to serve the common good.

During 1981 the principal issue affecting Church-Government relations was that of Paraguay's indigenous groups. One group in particular, the Toba Maskoy, received harsh treatment early in the year. The army evicted them from lands they had just possessed by virtue of a Presidential Decree of October 1980 which had sanctioned the appropriation of 10,000 hectares from the

Argentinian lumber, tannin and cattle company, Carlos Casado. Seven hundred Toba Maskoy people were transported against their will to an inhospitable location in the Paraguayan Chaco known as Km 220. Mgr Alejo Ovelar, the Bishop of the Chaco, described Km 220 as 'totally unfit for agriculture, being arid for half of the year and flooded the rest of the year'. Dr C. A. González, Professor of Law at the Catholic University, accused the government of genocide, alleging that the Toba Maskoy would die of starvation if confined to Km 220 against their will. In the same year the Church put forward fundamental criticisms of important legislation concerning the rights of Indian groups, which was making its way through Paraguay's parliamentary assembly.

Outside the field of Indian affairs, however, the only noteworthy activity on the part of the Catholic Church in 1981 was the mobilization of lay groups in a project designed to impart greater consciousness of 'National Reality and the Christian Mission'. In March 1982 the Archbishop of Asunción, Mgr Ismael Rolón, spoke of the violence suffered by Paraguay's poor and suggested that if the government did nothing about it, they would open the door to 'those obscure forces of international terrorism capable of rupturing social security and plunging the community into the chaos of fratricidal struggle'. *Patria,* the government newspaper, replied with a letter, supposedly written by an 'Indignant Catholic', which accused Mgr Rolón of using the name of God to incite violence. *Patria*'s indiscretion brought a wave of public sympathy and support for the Archbishop who, in the presence of the President, military chiefs, government ministers and diplomats, during the commemoration of the *Fiestas Patrias* (Festivals of the Fatherland) in May, delivered a homily on freedom of thought and expression and the need for tolerance, respectful dialogue and peaceful co-existence.

The Catholic Church in Paraguay is not, however, a monolithic institution. It embodies a number of competing theological forces and tendencies, which makes the current modus vivendi with the government an unstable one. One sector of the Church is receptive to the new Cold War mentality in international relations. Hence Archbishop Rolón's reference to the 'obscure forces of international terrorism' – words that belong to the President's vocabulary. On the other hand, the Bishops' Conference of

Paraguay met with the President of the National Conference of Brazilian Bishops in July 1981 to discuss and study the problems associated with the massive migratory flows of Paraguayans and Brazilians to Paraguay's Eastern Border Region, the location of Paraguay's rapidly expanding agricultural frontier. Since then a joint programme of action has been initiated, and the bishops met again in March 1982. As the Brazilian Church is one of the most radicalized churches in Latin America, the joint programme may have a considerable impact upon the Church in Paraguay, as it intervenes in one of the most poverty-stricken and potentially violent regions of the country. The potential for conflict between the Catholic Church and the Government remains high.

There are only just over 50,000 Protestants in Paraguay, representing about 2 per cent of the total population, but, as elsewhere in Latin America, Protestant work and ministry has four distinct sources or roots: pioneer missionary work among indigenous tribal groups, unreached by Roman Catholic missions; chaplaincies for North European and American expatriates; reproduction of churches among other ethnic minorities, e.g. Koreans and Slavic peoples; and direct evangelism among the partly secularized urban population. The American Bible Society was first on the scene, in 1856, and thirty years later the American Methodist Episcopal Church launched a missionary enterprise. But Wilfred Barbrooke Grubb, an Anglican serving with the South American Missionary Society, was the first European to make peaceful contact with the Chaco Indians. His work, which dates from 1889, led to the evangelization of the Lengua, Sanapana and Angaite tribes, and from the earliest years included co-operative and economic development projects as well as medical, educational, and evangelistic activities. The Mennonite communities which settled in the Central Chaco area in the 1930s attracted migrant Indian labour and some of their Christian leaders assumed a missionary responsibility towards the Churupí, Angaite and Lengua groups which came to live or were already settled in the area. The main aim of the Mennonites was, however, to get the Indians to settle down and become 'useful members of the Paraguayan nation', which meant, among other things, providing a plentiful supply of cheap labour. Six thousand Indians are now living – many of them in rudimentary workers' camps – on the fringes of the Mennonite

179

colonies. The other side of the picture is that Mennonite land settlement programmes have secured more than 30,000 hectares of land for indigenous communities.

The New Tribes Mission, a North American fundamentalist organization, have been responsible for a third initiative. They began work in the Paraguayan Chaco in the 1940s, and over the past thirty years have been active, notably amongst the Aché and Ayoréo Indians. Unfortunately, they have been open to the charge of cultural insensitivity and aggression in their missionary zeal. Survival International – an organization campaigning for tribal people's rights – is severely critical of the New Tribes Mission's methods, calling attention to what it describes as their crude methods of conversion, the repeated failures of their economic and social programmes, and their self-evident contempt for traditional Indian culture and religion. There are also disturbing accounts, supported by documentary evidence, of New Tribes Mission-organized manhunts which track down nomadic Indians in the dense scrub forest of the Northern Chaco with a view to their conversion and 'civilization'.

Towards the end of the nineteenth century the Paraguayan government allowed chaplaincy churches to be established for North European and American expatriates and immigrants. The Lutheran Church of Rio de la Plata was thus established in Asunción in order to minister to German-speaking people. The Anglican chaplaincy of Saint Andrew's had a parallel outreach to English speakers. In more recent years churches have been established in Paraguay to serve the Korean communities, and the largest Protestant church building in Asunción belongs to the Koreans.

The recognition by the Lambeth Conference of 1958 that the increasingly secular cities of Latin America were a legitimate and indeed urgent focus of evangelism for the Anglican Church, resulted in the beginning of urban programmes in Asunción and Concepción and the development of a bilingual school which has attracted some of the most influential families in the country. The Anglicans have also followed the Mennonites in land settlement work. Of the forty Indian communities to which the church most directly relates, four are newly settled on purchased land. Previously the Anglican central mission provided the only refuge in the

Lower Chaco area where Indian groups had any security of land tenure. The settlement projects of the Protestant churches do, however, arouse considerable controversy among those concerned with Indian issues. On the one hand, there can be no doubt that the medical work initiated by missionary societies, such as the Anglican South American Missionary Society, has done much to alleviate the suffering caused by pulmonary diseases and intestinal parasites – both common among undernourished Indians. It is also the case that the missionary presence has sometimes inhibited attacks on Indians by the military, ranchers and fur traders. There is evidence that in some instances severely disadvantaged groups, such as the Chaco Indians, have not only been introduced to Christianity but also enabled to survive, through the re-creation of socially cohesive groups. Missionaries point out that the Christmas and Easter festivals at the Anglican central mission of Makthlawaiya certainly have a religious significance, but they also effectively reinforce the integrity and continuity of the Lengua peoples.

Yet there are anthropologists who believe that a good deal of Protestant missionary activity results in the destruction of Indian culture and constitutes a greater threat to the Indian than the open contempt and hostility displayed by his non-religious neighbours. A Jesuit priest, Bartomeu Melia, who championed the cause of Indians in Paraguay until he was finally expelled from the country in 1976, put it this way: 'Many missions will be forced to recognize one day, albeit helplessly, that all they have done to help the Indians will have had no other effect than to lay the ground for an invasion by neo-colonial peoples who will try to get rid of Indians, either by eliminating them or by reducing them to marginal status. The map of the Americas is dotted with cities which we founded as missions in native territories and in which the Indian is today a stranger and a beggar.'

Although committed to highly specialized ministries, the Anglican Church remains a small minority, about 4,000 in total, with Indians constituting 90 per cent of its membership. For its outreach among people at opposite extremes of the social spectrum it still relies on a substantial expatriate missionary contribution. Its Paraguayan leadership is, however, increasingly influential, though interestingly its assistant bishop is a Chilean.

Unlike the Anglicans, other evangelical denominations were not deterred so long by the ruling of the 1910 Edinburgh missionary conference that Latin American cities were the unique preserve of 'our sister church of Rome'. Other Protestant attempts at urban evangelism predated the Anglican by at least a generation. In spite of early antagonism, the Baptists, Nazarenes, Pentecostals, Brethren, and Salvation Army all established churches in Asunción and other major cities and towns.

At the present time there are fifteen main Protestant denominations established in Paraguay, and many smaller religious groups. The Baptist churches, now with second- and third-generation membership, are theologically conservative and organizationally efficient: characteristics which they owe to their Southern Baptist parent churches in the United States. Among their institutions is a hospital in Asunción offering high standards of medical care. The Lutherans have concerned themselves with human rights issues. The Disciples of Christ, another denomination showing a pronounced emphasis on social concern, co-operate in an organization called the *Misión de Amistad*. This group promotes a land settlement programme among indigenous peoples in eastern Paraguay. Their work is not directly evangelistic: the Paí Tavyterá Indians retain their traditional religious customs and beliefs. The Mennonite missions, on the other hand, have combined evangelism with social ministries.

Evangelical leaders from other republics in the Southern Cone have played a significant part in the development of the Protestant churches in Paraguay. Juan Carlos Ortiz, a pastor from Argentina, spread the charismatic influence beyond the Pentecostal churches. Charismatic fellowships continue and attract professional as well as other social groups. In successive campaigns Luis Palau has succeeded in involving the majority of the non-Roman churches in concerted evangelistic effort. The Palau campaign held in September 1982 attracted the attention of the Paraguayan press, radio and television. Attendances at rallies totalled 155,000, and more than ten thousand people made professions of faith in response to the evangelist's preaching. A number of churches have reported that their congregations have doubled in number since the campaign. Even so, Protestant or Evangelical Christianity remains a minority movement within the country.

Chapter 8

Peru

Peru has long been recognized as a land of stark contrasts. Geographically it contains within its boundaries some of the most arid coastal desert in the world (the *Costa*), the spectacularly high and topographically diversified mountain area of the Andes (the *Sierra*), and vast expanses of Amazonian rainforest (the *Selva*). It suffers from a range of natural hazards, including extensive flooding, major droughts and the ever-present menace of earthquakes. Yet Peru is also blessed with a wide variety of natural resources including the world's most productive fishing grounds and large deposits of copper, iron ore, zinc and other minerals. Oil is to be found on the north coast and also in the Amazonian jungle.

The sharp contrast between this wealth of resources and the poverty of the mass of the population has led to Peru being described as a beggar sitting on a pot of gold. Average per capita income for the population of over 18 million people is only US $ 792 per year (1979), while in the highland area it falls to only US $ 160 per year – equivalent to some of the poorest nations in the world. The distribution of income is highly unequal, the top 20 per cent of households receiving 61 per cent of the total, and the bottom 40 per cent receiving only seven per cent. Average incomes in the capital, Lima, are some four and a half times greater than those in the rural parts of the country. It has been estimated that over a third of Peruvian families live in absolute poverty, with three quarters of this group living in the countryside. Infant mortality rates are among the highest in Latin America and are particularly severe in the *Sierra*. Overall, about a half of the Peruvian population has insufficient income to allow it to satisfy its basic needs. Ethnic differences between *indios* and *mestizos* continue to underlie a rigidly stratified class system that generates one of the most unequal distributions of wealth and income in Latin America.

The purely environmental difficulties faced by Peru are therefore formidable. Despite its size (496,000 square miles), which makes it the third largest country in Latin America, Peru has a highly restricted agricultural area. Eighty per cent of the surface area is virtually uncultivable, and three quarters of the remainder is unsuitable for anything except natural pasture. The remaining five per cent gives Peru one of the highest people/land ratios in Latin America. Yet, despite these obstacles, Peru has developed intensive agriculture and dense human settlement, both on the coast and in the *Sierra*. The coast, which represents twelve per cent of Peru's area, and was once the site of a series of sophisticated pre-Hispanic civilizations, now contains 47 per cent of its population and is the principal setting for Peru's industrialization and urbanization process. The adjacent highland area contains the same curious mix of inhospitable environments and dense human settlement. Rising to over 16,000 feet, the Andean *Sierra* includes glaciated peaks, steep-sided intermontane valleys and high-altitude plateaus.

A succession of regional states and empires developed in pre-Hispanic times, culminating in the remarkable Inca empire, *Tawantinsuyo*, stretching from present-day Ecuador to central Chile, and covering an area twice that of Spain. Although not apparently more advanced than preceding highland states, the Inca empire knitted together a web of pre-existing ethnic kingdoms under the *Pax Incaica*. Initially created by military force, the empire came to be sustained by more than mere coercive power. While levying tribute from conquered peoples, Inca rule was also characterized by the use of material rewards (for example, food, cloth and weapons) to loyal ethnic leaders and groups, as well as by the granting of substantial local autonomy over internal affairs. At the same time, the more centralized nature of the Inca empire was expressed by the organization of the state redistributive system, the construction of state storehouses, roads, waystations and other public works, state-organized colonization and resettlement schemes, and policies of cultural unification within the empire.

By the middle of the sixteenth century this empire had been swallowed into the yet vaster, transcontinental Spanish Empire. The new colonial society which developed in the post-Conquest period was qualitatively different from anything which had preceded it in the Andean era. One cause of this was the dramatic demographic collapse which followed conquest, reducing Peru's indigenous population from approximately nine million in 1520 to less than a tenth of this size a century later. This collapse was brought about primarily by epidemic diseases which swept across Peru throughout the sixteenth century, but also by warfare and unchecked Spanish exploitation in the first few decades of conquest. In these circumstances it is perhaps more surprising that so much of pre-Hispanic civilization and culture survived the onslaught of Spanish imperialism.

The chief social impact of Spanish colonialism was the creation of an ethnically divided caste society whose features have survived to the present day. The division between the white European colonists and the native Indians became a major fissure of colonial society, providing the basis for a rigidly stratified social order. Although miscegenation rapidly produced an intervening group of *mestizos*, and coastal labour needs were increasingly met by African Negro slaves, the distinction between the *blanco* and the Quechua-speaking *indio* remained, and remains, sharp. The two groups were culturally separated by language, dress, dietary habits and religion, as well as by the rural residence of the Indians and the urban orientation of the Spanish. More importantly perhaps, the two groups were stratified in terms of relations of domination and subordination. Crown policy aimed to integrate the Indian sector into the Spanish market economy. The Indians were to provide goods and labour to maintain this economy, while at the same time the native peasant community would be preserved as the essential basis for the survival of the Indian population and society. To this end the Spanish adopted a variety of coercive mechanisms to extract resources from the Indian population including forced labour, tribute payment and a rotating labour draft. Thus Indian labour became vital to the survival and expansion of the proliferating Spanish enterprises – estates, mines and textile workshops in particular.

However, this colonial system was not quietly accepted by the indigenous population. Open revolt was rare, though it occurred sporadically as millenarian movements seeking the restoration of a Golden Age. Resistance first took the form of fidelity to native traditions, especially to Andean cosmologies, and resistance to the spiritual conquest of Christianity. The external observance of Christianity was accompanied by the continuance of native modes of spirituality. The second major area of resistance was in the colonial legal system, which the Indians rapidly learnt how to exploit and manipulate for their own defence, playing off Spaniard against Spaniard. Although neither of these forms of resistance was able to alter the circumstances of colonial domination, they did at least temper its abuses and offer a degree of personal dignity.

Three centuries of colonial rule came to an end with Independence in 1824 – brought reluctantly to an uncertain population by external military leaders. Formal independence has not, however, erased the colonial legacy which remains in many aspects of Peruvian life. This legacy includes such diverse features as a dual culture, the orientation of economic life through the capital, Lima, a bureaucratic hierarchical tradition, the use of cheap Indian labour and the marginalization of the mass of the population from the process of development. Political power in the nineteenth century rested with local and provincial landowners, merchants, priests and professionals, who exercised almost complete control over their small fiefdoms. At the national level, a series of military *caudillos* succeeded each other in the presidency for short periods.

A period of economic growth during the middle of the nineteenth century was brought to an end by the disastrous War of the Pacific (1879–83), when Peru was occupied by Chilean troops, its coastal estates sacked, its nitrate-rich southern provinces annexed, and its national pride humiliated. Recovery from this war was slow because of the extent of the destruction, the exhaustion of the guano deposits, and a domestic political struggle which was only stilled by the victory of Nicolas Pierola in 1895. However, from that date Peru entered a phase characterized both by a long-run expansion of the export economy and by political stability, as civilian rule and a party system were consolidated. Peru's export sector was, and is, unusually diversified by Latin American standards. It includes sugar, cotton, oil, wool, copper and other mineral products. The ability to shift emphasis from one set of these products to another enabled the Peruvian economy to expand through to the Great Depression in the 1930s. Cotton and sugar cultivation was extended on the coast, along with oil production, while the *Sierra* was opened up for wool, copper, silver and coffee exports. It was during this period that the greatest expansion of the estate sector occurred, absorbing peasant and Indian community land, and forming massive plantations and large estates. Labour conditions on these estates were highly exploitative, and there were uprisings in the *Sierra* as well as widespread strikes of plantation workers on the coast. Politically, this period was marked by the organization of the civilian élite and the emergence of new class forces. Pierola's victory in 1895 laid the foundations for a quarter century of the 'Aristocratic Republic', during which time the export élite ruled through the *civilista* party. This period saw the centralizing of political power in Lima, a major increase in government expenditure, the introduction of direct elections, the reorganization of the army and the improvement of the urban environment. It also saw the emergence of the *indigenista* movement as a major intellectual force seeking to champion the cause of the Indian majority.

The 'Aristocratic Republic' was succeeded in 1919 by the eleven-year rule (the *oncenio*) of Augusto B. Leguía. During his dictatorship he sought to displace the *civilista* oligarchy from political, if not economic, power and to construct a *Patria Nueva* based on a coalition between the emerging middle classes, the industrial bourgeoisie and the urban masses. Having seized the presidency, Leguia embarked upon an ambitious programme of modernization, carried out by an expanding interventionist State and with the aid of American money. The Great Depression of the 1930s brought export growth and Leguia's *oncenio* to a close, and came to represent something of a watershed in many aspects of Peruvian life. By comparison with many other Latin American countries, Peru suffered less of a crisis at this time and recovered more quickly thanks to its diversified export structure. Nevertheless, the Depression produced mass redundancies, high urban unemployment and a fall in real wages. Waves of strikes broke out in Lima and in the centres of the export economy, while important new political movements vied for control of the working class. From 1930 onwards Peruvian politics entered a stage in which mass political participation became a reality, although women were only given the vote in 1956 and illiterates in 1980.

The principal party to emerge from this ferment was APRA (the American Popular Revolutionary Alliance) – a radical, populist movement, led by the charismatic Haya de la Torre, which became the key element in post-1930 political life. Yet despite considerable popular support throughout the period, APRA continually failed to reach government, and was continually frustrated in its bids for power – excluded by military coups, electoral fraud and the need to compromise with the established élite. In attempts to make itself more acceptable, APRA began to move increasingly to the right, dropping its opposition to US investment and playing down its commitment to nationalization and extensive land reform. This search for legitimacy and access to power led APRA into a closer and closer identification with the Peruvian establishment, forming tactical alliances with representatives of the oligarchy, including the very same military dictator who had suppressed the party from 1948 until 1956. But even this failed to ensure APRA's accession to power, the military intervening twice (in 1962 and 1969) to keep them out.

In the 1940s growing pressure from the middle classes, and the need to pre-empt some of APRA's programme, led conservative and liberal governments into expansionary policies. These finally collapsed into incoherent economic management, inflation and the alienation of domestic and foreign investors. A coup led by General Manuel Odría in 1948 put an end to these policies and to the legal activities of the APRA party, which again retreated to its highly organized underground structure. The new government enthusiastically turned to orthodox, free market policies based on renewed export-led growth, minimum government intervention and the encouragement of foreign investment. The economic results of these policies were spectacularly successful, although they were accompanied by repression of the labour movement. Exports grew rapidly from 1948 until the mid-1960s, and industrialization linked to export processing expanded strongly in the early 1950s. In the latter part of that decade broader government support began to be offered to a process of import-substituting industrialization, with lavish incentives to investment and substantial protection. The result was accelerated industrial growth, accompanied by a wave of direct foreign investment in manufacturing, so that by 1968 35 per cent of corporate sector output was foreign controlled.

The counterpart to this industrialization process was the rapid urbanization of Peru brought about by high rates of rural-urban migration. This focused in particular upon the capital, which expanded from half a million people in 1940 to 1.5 million in 1961 and to 5 million in 1980. Many of the migrants have been forced to leave rural communities by the pressure of population on the land, but most appear to have chosen to move, attracted by the possibility of industrial employment, the expansion of the public sector, better education for their children or simply by the higher standard of living of even the poor in the large cities. The consequence of this rapid urbanization process has been to put a severe strain on the capacity or willingness of city administrations to provide housing or basic services. From the 1920s onwards, but particularly in the post-war era, the solution adopted by the poor has been the invasion of unused land on the margins of the city. Here families construct their own dwellings, beginning with the flimsiest of construction materials, such as matting, and gradually improving the standard and size of the building. By 1960 these squatter settlements had come to represent one fifth of the population of Lima, and by 1981 almost a half. In other cities of Peru such squatter settlements represent an even higher proportion of the housing stock. Another aspect of the urbanization process has been the growth of the small-scale, 'informal' sector of petty traders, outworkers, employees in small workshops, domestic servants, skilled labourers, etc. In manufacturing as a whole this sector produces about one third of output but employs two thirds of the labour force.

One of the political responses to these social and economic changes, occurring in the late 1950s, was the emergence of a new political party which rapidly established itself as a major rival to the oligarchic parties and even to APRA itself. Led and held together by the architect Fernando Belaúnde, *Acción Popular* was a reformist party of middle-class, centrist tendencies. Narrowly defeated in the abortive 1962 election, whose results were cancelled by a military coup to prevent APRA coming to power, *Acción Popular* won the 1963 election when it ran with tacit military support. Committed to carry out a variety of social and economic reforms, Belaúnde found many of his initiatives blocked or watered down by the majority opposition led by APRA. The latter frustrated the implementation of an agrarian reform law, prevented tax reform and delayed funding for particular initiatives. Nevertheless, the first Belaúnde regime (1963–8) was notable for the creation of state enterprises, the expansion of the development banks, higher social expenditure, community self-help projects and large-scale construction activities. Belaúnde's term of office was also notable for the expectations it generated among the rural poor in particular. Immediately after he took office, large numbers of highland peasants took advantage of the apparent change in government policy to invade private estates in an attempt to reclaim expropriated lands. In 1965 a group of students and intellectuals sought to capitalize upon this by setting up guerrilla *focos* in various highland areas. They were swiftly defeated by concerted police and military action.

By the mid-1960s deepseated economic problems had begun to emerge, with a pronounced decline in private investment, a slowdown in export growth, a steadily worsening balance of payments situation, and a significant expansion of the foreign debt to more than US $ 700 million. These trends culminated in the 1967 devaluation of the sol by 40 per cent and the introduction of tardy deflationary measures. By this time, however, the legitimacy of the Belaunde regime had been badly eroded by charges of corruption, by splits within his own party, by the collapse of *Acción Popular*'s coalition with the Christian Democrats and by disillusionment with the pace of reform. The final triggering event for the overthrow of the regime was the badly mishandled, although largely successful, negotiation with the International Petroleum Company (an IPC subsidiary of Standard Oil of New Jersey) over the return of subsoil mineral rights from its operations on the north coast. The alleged disappearance of the crucial final page of the agreement created widespread suspicion of a sell-out of Peruvian interests.

The coup against Belaúnde in October 1968 was followed by twelve years of military rule (the *docenio*) which brought about a profound change in Peruvian political life. It inaugurated a unique period of military intervention, often described as 'the Peruvian revolution' because of the policies of the radical officers heading the government. These included the reform of highly unequal landholding structures, worker participation in industry, expansion of the state sector in strategic areas, a fully labour-managed economic sector, reform of education and the mass media, less foreign dependence, a new political system and an independent foreign policy with a strong 'Third-Worldist' flavour. In the First Phase of the 'revolution' (1968–75) laws were introduced to implement these reforms and the government had remarkable success in resisting élite pressures for moderation. In the Second Phase (1975–80) the military were, however, increasingly on the defensive as the economy disintegrated and pressures for return to civilian rule became irresistible.

The radicalized military government drew its initial strength from the new professionalism of the armed forces, the ideological influence of the military higher education college, especially its use of the model of dependency espoused by the United Nations Economic Commission for Latin America (ECLA), the experience of the 1965 counter-insurgency campaigns, the association of national security with national development, and disenchantment with 'corrupt' civilian politicians. The cumulative impact of these influences was to create a reformist consensus among a sufficiently large group of officers to sponsor a coup, and then to set in motion a 'revolutionary' process of reform. Although eventually the Peruvian experiment foundered on the rocks of international recession, economic mismanagement and over-ambition, the legacy of the period remains striking.

Six days after the Revolutionary Government of the Armed Forces came to power in 1968 the International Petroleum Company was expropriated and the military occupied its oilfields and installations. This was a dramatic move against foreign capital and represented the first of a series of clashes between the government and the United States. Nine months later the promulgation of a radical agrarian reform law promised 'land to the tiller'. Of all the military's actions, this is likely to be the one with the longest-lasting influence. Agriculture's poor performance was thought to be a consequence of the highly unequal land tenure system. According to the 1961 census 0.4 per cent of farms in the country accounted for 76 per cent of farmland, while another 83 per cent of farms held only 5.5 per cent of it. The 1969 law established that all farms larger than 150 hectares on the coast, and 35 to 65 hectares in the highlands, were liable to expropriation, as were all farms not managed by their owners. The land was redistributed to the rural labour force, either as individual smallholdings or, more usually, as production co-operatives in which the integrity of the former estate was maintained and the land farmed collectively. The reform redistributed nearly 40 per cent of Peru's crop and pasture lands, transferring ownership to one fifth of the agricultural labour force.

On the coast, where capitalist wage relations were most firmly established before the reform, 82 per cent of the land redistributed was held collectively but this proportion fell by half in the highlands. Yet, while the reform clearly had a major impact on landholding in Peru, it did not solve the agrarian problem. Production levels were scarcely affected and food imports continued to rise, thereby increasing Peru's food dependency. Seasonal labourers and the bulk of the smallholding peasantry did not benefit, and conflicts developed between these groups and the new landowners. In some cases this has resulted in the invasion of reform sector farmland. Furthermore the redistributive element of the reform in terms of income was relatively slight because the beneficiaries were already the better-off groups in the countryside.

The agrarian reform appears to be one of the few reforms for which the regime had a reasonably clear idea of what it wanted to do at the time of the coup. Most of the other major reforms implemented in the First Phase developed in a more ad hoc fashion, as the military defined its policies in relation to its more abstract goals, such as social justice, popular participation and the reduction of external dependency, or as circumstances called forth new responses. The State was expanded in an irregular but massive fashion, partly because of the military's belief that it should play a leading role, and partly because of the private sector's failure to come forward in the economic sphere. It also expanded as it inherited private sector 'lame ducks', such as the Prado banking empire and the fishing industry. By 1975 the state sector had come to represent 32 per cent of formal sector output, compared with 16 per cent in 1968, while foreign ownership had declined in the same period from 35 per cent in 1968 to 16 per cent in 1975. The State nationalized strategic industries, such as steel and chemicals, became responsible for export marketing and took over a number of important foreign enterprises, as well as renegotiating the terms under which foreign firms could operate in Peru.

Work place participation was promoted by a variety of measures designed to reform private enterprise as well as to create a fully labour-managed (Social Property) sector of the economy. 'Industrial communities' were set up in all enterprises larger than six employees, and each 'community' was to receive 25 per cent of post-tax profits (10 per cent in cash and 15 per cent as new share issues), with the intention that it would come to hold 50 per cent of ownership. As with the agrarian reform, however, this measure was to benefit those who already had a privileged position in the labour force. By 1975 3,500 'communities' had been formed but these embraced less than five per cent of the economically active population of Peru. In 1973 the government formed a National Commission of Industrial Communities which, to the government's dismay, then applied pressure for the further radicalization of the reform. This process, which had its parallel in agriculture, was also assisted by the appointment of left-wing civilian advisers and ideologues to the government. The government also intervened in the educational system, reorganizing the universities and restructuring the state sector of education to make it more relevant to Peru's developmental needs. For the first time Quechua was declared an official language, instead of Spanish alone. In foreign affairs the government followed a policy of non-alignment, establishing diplomatic relations with a number of Eastern European countries and becoming the first Latin American country, after Chile, to reestablish relations with Cuba.

Although the government claimed to be building a 'fully participatory social democracy', it became evident after a time that participation 'from below' was only to be permitted via government-sponsored and -controlled organizations. In 1971 the National System for Social Mobilization (SINAMOS) was set up in order to mobilize support for the government's policies and to channel mass participation in directions desired by the government. SINAMOS was also involved in community self-help projects, and training for self-management where it became identified with government attempts to control popular organizations. SINAMOS eventually became a major organization with over 5,000 employees, yet never succeeded in establishing its legitimacy as an authentic organ of 'popular participation'. Between 1973 and 1975 it was a target for anti-government opposition and was finally run down when the government became disillusioned with its performance. At the same time government-sponsored organizations were set up parallel to older institutions in the labour movement. A Workers Confederation of the Peruvian Revolution was set up to compete with communist and APRA-controlled labour federations, and the National Agrarian Confederation was established in competition with the left-wing Peruvian Peasants Confederation. The aim appears to have been to draw support away from the organizations controlled by the traditional political parties, but this goal was frustrated by the government's reluctance to grant the new institutions any significant degree of autonomy.

By 1975 the First Phase of the 'revolution' was in real difficulties. The economic situation began to deteriorate sharply with accelerating inflation, a huge balance of payments deficit, falling reserves and a growing burden of foreign debt. The world commodity boom which had supported the expansionary policies of the First Phase had also drawn to a close and the export sector as a whole was facing stagnation. The mushrooming state sector had begun to escape financial control and the military indulged itself in a spending spree on military hardware. The hoped-for oil wealth from the Amazon, which was intended to alleviate the situation, failed to appear in the quantities necessary, so Peru began to face an acute economic crisis. At the same time the failing health of President Velasco, combined with differences among the military, started to destabilize the regime. The combination of these events led to the bloodless coup against Velasco and his replacement by Morales Bermúdez.

The inauguration of the Second Phase marked the end of the reform element of the 'revolution' and the gradual withdrawal of many of the innovations introduced in the earlier period. The role of the 'industrial community' was reduced, 'Social Property' was virtually abandoned, some parts of the state sector were returned to private hands, and a more favourable attitude to the private sector was adopted. Nevertheless, the period 1975 to 1978 represented a major economic and social crisis for the whole nation. Attempts to introduce increasingly severe austerity programmes met with fierce resistance from those most directly affected. Successive economic teams attempted to cope with the deepening crisis represented by accelerating inflation, falling industrial output and rising unemployment. For two years the military attempted to handle the crisis by returning to more orthodox, but rather half-hearted, economic policies including price increases and devaluation of the sol. As the situation worsened, and first US private banks and then the IMF were called in to provide emergency loans, the government was trapped between the creditors' demands for greater economic stringency and the resistance of the working class. The latter was most vividly demonstrated in 1977 with a general strike which contributed to the collapse of negotiations with the IMF. Finally, in the face of imminent external bankruptcy, the government steeled itself to the introduction of severe measures. In May 1978 major price rises were approved, subsidies were removed, the sól was devalued, and government spending cut back. As before, the result was rioting in several major cities and a second general strike but, in the absence of any alternative, the government stood firm. As a result, an agreement was reached with the IMF, and the rescheduling of the external debt was successfully negotiated. The economic situation then began to improve, aided by increased oil exports, sharply reduced imports and rises in export prices, especially for minerals, but the cost of this adjustment process was very high. Unemployment rose to 8.5 per cent, real wages for both blue- and white-collar workers fell dramatically, while income distribution became even more unequal, protein and calorie intake declined markedly and per capita GNP fell by eight per cent between 1976 and 1978.

At the same time the government was also attempting to extricate itself from the overall situation by engineering a return to civilian rule. In 1978 elections were held for the Constituent Assembly which was to draft a new constitution prior to general elections in 1980. *Acción Popular* refused to participate in the elections for the Constituent Assembly, with the result that APRA won a substantial majority. By this time the military had reached a rapprochement with APRA and were in fact co-operating with them to ensure an APRA victory in 1980. The most remarkable characteristic of the 1978 elections, however, was the very successful showing of the left-wing parties who gained over a third of the votes, reflecting the increase in politicization which the First Phase had stimulated and which the Second Phase had brought on to the streets. Yet by 1980 both APRA and the left were badly fragmented. Haya de la Torre became seriously ill, and without his presence APRA began to divide between a conservative old guard and a more populist, social democratic group led by Armando Villanueva. Haya's death in August 1979 opened an acrimonious split between the two groups as they struggled for the succession. Villanueva's group finally prevailed, but at the cost of alienating the military and generating a highly unflattering campaign image. On the left, despite considerable efforts to achieve unity, the parties went into the general election as warring factions which offered no coherent alternative to the established political parties. *Acción Popular*, on the other hand, approached the election with a record unblemished by association with the military, with a charismatic and experienced leader and with a populist rhetoric attractive to many sectors of the population. The result was an overwhelming victory for Belaunde and *Acción Popular* in May 1980. Belaunde returned to the presidential palace after a twelve-year absence. The municipal elections in November of that year confirmed the dominance of *Acción Popular*, although the left made a good showing as a result of its decision to run as a united coalition (*Izquierda Unida*).

The return of Belaúnde was marked by the initiation of an economic recovery programme based on free market policies and a variety of monetary and fiscal measures. Subsidies and controls introduced by the military government have been removed, and prices have risen. In January 1981, for example, the prices of fuel and many basic foodstuffs rose by an average of 48 per cent. Inflation has remained high, reaching 61 per cent in 1980, 73 per cent in 1981 and 65 per cent in 1982, with no sign of an early fall. Domestic interest rates have been raised to reflect the level of inflation, and a mini-devaluation programme accelerated to a compound yearly rate of over 140 per cent by the first quarter of 1983. This tight monetary policy has also been expressed in persistent, if often unsuccessful, attempts to reduce public spending. The first three years of Belaúnde's government were in fact marked by a mounting budget deficit, created by ambitious plans for public works, road building, and other development projects, as well as higher expenditure on wages and salaries within the state sector. The numerous state enterprises, which the government is anxious to sell off as part of its privatization programme, also performed poorly. In an attempt to reduce this deficit, the government ordered cutbacks in a number of the investment projects, sharply increased public sector prices and applied a surcharge to imported goods. But it was eventually forced to turn to the IMF in June 1982 in order to obtain a US $ 960 million line of credit. The external debt has continued to rise, reaching a total of US $ 11.5 million by the end of

1982 – an increase of 16.5 per cent over the previous year and costing the equivalent of over 50 per cent of the value of exports in debt servicing. After windfall gains from higher export prices in 1980, the balance of payments has been hit by a slack demand for Peru's export products. Finally, the economy as a whole began to slow down in 1982 and actually contracted in 1983, with manufacturing in particular suffering from depressed consumer demand, rising costs and the tight monetary squeeze.

In the longer term the government has sought to increase foreign investment in the economy, with emphasis on the oil and mining industries. New investment regulations encouraged greater production and exploration in the oil industry. Other legislation has been concerned with some of the measures introduced during the First Phase of the *docenio*. A new Industries Law seeks to dismantle further the 'industrial communities', and the Agricultural Promotion Law of November 1980, while respecting landholding maximums, has opened the way to the breakup of the co-operative units and to the resurgence of private agrarian capitalism. The reaction of the labour movement to the poor economic conditions, and to the government's management, caused an increase in strike activity throughout 1982 and 1983.

The major political threat to the Belaúnde regime has not come, however, from either the military, which remains discredited, or the parliamentary left, which has entered a period of crisis, but from a highly organized guerrilla campaign waged by *Sendero Luminoso* (Shining Path). *Sendero* is a powerful movement with a strong base in the poor peasantry, particularly in the Ayacucho region of Peru. Its origins and organizational structure are still shrouded in mystery, and even the government security forces seem to have little information or understanding of the movement. *Sendero* started its armed actions in 1980 and has shown increasing military capacity, having plunged Lima into darkness a number of times through cutting the capital's electricity supplies, and destroying a large chemical works in the city. Evidence of its support in the Ayacucho area could be seen in the large attendance at the funeral of one of its militants in the city of Ayacucho, and the general strike there in January 1983.

The government has sent an estimated 12,000 troops into Ayacucho, and at the end of May 1983 declared a state of emergency. It also introduced an anti-terrorist law with severe penalties. There have been many reports of human rights abuses carried out by the security forces under the pretext of this law, but increased government repression is unlikely to solve a problem whose roots lie in the traditional neglect of the peasants of the *Sierra*. Many of the frustrations of this impoverished section of the Peruvian population have found expression in *Sendero Luminoso*. For the first time in the nation's history, the central government cannot afford to ignore the problems of the *Sierra*. Peru's political future may well depend on its response.

The Roman Catholic Church is an important force in Peru. The vast majority of Peruvians feel themselves to be Catholics, even though for many religion is restricted to the observance of the rites of passage and religious festivals. Though the Church has been deprived of many historic roles through the increasing secularization of State and Society, it continues to exercise influence in education, social work and in the maintenance of cultural values. At the popular level, church workers have had an impact in strengthening mass organizations, above all in the shanty towns but also in peasant communities, especially in the southern Andes. Many lay Catholics and pastoral agents participate in the parties of the secular left, creating a marriage of Christian faith and progressive/Marxist radicalism, similar in many ways to that found in Central America.

In 1532 there was a historic confrontation in the fortress city of Cajamarca between the Indian ruler, Inca Atahualpa, and the leader of the Spanish *conquistadores*, Francisco Pizarro. The Spanish party, 160 strong, included a Dominican friar, Vincente de Valverde, and it is said that when Atahualpa confidently entered the plaza of Cajamarca, borne on a golden litter and surrounded by thousands of Indian foot-soldiers, the friar held up a crucifix and a Latin breviary and called on the Inca to renounce his idolatry. He refused and a bloody battle ensued, during which Atahualpa was captured, and after an eight-month imprisonment was publicly executed by strangulation. A last-minute submission to Christian baptism spared him from burning at the stake.

Thus Christianity entered Peru, and as in other parts of Latin America, cross and sword, Church and Crown, were inseparable for the next three centuries. In fact, Catholic Christianity found fertile soil in the conquered Inca empire. During the decades immediately preceding the Conquest, the Inca rulers had deified themselves as children of the supreme sun god Inti, and when Atahualpa's mortality was so dramatically displayed this suggested to his subjects that the Christian God was altogether superior. The first canonized saint of the New World was St Rosa of Lima, a Dominican mystic in the Spanish tradition; she was soon followed by the mulatto Martín de Porres, son of a Spanish hidalgo and a Negro slavewoman − a saint who enjoys great prestige today, especially among the urban poor. In the person of St Toribio de Mogravejo, a sixteenth-century Archbishop of Lima, the dispossessed natives of the Andes found a strong defender, with affinities to his more famous contemporary Bartolomé de las Casas.

In the struggle for independence churchmen were to be found on both sides. The aboriginal Tupc Amaru II (after whom the modern Tupamaros of Uruguay are named) almost succeeded in toppling Spanish power and restoring Inca rule in the 1780s; he was accompanied by a field chaplain and the sincerity of his Catholicism has never been questioned. When the Peruvian Republic was born in 1829 few changes were introduced for the majority of its citizens: the Catholic Church continued to enjoy state protection and only towards the end of the nineteenth century were a few Protestant missionaries allowed into the country.

Today almost 96 per cent of Peru's heterogeneous population are baptized Roman Catholics. The 1980 Constitution recognizes the separation of Church and State, but mentions the 'special position' occupied by the Catholic Church in the life of the nation. This 'special position' is not merely a recognition of numerical strength, but also of the substantial contribution to health, education and culture still made by medical missionaries, teaching nuns and religious communities. Church attendance is, however, relatively low, especially in urban areas: a census taken in Lima in 1967 indicated that only 20 per cent of Catholics attended Mass, of whom 60 per cent were women and girls. As a result of a pastoral reorganization carried out in 1972, the dioceses are now grouped in nine zones, each of which has its own assembly. There are 51 bishops, just over 2,000 priests, and about 2,000 men and 5,000 women in religious orders. There is an important Faculty of

Theology at Lima, associated with the Pontifical Catholic University of Peru, which has about 200 students – women as well as men, laity and clergy. In addition to this there are four 'research and social action' centres, concerned with Church and Society issues, and there are fourteen Catholic radio stations.

As early as 1958 a Peruvian Episcopal Assembly, influenced perhaps by the general reformist sentiments of the time, criticized social inequalities and called for reforms. Subsequent distancing of the Catholic Church from the oligarchy went hand in hand with a growing identification with the rural and urban poor. The Second Vatican Council, followed by the Latin American Episcopal Conferences (CELAM) in Medellín and Puebla, also had a profound influence on the Church in Peru. A great influx of foreign priests and nuns (especially from Spain and Canada) during the 1960s and 1970s, to cope with the large increase in population caused by the population explosion, was of crucial importance in the communication of new ideas about the role of the Church in society. About 60 per cent of Peru's priests, and the same proportion of monks and nuns, are still foreign born.

In 1968, ONIS, a movement of progressive clergy, was founded and the Medellín conference, in which the Peruvian delegation took a decisive part, gave official blessing to many of the innovations taking root in Peru – the attempt to understand society in scientific terms, the theme of liberation, and 'the option for the poor'. In January 1969 the Bishops' Conference undertook to put the Medellín recommendations into practice, and during the following years the Catholic Church backed the government reforms and supported peasants, shanty town dwellers and workers in their struggles. The year 1971 saw the publication by the Peruvian bishops of 'Justice in the World' – the most radical episcopal document ever produced in the Americas – which, after a prophetic denunciation of the ills of Peruvian society, with particular reference to the extremes of wealth and poverty, went on to sound a clarion call for 'a new social order based on Christian, humanist socialism'.

In the same year *A Theology of Liberation*, by the Peruvian diocesan priest Gustavo Gutiérrez, was published in Lima. Influenced heavily by the author's parallel studies of sociology, psychology and economics, the book urges the need for a greater decentralization (and consequently a greater regionalization) in the field of theology, while preserving the catholicity of the Church's organization. There was also a meeting of 2,000 Catholics which gave birth to the *Iglesia Solidaria*. This movement, which united priests, monks and nuns, students and workers and grassroots Catholic community groups, later became known as 'Faith and Action in Solidarity' and remains an important force within the Church. Progressive clergy and lay Catholics aimed to construct the 'Church of the People', creating grassroots communities, *Comunidades Eclesiales de Base* (CEBs) designed to promote both theological reflection and radical social action. An annual Theology Summer School still attracts thousands of participants from all over Latin America. The period 1968–73 confirmed the distancing of the Church from the dominant classes and represented an advance towards the alternative option – an alignment with the working people and their efforts to transform society. With a reformist government in power and a low level of class conflict, radicalization was considered to be less controversial and not necessarily 'subversive', and could take place with the guarded approval of the government and the grudging acceptance of business and landowning interests.

After 1973, however, the situation changed. The government's move to the right caused some sectors of the Church to retreat from earlier positions, while others deepened their identification with the oppressed. In 1976, the government having abandoned all pretence of reform, social protest increased sharply. The participation of the urban poor in the 1977 general strike reflected the years of church work in the shanty towns and demonstrated the importance of the *Iglesia Popular*. In 1978 committed Catholics were active in the mass mobilizations, with the CEBs providing important support for those in the struggle. In these years progressive bishops spoke out many times on issues of justice and human rights. In the course of 1979 social tension lessened and mass activity declined. The return to democracy created new political conditions in which Catholic social activists concentrated on long-term educational and organizational grassroots work and on expanding the network of CEBs. Within the hierarchy, the attitude towards the ideas of the *Iglesia Popular* continued to cool, and tolerance came to replace support. Nevertheless, in line with the conclusions of Puebla, where once again the Peruvians played a key role, the hierarchy firmly placed human rights at the centre of the Church's concern. In 1981 the bishops denounced the official use of torture. The violence of the government's counter-attack, supported by the right-wing press, revealed their concern to silence the Church on political matters. The government also objected to criticism of the consumerism and growing inequality resulting from its policies. The Roman Catholic Church is now much more heterogeneous than it was a decade ago – tendencies range from the ultra-conservative *Opus Dei* group, through conservatives and progressives to the radical ONIS activists – and the balance of forces has shifted; but at the 1982 Bishops' Conference *Opus Dei* failed to get any supporters elected to office, and well-known progressives continued in positions of responsibility. The relative social peace of 1980–1 is now coming to an end, and pressures on the Church from different social and political forces are intensifying. The government and the privileged classes are attempting to win over sectors of the Church to the defence of the status quo, while seeking the marginalization of the radicals. Meanwhile the 'poor and oppressed', now more self-confident, organized and articulate, are placing greater demands on the Church to live up to its avowed mission to support them. The hierarchy may perhaps become more conservative, but the progressive current is too well consolidated to be pushed aside, and church structures have been sufficiently democratized to ensure the 'lowerarchy' a degree of autonomy. The dynamism in the Church comes from the association with working people, from the several thousand CEBs and from the Catholic activists working in grassroots organizations. Should Peru become a more authoritarian society, as seems likely, with intensified social conflict, the Church will become more divided, but a significant sector will speak out against injustice and align itself even more closely with the cause of liberation.

The religious monopoly of the Catholic Church was maintained for 350 years, and not until 1915 were Protestants allowed to worship in public. Protestantism was in fact virtually unknown in Peru until the arrival, towards the end of the nineteenth century, of a new wave of immigrants from Northern Europe, which led to the founding of the Baptist, Methodist, and Lutheran churches. An Anglican presence had been established in 1849. Until the 1950s the historic churches worked principally with their own English-

and German-speaking immigrants and were served by immigrant pastors and ministers, but they are now more Peruvian, as well as more actively evangelistic. The historic European churches were followed in the 1920s by the North American churches, reflecting the greater general involvement in the region by the USA since the beginning of this century. But the mainstream Protestant churches remain a tiny minority of the Peruvian population, the largest being the Methodist with a membership of about 4,500.

The influence of the Catholic 'Theology of Liberation', and of the ecumenical stirrings of the latter decades, has varied greatly from church to church. The Anglican Church is markedly ecumenical in its social commitment to the marginalized urban inhabitants, the Lutherans only slightly less so. The mainstream Baptist and Adventist churches are much less enthusiastic about inter-church contacts, whereas the Methodist Church in Lima (of US origin) has played the major role in the establishment of two social/educational institutions – CELADEC (Latin American Evangelical Committee for Christian Education) and SEPAS (Peruvian Evangelical Service for Social Action). The Methodist and Lutheran churches are active participants in the National Ecumenical Committee, which draws together representatives of different faiths, including Catholics and Jews.

The last ten years have seen important changes in the attitude of the historic churches towards social injustice and underdevelopment. There is a greater questioning of the model of economic and political development prevalent in most Latin American countries and of the economic, political and cultural domination of the USA. There is also a greater awareness of the dangers of patronizing attitudes and high-powered assistance projects which can only produce a new crop of 'rice Christians'. SEPAS is supporting community development projects such as income-creating workshops and nutrition programmes. The historic churches, especially the Methodists, have also become involved in human rights campaigns and have given support to refugees from other Latin American countries. This change of attitudes has not always been easy for the largely middle-class congregations that make up the historic churches, and disagreements have been not infrequent in recent years (the Methodist Church was even suspended from the National Evangelical Council), but there seems to be a determination by them all to continue along the path of greater involvement in the total life of the Peruvian people.

Numerous independent churches and sects have sprung up in Peru since 1915. Most are small, relatively democratic, evangelical bodies run by nationals, and are mostly urban in character. Many of them participate in inter-church social action programmes, though their main aim in doing so is the recruitment of new members. The more fundamentalist groups are now the most important Protestant churches in Peru, in terms of membership and influence. Especially important are the Pentecostal and Adventist, who together comprise the great majority of the Protestant population. More recent arrivals in the Pentecostal tradition are the Nazarenes and the Pilgrims, both of US origin. The total membership of all these fundamentalist churches is now approaching 700,000. Most started work in Peru after 1945. Almost all originated in the USA and maintain close contact with their mother churches; much of their work is directed and carried out by US citizens. They tend not to collaborate with other churches, one notable exception being the Adventist Church, which does participate in the National Ecumenical Committee.

Peru's deteriorating economic crisis and growing political radicalization are reflected in the resilience of *Sendero Luminoso* and the victory of the left in the municipal elections of November 1983. The strain imposed on the churches is already evident: while many priests and nuns working among the poor are still struggling to work out a 'preferential option for the poor', the right-wing backlash is gathering strength, with landowners in the *Sierra* attacking the Catholic Church wherever it has taken practical steps to educate or organize the *campesinos*. Fundamentalist and Pentecostal churches, as well as charismatic Catholic movements, will prosper in this atmosphere of uncertainty and division – offering a threatened people the comfort of total belief and respectability.

Chapter 9

Mexico

Mexico, with over 70 million people, is, after Brazil, the second most populous country in Latin America, and the third largest by area, extending over 761,602 square miles. It has a varied natural base, ranging from the northern deserts to jungles in the south, with a great highland plateau of 3–8,000 feet elevation in between. Mexico has a long pre-Colombian past which included two great civilizations – Aztec and Mayan – and may have had some 20 million Indian peoples at the onset of the Spanish Conquest led by Cortes in 1519. An estimated 10–12 million of these inhabited the high plateau region of central-southern Mexico, while Tenochtitlan, the capital of the Aztec empire until its destruction by the Spanish in 1521 and now the site of Mexico City, had just over one million people. By contrast, the more arid northern part of the country, which then included the present day States of California, Texas and much of south-west USA (ceded to America after the war of 1846–8), was more sparsely populated by dispersed Indian settlements.

The devastation of conquest, followed by centuries of colonization and intermarriage with Europeans, reduced the pure Indian population so that today most Mexicans are of mixed (*mestizo*) stock. Broadly speaking, Mexican culture is an amalgam of Spanish and Indian elements, although the indigenous component remains a strong feature. During the nineteenth century, leaders of Indian stock (or often, *mestizos* defending Indian interests) were particularly influential in both the movement for independence (from 1810) and in the early post-independence period (from about 1824) until Porfirio Diaz assumed presidential power in 1876. It was the efforts of men such as the Indian Benitio Juarez, who became President in 1867, which helped to keep Mexico united. Under the Diaz dictatorship (often referred to as the *porfiriato*) which lasted from 1876 until the revolution of 1910, Indian interests were, however, eroded substantially. And despite relatively liberal official attitudes towards racial discrimination and indigenous cultural values since the revolution, Mexican society has been essentially dominated by those of Spanish-speaking European stock. This trend has been reinforced by a heavily centralized political structure and an educational system in which only Spanish is taught in schools. Nevertheless, it was estimated that by 1970 about two per cent of the total population still spoke only an Indian language. About a fifth of the national population still display Indian traits of one kind or another.

Mexico is one of the few Latin American countries, along with Bolivia, Cuba and – more recently – Nicaragua, to have experienced a profound social revolution. This took place during almost a decade of civil war dating from 1910, and it began largely as a reaction to the continuation of the Díaz dictatorship. For 35 years, Porfirio Díaz had presided over an expansion of the Mexican economy, but at the cost of considerable foreign, notably US, penetration and the reinforcement of social inequalities. In particular, he had ignored the lot of the peasantry who at that time accounted for about three quarters of the total population of 15 million. On the eve of the revolution, 96.6 per cent of rural families were landless. The large landowners, or *haciendados*, were the backbone of Díaz's support. When the immediate objective of forcing Díaz out of office had been achieved, within a year, the revolution gathered further momentum. While there was no completely dominant ideology driving it forward, perhaps the notion of 'Land and Liberty' (*Tierra y Libertad*) best captures the popular demands, and to this end a redistribution of land was a central goal. Through the spontaneous efforts of local military leaders – including the legendary figures of Pancho Villa and Emiliano Zapata – Indian and *mestizo* peasants rose up in revolt against large landowners, including the Church, and foreign interests. The hostility to the grip of the Roman Catholic Church over the largely illiterate peasantry was particularly intense amongst certain of the revolutionary leaders. In the 1920s, after the revolution, there were several persecutions of the Church and attempts to limit the number of priests and prohibit foreign priests. In 1928, these attacks aroused a Catholic revolt – the Cristero rebellion – which was encouraged and often led by priests but whose base was illiterate, conservative peasants. Seventy thousand died during the rebellion.

In many respects, the interlinked issues which were exposed during the revolution itself, e.g. land reform, economic nationalism, and political continuity/stability, have been central to post-revolutionary ideology. Yet, on a political level, events since 1910, and more particularly from 1929 when the Institutional Revolutionary Party, the PRI (*Partido Revolucionario Instituciónal*), was established, have increasingly eroded the revolution's popular base, and the reforms it set in train. Indeed, it might be argued that by the signing of the new constitution in 1917 a revolutionary élite began to consolidate and extend its control over Mexican society. Initially, this involved the suppression of armed rebellion and, where necessary, the buying off of rebels by the government. General Obregón (President 1920–4), when asked about his success in discouraging rebellion, replied, 'I know of no General who can withstand a broadside of 50,000 pesos.' Some critics of the system believe this method of maintaining stability is still rife in Mexico, but that the price has risen.

Following the assassination of Obregón, shortly after his re-election to the Presidency in 1928, the Mexican revolutionary élite set up the Revolutionary Party (PRI) in order to solve internal differences, and, in the short term, to dissuade supporters of former president Obregón from rebellion. Within a few years of its formation, under the presidency of Lázaro Cárdenas (1934–40), the party encouraged the setting up of workers' and peasants' organizations, and their incorporation into the Revolutionary Party. The PRI came to represent three major social groupings – peasants, organized labour, and the middle class. Thus, from an early stage, the party became, in theory at least, a 'mass party'. Cárdenas also promoted some fairly radical changes, including the nationalization of the railways (1937) and the oil industry (1938), the latter formerly controlled by US and British companies. He also extended land reform, which, although it had been introduced in 1915, had not been fully implemented. Since the 1940s, the growth of larger-scale, 'modern' industry, encouraged by government policies, and the commercialization of agriculture have emerged as the central platform of Mexican development strategy.

Formally, the Mexican political system which has evolved since the revolution is democratic, federal and constitutional; in practice it is centralized, authoritarian and presidential although it does have some democratic characteristics. The Presidential term is six years (the present President, Miguel de la Madrid, took office on 1st December 1982) and no man may serve more than one term. The outgoing President chooses his own successor, after consultation with key political leaders, though it does not follow from this that the new man will faithfully follow the lines laid down by his predecessor. Rather, each new Mexican President is determined to be his own man, and one can detect something of an alternation in the way in which each has wielded power, with a notably right- or left-wing President being followed by a reaction. It should, however, be noted that the swing from left to right and back is minimal at the level of real policy, as opposed to rhetoric. The system remains fundamentally conservative. The six-year term also leads to the well-known 'presidential cycle'. In his first year the President is comparatively weak, as a number of figures surviving from the former regime remain at their posts. In the second, third and fourth years of his term the President is fully in command and the key decisions of his administration will be taken. By the fifth year attention begins to turn towards the succession; the successor is generally nominated around the middle of this year and then the President begins to lose his power as attention gravitates towards the new man.

It is sometimes said that the only limit placed on the power of the President is that of the six-year term of office. Formally, the President is elected by popular vote. In practice, there is never any doubt that the official candidate will win; in 1982, de la Madrid polled 71.6 per cent of the vote – which meant that the opposition vote in that year was unprecedentedly high. Each Mexican President is the head not only of government (and the State) but also of the official party – the PRI. Unlike, for example, the USSR, the party is far less important than the formal state bureaucracy, although it has the task of contesting elections for President, state governor and Congress. In a sense this is no real hardship since no opposition candidate has ever won so much as a governorship. But the Mexican élite like to see a high electoral turnout and expect the PRI to secure it. The opposition is guaranteed some congressional representation under legislation favouring minority parties, and it occasionally wins municipal elections in the provinces, but opposition parties operate more as pressure groups than as serious contenders for national power. Their relatively weak financial and numerical base, and lack of political patronage, limits their scope for action. The main opposition parties are PAN, a right-wing Catholic party, and a variety of minor fringe parties on the left. The Communist Party is probably the most important of these; in 1980, it dissolved itself to form PSUM (United Mexican Socialist Party) in coalition with two or three other groups.

The limitations on the influence of these opposition parties do not apply, however, to the few very rich and economically powerful private sector interests whose wealth has been enhanced by the development model pursued. Several important families control a well-organized network of business interests, and certain sections of the media, all of which actively seek to influence government policy. Over the last 40 years new sources of potential political conflict have arisen within the upper echelons of Mexican society, among these private sector groups and certain sectors of the middle class, but also in the increasingly important state sector, typified by Pemex (the state oil concern) and other public corporations. These new elements have added further complexity to the political structure, but dissent is still channelled through the PRI which dominates the political scene. Unlike most Latin American countries, the Mexican military have been eased out of direct political power. The last military President (General Avila Camacho) left office as long ago as 1946. But the military may be used as a supplementary police force when required, as in the 1968 student demonstrations in Mexico City or in clashes between peasants and landowners. During the last few years extensive modernization and expansion of the armed forces have been under way, stimulated by the political turbulence in Central America, not least the civil war in Guatemala, close to the Mexican oilfields.

Despite Mexico's reputation as one of the least repressive countries in Latin America, human rights are not always respected. Trade union or peasant action which might be potentially damaging to the PRI is often stamped upon. Recent Amnesty International reports have documented irregular arrests and the use of torture to obtain confessions (which in turn are used as the basis of evidence for convictions). Independent sources in Mexico estimate that 400 prisoners have disappeared. Political murders and assassinations also take place, left-wing political activists often being singled out. One notable example in 1980 was the murder of Núñez Acosta, mayor of the only Communist-controlled town in Mexico, Juchitán (Oaxaca), in which the PRI was widely suspected of being involved. Similarly, despite the redistribution of land and setting up of the *ejido* system after the revolution, land tenure disputes are common, since redistribution has often been grossly unequal, and peasants are frequently unable to gain access to the land. Illegal occupation of land may result in forcible eviction or murder.

In comparison with the majority of Third World countries, contemporary Mexico does not rank among the poorest. This was so even before it became an oil exporter in the mid-1970s. In 1980 the country's average per capita GDP was put at US $ 2,090 by the World Bank – a level similar to that of Brazil (US $ 2,050) and Chile (US $ 2,150) but roughly double that of neighbouring Guatemala (US $ 1,080) or Peru (US $ 930). In the same year many countries in tropical Africa and Asia registered per capita incomes of between a tenth and a half of the Mexican figure. Nevertheless, the contrast between the per capita income of Mexico and that of highly developed economies such as the United States – and even the United Kingdom – is striking. The US level, at US $ 11,360, was over five times that of Mexico, and the UK's, at US $ 7,920 almost four times greater. It is not surprising therefore to find that over the years tens of thousands of Mexicans have migrated north across the 2,000-mile border with the USA, illegally as well as legally, in search of jobs and higher incomes. During times of economic expansion the US authorities have tolerated high levels of seasonal, temporary and longer-term migrant labour, but the recessionary climate of recent years has brought a tightening of border surveillance. Internal migration is even more common, in response to the highly unequal distribution of income within the country. In the late 1970s less than one quarter of the total national household income went to some 60 per cent of the population, and today the number of Mexicans surviving at the margins of basic subsistence is still considerable – totalling perhaps 14 million, i.e. one fifth of the population – with many millions more in a highly precarious position. About 40 per cent of the total labour force earn only the minimum wage, with peasant farmers, many of Indian stock, and migrants to the towns and cities among the worst affected groups. In rural areas, minimum wage legislation is not always enforced and a recent study showed that 1,750,000 farm workers were underpaid. The growth of largely urban-based manufacturing and commercial activities, sponsored by government policies, has drawn more and more people into a variety of non-agricultural occupations during recent decades. In 1960 55 per cent of the labour force was still engaged in agriculture, but by 1980 the proportion had been reduced to 36 per cent, with corresponding rises in the industrial and service sectors. These changes involved large-scale internal migration – up to 1.3 million peasants a year have been leaving the countryside for towns and cities – and there have been rapid rates of natural population increase, averaging 3.5 per cent annually in the past 25 years. Thus 67 per cent of the people now reside in urban centres, with a larger proportion of urban dwellers now living in larger-sized cities. In 1960 there were only three cities of over 500,000 people (Mexico City, Guadalajara and Monterrey) but twenty years later there were seven, two of which (Ciudad Juárez and Tijuana) are located along the northern border. The rapid growth of these border cities is linked to special government programmes devised to attract subsidiaries of US firms to locate labour-intensive parts of manufacturing industry there. By 1982 there were over 600 firms – the *maquiladoras* – employing over 125,000 people in this area. Together these firms, which produce for export, were the second largest net earners of dollar foreign exchange after Pemex, the state oil company.

The dramatic scale of the urban explosion, and its associated social costs, is graphically illustrated by the country's capital, Mexico City, and its sprawling metropolitan area, where one in five Mexicans now live. The population of this city has always been large, but between 1970 and 1980 it grew from eight to fifteen million. If recent growth rates continue, the city will have a population of 32 million by the year 2,000. The provision of shelter, services and jobs has not kept pace with this phenomenal growth. Public housing and other utilities have never been well developed, and though there have been improvements during the past twenty years, through federal and local authority schemes, the scale of building has been insufficient to replace old, substandard, often dirt-floor dwellings, let alone provide for the influx of newcomers. The level of rent or mortgage payments needed in many public schemes is beyond the income capacity of the majority of the city's population. Many low-income urban dwellers build their own wooden shacks on poor land or hillsides, or sometimes slightly more durable single-storey concrete and mud houses with one or two rooms. Employment opportunities are also scarce. In Mexico City only three out of five people in the work force have full-time jobs. The rest survive through some sort of marginal work, ranging from selling (or producing) cheap goods, foodstuffs and cigarettes to recycling waste materials. In Mexico as a whole 30–40 per cent of the labour force is estimated to be unemployed or under-employed.

In the rural areas, where 26 million people still attempt to live and work, large numbers of peasants are without land or have insufficient land to make a living. The farmers on communal lands, or *ejidos*, are particularly impoverished. The increases in agricultural output in recent years have been confined to the newly-opened irrigated lands and larger plantations, especially in the north-western part of the country, where costly river basin schemes have been implemented. The level of malnutrition in the rural areas is very high: in 1980, an estimated 19 million people still had a daily calorie and protein intake below the minimum required. The seriousness of the situation led President López Portillo to announce during that year a policy aimed at improving the nutritional level of an estimated 50 per cent of Mexican people, and benefiting some smaller-scale agricultural producers outside the irrigation zone.

These policy 'innovations', known as SAM (*Sistema Alimentaria Mexicano*), have not, in fact, come to fruition owing to the country's mounting debt problems during 1981–2. They have, however, exposed fundamental weaknesses in the Mexican development model. The rural sector has for many years been used to shore up the urban-industrial system. Irrigation schemes absorbed some 75 per cent of government investment in agriculture between 1945 and 1980, and costly 'Green Revolution' techniques (high-yielding varieties of wheat, expanded use of fertilizers, etc, often underpinned by the interests of foreign agribusiness multinationals), enabled new lands to be brought into production and foreign exchange earnings from grain exports rose. Thus for much of the period between 1945 and 1970 agriculture was able to contribute a surplus to the economy. But this surplus was in large measure linked to the widening of the income gap between urban and rural sectors, and specifically through low wages to agricultural workers. At the same time the emphasis upon irrigated agriculture and high-technology farming techniques created new imbalances between the irrigated zones and the rain-fed regions where productive land area and output were declining as the population increased rapidly. During the course of the 1970s these and other factors combined to accelerate a crisis in Mexican agriculture. The sector's average growth rate (two per cent) in that decade, was one per cent below that of population growth; hence there was a shortfall in the basic food supply. Between 1970 and 1980 it was necessary to import food grain equivalent to almost one fifth of home production, and it was projected that during the 1980s food imports would need to grow by 12 per cent every year, thus using up an increased proportion of foreign exchange revenues.

By Third World standards, Mexico's success in extending its economic base through industrialization has been spectacular. The most recent round of industrial expansion dates from about 1975, after the discovery of major oilfields in the south-east coastlands of Campeche Bay, offshore and onshore of Chiapas State, once the territory of the ancient Maya civilization. These fields are further south than the longer-established oilfields of the interior coastal zone between Tampico and Veracruz. The opening up of the new reserves coincided with a period when Mexican economic growth had slowed from 7–12 per cent to about 2–3 per cent per annum, but when world oil prices had risen considerably under the impact of OPEC policy in 1973–4. While Mexico was not a member of OPEC it did take advantage of the higher oil prices it advocated. The increased revenues from oil thus paved the way for more rapid growth in the later 1970s when a number of the world's developed countries, including much of Western Europe and the USA, were caught in a phase of recession exacerbated by rising energy costs.

For some thirty years prior to this new wave of expansion, Mexico had undergone substantial industrialization, largely to serve the domestic market. The economic infrastructure had been expanded and upgraded, the network of paved roads grew, and the country's capacity for production of intermediate products in the steel and chemical sectors increased. A wide range of consumer goods including cars and trucks, TVs and refrigerators were also produced. An estimated 70 per cent of Mexican industry was concentrated in the three major cities of the central plateau – Mexico City, Guadalajara and Monterrey – while the northern border towns were opened to US export industries. This industrialization strategy relied heavily upon foreign direct investment (FDI), loans, imports of capital goods and technology. All of these were obtained largely from developed countries, but disproportionately from the USA, and through the greater involvement of transnational enterprises in the economy. These developments meant that Mexico became more closely integrated into the international economy dominated by its northern neighbour. At the same time external dependency and vulnerability were enhanced by continued reliance on raw material exports for foreign exchange. While exports of manufactured goods have been an important item in foreign trade since the late 1950s, and from 1960 accounting for some 20 per cent of export revenues, the country's export performance remained strongly tied to revenues from primary products such as coffee, cotton and sugar, whose prices are susceptible to wide fluctuation on international markets. Consequently, by 1975 the country was involved in a range of deep financial obligations – reflected in an enormous debt of over US $ 14.3 billion, exceeded only by Brazil (US $ 21.2 billion) on a world scale, and with annual debt service payments of over US $ 2 billion per annum.

The discovery of new oil resources in 1974–5, followed by an export surplus and high international oil prices, introduced dramatic elements which were initially to bring about a rapid economic upturn. The increase in oil revenues, from US $ 138 million in 1974 to US $ 9.2 billion in 1980, meant that petroleum for the first time began to account for some 70 per cent of foreign exchange earnings. At the same time, the country's international credit rating was strengthened, and the government was able to embark on a massive spending programme to intensify the industrialization process. For example, steel capacity was to be more than tripled from 7 million to 24 million tons by 1990, while petrochemical capacity was to be more than doubled (from 9 million to 23 million tons) and a domestic capital goods industry was to be built up. An ambitious project to decentralize industry was also announced.

These plans for industrial expansion required further imports of capital goods and raw materials; by 1980 these accounted for 87 per cent of total imports. Manufactured imports quadrupled in value and tripled in volume between 1976 and 1981. On the basis of its potential oil revenues, Mexico was able to borrow large amounts from international financial sources to pay for these imports. After 1977 Mexico became the recipient of the largest annual amounts (among non-OPEC, less developed countries) from the Euro-currency markets, contracting loans of between US $ 6 billion and US $ 8 billion per year from 1978 to 1982 inclusive. Foreign investment, particularly from West Germany and Japan as well as the United States, also increased. This external financing enabled the Mexican economy to achieve extraordinary growth rates at a time when world economic growth had slowed to about half its previous rate. Even excluding oil, Mexico's national production increased at a rate of 8 per cent a year between 1978 and 1981, and about 500,000 new jobs were created on average every year during the five-year period.

But this growth was achieved by accumulating debts which by 1982 amounted to a massive US $ 85 billion; Mexico overtook Brazil for a while as the world's largest debtor. At the same time international oil prices began to fall as the world recession deepened. Mexico reduced its oil price in line with OPEC producers in 1981, on the authority of the director of Pemex, who was subsequently dismissed. The fall in export earnings contributed to a balance of payments deficit which by 1982 had reached crisis proportions. That year Mexico sent shock waves through the international financial system when it announced it was unable to meet its debt payments. The peso was devalued, exchange controls were introduced for the first time in recent Mexican history, and the domestic banks were nationalized. These steps were essential measures to stop the massive capital flight; between January 1981 and September 1982 an estimated US $ 14 billion left the country. Inflation soared. The international financial community hastened to produce a rescue package, terrified of the implications for the international banks should Mexico be forced to default. But the price the international bankers ask for a rescheduling agreement is high, and includes the negotiation of an economic adjustment programme with the IMF. IMF austerity programmes have profound implications for the poor of the country concerned; they usually include cuts in public expenditure, including subsidies on essential consumer goods, a wage freeze, and steps towards import liberalization. Some maintain that the price is too high and could result in a massive social explosion and political chaos. In such circumstances no austerity package could be sustained and the government would soon be unable to pay even interest payments on loans. Some argue that Mexico should not succumb to the bankers' demands but should join with other debtor nations in imposing its own terms.

There have also been suggestions that one consequence of Mexico's increasing economic vulnerability and dependence on US economic assistance may be in the field of foreign policy. Mexico has traditionally had the most independent foreign policy in Latin America, refusing to break off diplomatic relations with Cuba when the rest of the region followed the United States directive. A progressive stance on foreign policy issues has undoubtedly served its purpose in terms of Mexican internal politics, giving the government a radical image which is hardly mirrored in its treatment of the profound socio-economic problem within the country. This has been seen particularly in Mexico's position on the conflicts in neighbouring Central America. The Mexican government's support for the Sandinista revolution was very popular within the country, as is its willingness to distance itself from current US policies towards El Salvador by supporting FDR-EMEN. Mexico has played an active role in seeking a negotiated solution to the civil war in that country and has opposed escalating US involvement in the region. Its position has been very important to the revolutionary forces within the region, although most recognize that the Mexican government is essentially pursuing its own interests. These involve primarily a desire to see stability on its borders and to prevent the regionalization of the Central American war in a way which could involve Mexico itself.

Mexico is more cautious, however, when it comes to its most immediate neighbour, Guatemala. Guatemala borders on Mexico and some of the problems over land ownership, which are the origins of that country's social conflict, are not dissimilar from problems in southern Mexico. The flow of refugees from Guatemala has therefore presented the Mexican government with a dilemma. Its response has been ambivalent; little assistance has been given to the refugees, although they have been allowed to set up squalid, makeshift camps in Chiapas. However, there have been cases of soldiers in the area attacking the refugees and even sending them back to Guatemala. Although such incidents declined in 1983, they reflect the nervousness of the local authorities at the implications of events in Guatemala for Mexico's internal politics.

So far, however, there have been no signs of major shifts in Mexican foreign policy as a result of the economic crisis. But nothing can be said with certainty about the country's future. Mexico's GNP fell by 3 per cent in 1983, after a minimal rise in 1982; real wages have already fallen substantially as inflation nears 100 per cent, and unemployment will certainly rise further as the recession bites deeper. In this situation, the Mexican political system will face a real test of its traditional skills in managing social conflict. Its performance will be nervously watched by the world bankers.

Mexico has perhaps the strongest Roman Catholic Church, and certainly the strongest anti-clerical history, of any in Latin America. Ninety-five per cent are baptized Catholics, 80 per cent are confirmed, and 77 per cent married in church. From the time of the Conquest, the church hierarchy (although not necessarily the priesthood, and still less the body of worshippers) came to be strongly identified with Spain and the Empire. By the early part of the nineteenth century there was an archbishop, eight bishops, 1,703 parishes, and 254 monasteries and convents. During the nineteenth century the church hierarchy also showed its 'reactionary' credentials by supporting Maximilian's attempt to restore imperialism to Mexico. At the same time, and continuing into the early twentieth century, Mexico's progressive modernizing élites described themselves as atheist and were, in many cases, actively anti-clerical.

The élite, which at the end of the 1920s constituted itself into the official Revolutionary Party, opposed the Church for several reasons. It had supported the Spanish Empire and the attempted imperial restoration by Maximilian; it was seen as an ultra-montane force at odds with the new emphasis on Mexican nationalism; at another level, the Church was a competitor with the Revolutionary Party for popular support and political legitimacy – once or twice prior to 1920 the Church had supported candidates for political office in Mexico and these had won convincingly; finally, there was the lure of church property – the Revolutionary Party was attempting to build a political base by a policy of distributive reforms, including land reform. In many places the Church endured persecution silently but, for a few years during the 1920s, Catholic rebellion spread – particularly through the Bajio area of western Mexico. In 1929 the church hierarchy agreed to a compromise peace at a time when, according to some later historians, the Catholic rebels might have won. But, in any case, the compromise was not really put into effect and official anti-clericalism came to an end only when Cárdenas announced a new policy (of ignoring the Church and waiting for its influence to wither) in 1938. At that time national unity was considered vital, following the expropriation of foreign oil companies (an act supported by the Catholic hierarchy), and the revolutionary élite began to move to a less radical position on a variety of other issues.

Since 1940 there has been a kind of *modus vivendi* between Church and State in Mexico. The earlier anti-clerical laws have not been repealed but they are no longer observed, and although the official party, which continues to dominate the electoral process, remains officially atheist most of its leading members are Catholics. The President, Miguel de la Madrid, is a practising Catholic and his wife is said to be a member of *Opus Dei*. The largest official opposition parties (PAN and PDM) are both explicitly Catholic in the sense that they derive their inspiration from traditional Catholic teaching on social and political issues. PAN was founded in 1939 as an alternative to the Revolutionary Party and, although still very much a minority party, it has recently increased its electoral strength: at the last election, it won about 20 per cent of the vote for Congress and 16 per cent for the Presidency. PDM, smaller and more militant, has recently performed well in local elections, particularly in the Bajio area where political Catholicism remains strong. Yet many, probably most, Mexican Catholics still vote for the government party.

Church education in Mexico – where half of the entire population are under the age of sixteen – is widely recognized as being of high standard but also expensive. Around one tenth of Mexican children are privately educated, overwhelmingly in Catholic schools which tend to attract middle-class children whose parents are concerned to protect them from the 'massification' (a literal translation of a widely-used Mexican word, denoting deterioration under pressure of numbers) of so many state-run institutions. The Jesuit-run university, the Ibero-Americana, unquestionably provides good education, and is able to charge high fees to relatively wealthy parents who fear the corruption of their sons, and even more particularly their daughters, in the 400,000 student national university. There are, it is true, scholarship programmes which do something to make the Ibero accessible to poorer students, but the university overwhelmingly exists for children of, and entrants into, the professional middle class. Some Jesuit schools, including the Instituto Patria in Mexico City, have however been closed and their resources transferred to educational work in the slums. The Church's influence is rather less on 'moral' issues. Abortion, it is true, is illegal in Mexico but contraception is quite widely practised. Marriage is civil as well as religious, the civil ceremony being highly ritualized and 'religious' in tone, if not in formal significance. Divorce is civil and quite common, particularly among members of the middle class. Very many divorced (and remarried) people still think of themselves as Catholics.

In general, the Catholic Church's position within Mexican society has changed since 1940 but hardly weakened, even though attendance at Mass has fallen dramatically. The credibility of the official party's ideology has come close to disintegrating at various times since then (not least during the economic crisis of 1982), while the Church remains the obvious institutional alternative, no longer for political power but certainly for moral allegiance. And it is certainly strong enough to take a more active role in political affairs some time in the future. The Church's hierarchy in Mexico tends to be conservative, and was influential at the Puebla Conference of Bishops which partially reversed the more radical line set out for the Church in the earlier conference at Medellín. A conservative outlook is perhaps inevitable in a country with Mexico's anti-clerical revolutionary traditions and where the government is officially atheist and 'on the left'. It is also the case that abuses of human rights are less blatant in Mexico than in certain other Latin American countries; though this does not take away the need for the Church to speak out on this particular issue. The Catholic Church has remained close (particularly through its provision of education) to the newer business and professional classes which have emerged in Mexico since the Second World War. A small but powerful plutocracy provides generous funding for the Church – the so-called 'Monterrey group', for example, helped finance the construction of the new (and architecturally splendid) shrine of the Virgin of Guadalupe. This shrine, where the national character of Mexican Catholicism is emphasized, is located in the northern outskirts of Mexico City. Vast crowds attend the Sunday services and the whole of the surrounding area is rather like a medieval fair, occupied by people selling religious symbols as well as secular goods. The communal nature of Mexican churches is also experienced in the atmosphere of many places of worship outside the capital city, particularly in small towns where the churchyard provides a focal point for gatherings, sometimes to the disgust of the local political authorities.

While the great mass of the faithful are, then, still traditional Catholics, with many bishops and priests content to minister to the popular religiosity inherited from previous generations, the Catholic Church in Mexico has inevitably been affected by Vatican II. Serious efforts have been made to discern 'the signs of the times' and to respond to the demands for social justice and development – within the present economic and political system. A relatively small sector of the Church has gone beyond this, drawing its inspiration from Medellín for its theological reflection, its involvement in social action, and its challenge to the very basis of Mexican society. Best known among the minority of progressive bishops is Don Sergio Méndez Arceo, who retired in 1983 after thirty years as bishop of Morelos. During his ministry the cathedral at Cuernavaca became famous for the liturgical use of the art and music of Mexican folklore, and Cuernavaca itself housed study centres where many found, under the stimulus of men like Ivan Illich, their basic perceptions of Church and Society turned upside down. In Mexico City, the Centre for Theological Reflection run by the Jesuits has an extensive publishing programme, and the Centre for Social Communications (CENCOS), one of the country's principal ecumenical organizations, acts as a switchboard for the flow of radical ideas and information. Among Mexican liberation theologians with an international reputation are José Miranda, Raúl Vidales, Enrique Dussel and Luis del Valle. Nor is the Mexican Church without its martyrs in the struggle for social justice. The persecuted Church of ← the 1920s, suffering at the hands of an 'atheist' State, was immortalized by Graham Greene in *The Power and the Glory*; it is not so widely recognized that half a century later bishops have been the target of abuse for their protests against the violation of human rights, and that in 1977 two priests were killed because of their work among the slum dwellers of Chihuahua and Mexico City. In tribute to one of them, Father Rodolfo Escamilla, Don Sergio Méndez and seventy priests led a procession of 5,000 people to the Guadalupe Basilica in May of that year.

The history of Protestantism in Mexico begins almost as soon as the country was conquered by Spain. No sooner had the first Spanish settlers arrived than the Inquisition had to concern itself with Esteban Moral, a Moravian Hussite who was banished from Mexico and ordered to face a trial for 'heresy' and 'Lutheranism' in Seville. There were others who underwent similar experiences during the 300 years of Spanish colonial rule. These Protestants came to Mexico not as missionaries but simply as individuals interested in living in the New Spain, or exploiting its potential as smugglers, pirates, slave dealers and merchants.

After Mexico became independent in 1821 there was a modest influx of foreign Protestants. Some were diplomats, especially British and American, who usually lived in Mexico City. Others were merchants and miners who spread over the country. These were the people who at first made a deliberate, albeit modest, effort to convert some Mexicans to Protestantism by means of services held in their homes. James Thomson, a famous Scottish agent of the British and Foreign Bible Society, went to Mexico in 1827 but was obliged to withdraw in 1830 because non-Catholic religious activity was forbidden. The invading American army in 1843 included some soldiers who held Protestant services in Spanish and gave Bibles to the people, but it was not until freedom to worship had been granted in 1860 that the first Protestant missionaries began to arrive in Mexico. At the same time a number of former Roman Catholic priests tried to establish an indigenous Mexican Episcopal Church, which flourished for a time but then dwindled and is now one of the smallest Protestant churches in the country. Methodists, Congregationalists, and Friends came between 1870 and 1880 and were followed by Baptists, Presbyterians, Anglicans, Seventh Day Adventists, Disciples of Christ and others. At the beginning of the twentieth century all the Protestant churches in Mexico were governed by foreign missionaries and most of their support came from abroad. In 1916 the Protestant community in Mexico numbered about 50,000, half of them being Presbyterian, and a quarter Methodist.

The Protestant picture in Mexico is now very different. According to the 1980 census, 2.5 million out of a total population of 69 million declared themselves Protestant, and another 1.5 million said they had 'another (non-Catholic) religion'. This latter category included Mormons, Jehovah's Witnesses, some Seventh Day Adventists and other non-classified Protestants. Pentecostalists, of whom there were only a few in 1916, now constitute about two thirds of all Protestants in Mexico; the historic churches that came between 1861 and 1900 account for about 20 per cent; Seventh Day Adventists and similar groups account for about 8 per cent; and the rest are divided into many smaller groups, some so-called 'Faith Missions', most supported and directed from the USA, and about two thousand non-affiliated congregations in which there are many charismatics. The flourishing Pentecostal churches are reversing a trend by sending missionaries abroad, especially to the United States, to other parts of Latin America and even to Europe, particularly to Spain and Italy.

The status of all the churches in Mexico, Catholic and Protestant, has to be seen within the context of Mexican history, especially the fact that as soon as freedom of religion was granted it was also immediately and effectively curtailed, and as a consequence Mexico has some of the most stringent laws against religion in the world. Among other things, all church property becomes state property, clergymen cannot vote or be elected for any public office (as a consolation, they pay no income tax), even the wearing of clerical garb in the streets is forbidden, as is the holding of services in any place that has not been previously authorized. Sermons must not include political references, and church publications must not mention even the names of government officers, either critically or favourably. In practice, these laws are broken every day, in keeping with the custom inherited from colonial times of 'obey but do not fulfil' the law. The original intention of the laws was to strip the Catholic Church of its political and economic power, its monopoly of education, its ownership of large areas of land, including cemeteries, its hospitals and even its control of the Civil Registry, for all births, marriages and deaths were at that time recorded only in church registers. When the Protestant churches began to appear in the Mexican landscape the same laws were applied to them, but both they and the Catholic Church found ways of circumventing them. Thus it was possible for the Protestant churches to run schools where many members of the political and economic élites were educated, though not converted; hospitals where better medical facilities were offered than those available at either government or Catholic hospitals; and 'social centres' where many services were offered to the whole community. Politically, all Protestants identified with liberalism, which in many cases meant anti-Catholicism.

The foreign missionaries, mostly Americans, who established Protestantism in Mexico were, it seems, mainly interested in inculcating into their converts their own religious, social and moral values and those of the sending churches. Recent studies have shown, however, that many of the pastors and church members converted and educated by these missionaries were keenly interested in correcting the unjust conditions then prevailing in Mexico, and in not a few cases they even took up arms against the government that was overthrown by the 1910 revolution. This was part of a genuine effort to improve the conditions of great masses of destitute people in the country. Some of these pastors and laymen also became officers in the governments which came into power after the revolution and were especially influential in the educational field.

Conditions are now very different. The government has taken out of the hands of the churches most of the programmes for which they were responsible for many years. In most instances, the government schools now offer a better education than Protestant church schools. Hardly any of the private or church hospitals can offer medical services of the same quality as the government hospitals, although the Seventh Day Adventists conduct a superb medical and educational programme, including trade schools, regular schools and even a university. They combine this work very skilfully with the winning of new members, mostly middle- and upper-class – something the historic churches were unable to do – and a very large percentage of rural farm communities all over the country have Protestant leaders.

There are other fields in which the churches could be of help to the community, but most Protestants refuse to enter them. In many cases this is because the law forbids it and has relegated the churches to a legal limbo. In other cases the churches are interested mainly in their own numerical growth, which is the only way their survival as institutions can be guaranteed. Many churches feel they are called to do only 'spiritual' things, which means saving souls. They believe that conversion will inevitably bring social and economic improvement. In the midst of all this, however, a new social consciousness is being created and new ways are being sought of surmounting the obstacles bequeathed by the last century, the legal barriers and the undue emphasis on the 'spiritual' or other-worldly side of the Christian life. When, for instance, a crisis of authority developed in Mexico in 1968, in the aftermath of the student riots in Paris, some of the Methodist youth took to the streets over a particular case of government repression, and later debated the issue in a theological context in their church's publications, and in public and private meetings.

Since 1980 a new challenge has come to Protestants from sociologists, educationalists and politicians who are accusing them of being instruments of penetration by American imperialism, and of destroying Mexican culture, including the traditional structures of society. Newspapers frequently publish new charges against Protestants, and the Senate has appointed a commission to investigate the Protestant 'sects'. A recently published book, *A Gospel According to the Dominant Class*, suggests that Mexican Protestants, by preaching the acceptance of suffering as God's will in a way that disarms social action against poverty, actually encourage the dominance of the Mexican masses by North American imperialism. A small minority of Protestants, including some members of staff of the Baptist Seminary in Mexico City, share this viewpoint. Others reject the charge, claiming that Mexican Protestants are not simply aiming at church growth; they are also looking for new ways to prove their relevance in a society experiencing change and upheaval. While the effect of some sects is divisive and damaging to a community's sense of identity, they claim that a new awareness is emerging among other Protestants of themselves not as a separate group but as an integral part of the nation with a special contribution to make to its progress.

Chapter 10

Central America

Nicaragua's Sandinista revolution catapulted Central America into the world's headlines in July 1979. Since then, it has returned again and again: the escalation of the civil war in El Salvador; the assassination of Archbishop Oscar Romero; the covert 'warfare' of the CIA against Nicaragua; persistent human rights violations and the massacre of entire Indian communities in Guatemala. The events of recent years are, however, but the culmination of a long history of suffering, the roots of which stretch back to the Spanish Conquest.

Central America is the collective name for the republics of Guatemala, El Salvador, Honduras and Nicaragua. Costa Rica is often added, but the Costa Ricans consider themselves separate. Panama too is a different entity: it is the isthmus cut by the Panama Canal. Populations are small: Guatemala – seven million; El Salvador – five million; Honduras – three million; Nicaragua – three million; Costa Rica – just over two million. For the vast majority of the people who live in these republics the present crisis is part of their daily lives – a pattern of poverty, misery and squalor. In Guatemala, average life expectancy is 54 years; over half of the population are illiterate. In El Salvador only 15 per cent of the population live in houses with running water, 70 per cent of the homes have earth floors and 66 per cent have no electricity. In Honduras, the second poorest nation in the Western hemisphere after Haiti, 70 per cent of the children suffer some degree of malnutrition, and infant mortality runs at 128 deaths for every 1,000 live births. Only Costa Rica, with the highest per capita income in the region, can claim that its people live relatively decently. Yet even Costa Rica is threatened by the deep economic crisis of the region, and the future of its welfare programmes and social security system is in doubt.

Geographically the five republics have much in common, sharing the same tropical climate and mountainous terrain in the narrow strip of land which separates North and South America. The populations of Nicaragua, Honduras and El Salvador are mainly *mestizo*, of mixed Spanish and Indian blood; in Guatemala, the majority of the population – 65 per cent – are Mayan Indians speaking twenty-three different languages between them; in Costa Rica the population is predominantly white, of European descent. Both Nicaragua and Costa Rica have small enclaves, on their Caribbean coasts, of English-speaking Caribbean blacks. Nicaragua also has a population of some 75,000 forest Indians living in the tropical lowlands of the Atlantic coast.

The Indians of Central America are largely descended from the Mayan civilization. The Spanish Conquest more than halved their number, which in the early part of the sixteenth century is thought to have been between 12 and 15 million. Estimates vary of the number who died as a result of disease, wars, forced labour and the cruelty of the *conquistadores*. Eric Wolf calculates that between 1519 and 1650 eight to ten million Indians died. A way of life perished as the Conquest took hold of Central America. In his book *Sons of the Shaking Earth*, Eric Wolf examines the impact of this process:

> The Indian before the Conquest had been a cultivator, a seedplanter. The conquering Spaniard became a mining entrepreneur, a producer of commercial crops, a rancher, a merchant. The strategic economic relationship of the pre-Conquest united Indian peasant and Indian lord, tribute producer and tribute consumer. The goal of the Indian noble was to consume weath commensurate with his social position. The Spanish colonist, however, laboured for different ends. He wanted to convert wealth and labour into saleable goods – into gold, silver, hides and wool, wheat and sugar cane. Wealth to him meant wealth invested in Spanish goods, capital multiplying miraculously in the process of exchange. He wanted to organize and press the human resources under his command to pay his debts, enlarge his estate, to take his place among the other men grown rich and powerful in the new utopia.

The Spanish *conquistadores*, who had come in search of gold and silver, soon occupied the best lands and formed large estates (*haciendas*) to raise capital and crops for export. Their Indian workers were the survivors of the battles of the Conquest, forced to work as slaves or as peasant farmers who had to hand over a proportion of their crop as tribute. Spain maintained a strict monopoly of trade with Central America; the great fleets which set sail from Panama for Cadiz offered rich pickings to English pirates in the Caribbean. By the beginning of the nineteenth century, the social patterns initiated by the Conquest had hardened into a class system which gave power and wealth to a small, landowning élite. The mass of the Indians who lived in what is now Guatemala had been reduced to abject poverty and were confined to their communities in the western highlands: they were forced to work on the large estates under a system of compulsory labour or they were tied directly to the estates by 'debt peonage', a form of servitude by which Indians were obliged to pay off their debts to the landowner by labour. The mounting debts always exceeded what could be earned from work, so it was a form of lifelong slavery. Indians who came to adopt Spanish ways and language, and those of mixed Spanish and Indian descent, were known as *ladinos*. They were landless but free labourers and enjoyed a status considerably superior to that of pure Indians. The distinction between pure Indian and *ladino* is still as sharp today as it was in colonial times. At the top of the pyramid was the *criollo* (creole) élite of Spanish descent, the landowners and merchants who controlled commerce and finance. In Nicaragua, Honduras and, to a lesser extent, El Salvador, however, the Indians did not survive the rigours of the Conquest and were not therefore able to form a separate, identifiable group in the population.

Independence, declared throughout the region in 1821, was won easily from a Spain weakened by the Napoleonic Wars. It was not the result of any revolutionary movement but simply of the *criollo* élite's desire to trade freely with foreign, particularly British, merchants. Independence was followed by a Federal Republic of Central America, but this broke up in 1838 and from then onwards the five states governed themselves independently. By 1850, coffee was beginning to change the traditional patterns of exploitation. Demand for coffee from the industrializing countries of Europe and from the United States offered new opportunities for enrichment.

For the Indians and the poor, however, the coffee boom was another turn of the screw. Coffee grows best on the less humid uplands away from the traditional plantation lands nearer the coast; it was here that the Indians had settled after the Conquest, continuing to cultivate their holdings as common land. In both El Salvador and Guatemala the governments passed laws outlawing communal ownership and requiring all land to be held privately and by individual title. So the Indian populations lost their traditional communal holdings. Those who retained individual holdings, tiny subsistence plots known as *minifundia*, were legally obliged to work for the coffee plantation owners during the harvest season. Many individual owners lost their land soon after as they fell into debt. In El Salvador, where population pressure and the hunger for land was greatest, wage labour quickly replaced the more feudal landlord-peasant relationship which had obliged the peasant to provide his labour in exchange for land.

Nicaragua followed a similar pattern. Here too the government passed a series of laws which drove communal landholders off their land. Nicaragua's strategic position on the isthmus eventually attracted foreign attention and changed its history: the combination of rivers and huge inland lakes making it the crossing point from East to West for thousands of fortune hunters in the California gold rush of 1848. Sixty years later the proud nationalism of Nicaragua's modernizing but dictatorial president, José Santos Zelaya, spurned American offers of a canal treaty, thus precipitating the intervention of the US marines.

In Honduras, bananas, rather than coffee, became the major crop. In colonial times Honduras was a backwater and did not develop the plantation crops which confirmed the power and wealth of the élites in El Salvador and Guatemala. Instead, it was the American banana companies, the best known being the United Fruit Company, which became the major economic force in the country, controlling its major exports, making alliances with local landowners and intervening in political life to promote and defend their interests.

Costa Rica developed differently. It had no mineral resources and was not heavily populated by Indians. Land was plentiful, so settlers had to provide their own labour, and the small family farm geared to subsistence became the norm. For this reason coffee had a different impact on Costa Rica: the larger landowners who had the resources to create coffee plantations had no readily available source of cheap labour and were forced to offer higher wages to draw independent peasants from their land to work on the plantations. The change in the pattern of land ownership was dramatic, for many small farmers left their land – tempted by the relatively high wages of the plantations and the prospect of a regular income. By 1864 over half the peasantry had become wage labourers and by 1871, when coffee production had increased fivefold, 71 per cent of the rural population were landless labourers.

By the beginning of the twentieth century the United States had already emerged as the dominant power in the region (now known as the Caribbean Basin) following its victorious war with Spain, which ended with the annexation of Puerto Rico and the establishment of a puppet regime in Cuba. American investments in Central America grew, the United Fruit Company gained control of huge tracts of prime land in Guatemala and Costa Rica, and American bondholders quickly came to own public utilities, railways and electricity monopolies. Nicaragua was, however, the only country of mainland Central America to experience military intervention by the United States in the early years of this century. In 1909, when President José Santos Zelaya dared to enter into negotiations with foreign powers, with a view to siting an inter-oceanic canal in Nicaragua, the Americans supported a successful rebellion.

Three years later, when it seemed that the more amenable Conservative government was in danger of being overthrown by another rebellion, the United States intervened in force and occupied Nicaragua with 2,700 marines. With one brief interruption the US marines remained until 1933. The nationalist leader, Cesar Augusto Sandino (the hero and inspiration of today's Sandinistas), waged a prolonged and successful guerrilla war against them, vowing that he would not lay down his arms until the marines withdrew, but by the time they left the Americans had trained the Nicaraguan National Guard to replace the marines as an efficient fighting force. Sandino agreed to sign a peace treaty, only to be murdered and buried in an anonymous grave by the National Guard, acting under the orders of its first, American-appointed, commander, Anastasio 'Tacho' Somoza. In 1936 Somoza deposed the President and set up the family dictatorship which ended in

July 1979. Elsewhere in Central America no intervention was necessary: the local élites formed an alliance with their own armed forces, the American plantation companies and the US government itself.

The economies which brought immense wealth to the élites were, however, fragile, because they depended on one or two export crops. The Great Depression of 1929 laid bare this weakness. At that time 100 kilograms of coffee fetched US $ 15.75 in New York; by 1932 the price had dropped to US $ 5.79. The worst effects were felt by plantation workers whose wages were cut below subsistence levels. In El Salvador, where the coffee pickers had begun to organize in militant unions, the Communist Party launched a rebellion. It was a desperate and bungled move: *campesinos*, armed only with hoes and machetes, occupied a few coffee centres in the west of the country. About 30 people were killed. Within days these towns had been retaken by the army which then set about executing all suspects. At least 20,000 *campesinos* were killed, perhaps as many as 30,000. The unrest caused by the slump brought military dictators to power in El Salvador (General Maximiliano Hernández Martínez, 1931–44), in Guatemala (General Jorge Ubico, 1931–44), and in Honduras (General Tiburcio Carías Andino, 1931–48), and it was not until the economic recovery brought about by the Second World War effort of the United States and the fashionable revival of democracy that these dictators' regimes came to an end. In El Salvador it was the American ambassador who advised Hernández Martínez to resign; elections were planned but, with the reforming candidate clearly foreseen as the victor, a military coup placed another general in power.

In Guatemala, however, the small middle class, frustrated by the stranglehold of the élite over economic opportunity and political life, spearheaded a successful rebellion against Ubico and were able to organize elections. Under Juan José Arevalo (1944–9) and Jacobo Arbenz (1949–54) Guatemala enjoyed ten years of democracy. For the first time this century human and civil rights were respected, all forced labour laws were abolished, and the right of labour to organize was recognized. Behind these reforms was the view expressed by Arévalo's Minister of Labour: 'A capitalist democracy ought to compensate with the means at its disposal, some of which are legislative, for the economic inequality between

231

those who possess the means of production and those who sell manual labour.'

President Arbenz was a practical reformer who wished to 'modernize' Guatemala. A priority was agrarian reform, to bring into cultivation neglected land on the large estates which he regarded as remnants from a feudal past; this reform would give employment to land-hungry peasants and lay the foundations of a modern market economy. The agrarian reform law of 1952 was a cautious document affecting about 16 per cent of the country's total idle cultivable land in private hands. Schlesinger and Kinzer, in their history of the United Fruit Company, *Bitter Fruit*, describe the law as '... more moderate in almost every respect than the Mexican agrarian reform bill that preceded it by over a decade, and in fact would have been acceptable under the American Alliance for Progress seven years later'. But this was the era of the Cold War. The United States was ready to see Communism in any attempt to bring about change in the Americas. The inclusion of some of the United Fruit Company's uncultivated land in the agrarian reform convinced the US government still further that the Arbenz government was infiltrated by Communists. But for those Guatemalans who knew the details of United Fruit's involvement in their country, the agrarian reform decree affecting United Fruit – 386,901 out of a total of over 500,000 acres – was a just and sensible move to regain control over the country's resources. One American historian has written:

> For many Guatemalans the United Fruit Company was the United States. ... In the past UFCO and its sister companies had bribed politicians, pressured governments and intimidated opponents to gain extremely favourable concessions. To the Guatemalans it appeared that their country was being mercilessly exploited by foreign interests which took huge profits without making any significant contribution to the nation's welfare. In the eyes of many Guatemalans, the foreign corporations had to pay for their past crimes and for the years in which they had operated hand-in-hand with the Estrada Cabrera and Ubico dictatorships to exploit the Guatemalan people.

In 1954 the Arbenz government was overthrown by a military coup organized and financed by the CIA. The government installed by the coup immediately set about undoing the reforms of the Arbenz government, and went on to ban labour unions, peasant federations and agricultural co-operatives. This signalled to repressive regimes throughout Latin America that the United States was prepared to help them resist any reform as long as they acted in the name of anti-Communism.

The Costa Rican experience is, again, different from its northern neighbours. A middle class developed earlier in Costa Rica than elsewhere, as small farmers moved to the towns after the expansion of coffee cultivation at the end of the nineteenth century. Their influence in the state bureaucracy which expanded in the first decades of the twentieth century contributed to the formation of a much more pluralist society. The growing strength of the middle class coincided with the decline of the coffee 'aristocracy' and paved the way for the populist administration of President Calderón in the 1940s, which recognized the right of workers to collective bargaining and laid the foundations of Costa Rica's social security system. But it was the revolution of 1948 which led to eventual agreement between the middle class and the coffee aristocracy, and established the national consensus for the democratic political system which distinguishes Costa Rica from its neighbours. The army, seen by the middle-class reformers as a possible instrument for conservative interests, was abolished; the Communist Party was banned and its unions disbanded. The State assumed a major role in Costa Rica's economic life, both as consumer and as investor, stimulating the development of industry, while agricultural exports retained their crucial role in the economy and remained in the hands of the landowners.

The Cuban revolution in 1959 gave a new impetus to American attempts to control the course of events in its 'backyard'. A concern to prevent further Cubas lay behind the formulation of the Alliance for Progress, which was the Kennedy administration's answer to social unrest in Latin America. Its objective was to prevent revolution from below by reform from above, and it had important implications for Central America. An essential element in the Alliance for Progress was its commitment to agrarian reform, 'leading to the effective transformation, where required, of unjust structures and systems of land tenure and use'. It soon became clear, however, that the landowners were not prepared to

233

submit to even a marginal curtailment of their privileges, and that the United States was prepared to overlook its commitment to agrarian reform if the landowners were prepared to settle for modernization, that is, diversification of their landholdings into cotton, sugar cane and beef cattle, and the mechanization of production, financed by soft development loans.

Efficient, modern landowners producing for export benefited under the Alliance for Progress, but the expansion of land under the new export crops and beef cattle displaced peasant farmers who produced maize and beans, the local staples, for the domestic market. At the same time, mechanization reduced the opportunities for employment of those who lost their land. In El Salvador between 1961 and 1971 the number of *colono* (share-cropper or tenant farmer) plots declined by 70 per cent to make way for cotton plantations. The proportion of the rural population without land rose from 12 per cent in 1961 to 29 per cent in 1971, and 41 per cent in 1975; by 1980 this figure was estimated at 65 per cent. In Nicaragua some 15,000 jobs were lost in the agricultural sector as the small holdings on the Pacific coast gave way to cotton and sugar plantations. A similar process was under way in the cities. New investment in industry increased output but created few new jobs because modern, labour-saving technology was used. The creation of the Central American Common Market (CACM) boosted this trend and, by creating a larger market, enabled the new industries to take advantage of economies of scale.

Nothing was done to reduce the extreme inequalities of income in any of the Central American republics, although this would have been a far more effective step towards the creation of a mass market capable of sustaining modern industrial economies. In the 1950s and 1960s development experts predicted that industrialization would be pushed forward by a 'modern' and dynamic class of entrepreneurs whose enlightened and reforming ideas would displace the 'feudal' attitudes of the traditional landowning élite. This turned out to be a pipedream of the academic architects of the Alliance for Progress, for the landowning élite as a class were not feudal and backward-looking fuddyduddies: they controlled the banks and had privileged access to the state-controlled credit institutions, and actively sought new opportunities to increase their profits and wealth.

There was a short-lived industrial boom between 1960 and 1970: industry increased its contribution to Gross Domestic Product in the region from 13 to 18 per cent. The process was flawed, however, because it was geared to the drive for profits of both locally-owned and multinational companies, rather than the needs of the majority of the population. Imports were increased, foreign companies established assembly plants to re-export goods – thus draining further the balance of payments – and, since the industrialization was intensive of capital, rather than labour, relatively few jobs were created. Another problem with the industrialization process was its unevenness in the region. The CACM had been created without taking into account the differences between the individual countries of Central America. Guatemala, El Salvador and Costa Rica were able to benefit from it, but the more backward countries, Nicaragua and particularly Honduras, found themselves flooded with the cheaper, more efficiently produced goods of their neighbours. The regional tensions which resulted from this imbalance were responsible for the war – the so-called 'football' war – which broke out between Honduras and El Salvador in 1969 and which signalled the breakup of the CACM.

Until this war Honduras, more backward and less densely populated, had acted as a safety valve for land hunger in El Salvador. Many Salvadoreans had found a livelihood as small farmers in Honduras, where land was more abundant and rents cheaper. But Honduras too had undergone changes in the post-war period which made the Salvadorean settlers convenient sacrificial victims for the Honduran government in its efforts to deal with growing internal tensions. Honduras went through a process of agricultural expansion and innovation in this period which, though led by the foreign fruit companies, also included the local landowning élite. In the late 1940s the fruit companies began to improve transport and to give financial and technical assistance to stimulate the development of cattle raising in the south and north of the country, and the cultivation of cotton and coffee. As cotton, coffee and beef exports began to grow, land increased in value, and commercial large-scale farmers started to encroach on the lands of subsistence peasants and to seek access to land that was still owned communally or by the State.

There were other pressures on the land: the population of Honduras doubled between 1950 and 1974; labour rationalization and mechanization on the banana plantations made 19,000 workers jobless by the end of the 1950s so that they too had to look to the land for survival. The dismissals in the plantations were preceded by the banana workers' strike of 1954 – a significant event in Honduran history – as a result of which the workers were able to force the government and the fruit companies to recognize their right to organize rural trade unions. Representatives of the most conservative forces of the US labour movement, together with the Inter-American Regional Organization of Labour (ORIT), were sent to Honduras to mediate in the strike. They secured the removal of the most militant strike leaders and their replacement by known anti-communists, but subsequently helped to set up fifteen unions in Honduras.

Similar tactics were adopted to deal with the peasant movement, which by 1960 was the best organized in Central America. The same US labour organizations established a parallel union to undermine the radical peasant organization FENACH, and a military coup in 1963 led to the total destruction of FENACH. But the militant traditions of the peasant and banana workers were not eradicated. The traditional political system offered very little means to improve their lives. The Liberal and National parties, which dominated the scene, represented almost exclusively the interests of the landowners and cattle ranchers, and industrialists linked to foreign capital. The workers and peasants began to express their demands through their union organizations, even when the major federations were still influenced by ORIT and the CIA-linked American Institute of Free Labour Development (AIFLD).

The war between El Salvador and Honduras was one of the consequences of the militancy of Honduran peasant organizations. Since the 1950s the banana companies' response to growing union pressures had been to mechanize and shed labour, and also, wherever possible, to transfer responsibility for production to small farmers working with credit and technical assistance provided by the companies. In July 1968 the military government of Honduras, acting on American advice, passed an agrarian reform law as a response to signs that the peasant movements were on the point of organizing land seizures. The law dictated that national land was to be used in preference to private land, and so the government looked to the land, usually national, improved and brought into cultivation by the Salvadorean settlers. The first expulsion orders affecting Salvadoreans coincided with an inflammatory press campaign against them and two football matches between the two countries. Threats and maltreatment of Salvadoreans in Honduras provoked a deluge of refugees back to El Salvador, and on 14th July the Salvadorean army invaded Honduras, inflicting a humiliating defeat on the ineffective and badly trained Honduran army. After five days the Salvadorean advance into Honduran territory was halted by American pressure. The Central American Common Market lurched towards crisis as El Salvador and Honduras immediately barred entry of each other's products, and Honduras closed to Salvadorean goods the overland route to Nicaragua and Costa Rica.

Peasant militancy continued to grow in Honduras. In 1974 the destruction of nearly 60 per cent of the country's agricultural land by Hurricane Fifi led the peasant movements, in desperation, to take radical action including land seizures. Pressure from the peasants persuaded the government of General Lopez Arellano to carry out a new agrarian reform which promised to distribute almost 1.5 million acres to 120,000 peasants. The hostility of the landowners was intense, and when it was revealed that Lopez Arellano had accepted a bribe of US $ 1.5 million from United Brands (previously United Fruit), he was deposed by a coup, and a new military government halted the agrarian reform. The largest peasant movement, the UNC, continued to press its demands and in May 1975 seized 128 farms throughout the country; it then led a hunger march on the capital. An army unit attacked some of the marchers in Olancho and killed 14 of them, including a Colombian priest. Although, subsequently, there was a decline in activity among the Honduran peasants, the existence of a strong union tradition has given a particular character to the struggle of these peasants for land and economic rights. The relative economic and political weakness of the landowners, and the corresponding strength and relative independence of the army – manifested in its openness to some degree of reform – are other factors which distinguish Honduras from the other countries of the region. The sharp and violent polarizations which became evident in the 1970s in Guatemala, El Salvador and Nicaragua have been delayed in Honduras.

In Guatemala guerrilla organizations first appeared in the 1960s, attempting to reproduce the Cuban experience by establishing rural *focos* or insurrectionary centres in the mostly *ladino* eastern part of the country. They were quickly eradicated in 1966–8 by a counter-insurgency campaign, led by Colonel Arana and co-ordinated and assisted by the United States. Some 8,000 peasants were killed during the campaign in an attempt to eliminate a few hundred guerrillas, and afterwards terror emerged as a technique of government, with death squads dedicated to the torture and murder of suspected opponents of the status quo. This repression prevented any resurgence of political activity until the early 1970s. Like their Salvadorean counterparts, the Guatemalan ruling élite held regular elections but ensured by fraud that their own candidate, always a general, emerged the victor.

A turning point came with the devastating earthquake of February 1976 which killed 25,000 and injured 100,000. The devastation was enormous and the traditional houses of the peasants, built with heavy adobe blocks and roofed with tiles, proved to be death traps. Foreign aid workers poured into the country; they were familiar with the Guatemalan government's record and suspicious of its intentions, so they worked directly with the earthquake victims. As a result, communities organized themselves, chose leaders, and formed co-operatives, health communities and education groups. Guatemala became a forcing house of grassroots development – and the new methods were successful: the questioning, discussion and reflection which led from apathy to community organization moved on to a questioning of the Guatemalan social and economic system. Peasant and union organization gained momentum during this period.

Although assassinations and disappearances diminished under the presidency of General Laugerud, his government never brought the death squads under control. There was a resurgence of killing after the earthquake – often of petty criminals but also of union and peasant activists. The Guerrilla Army of the Poor (EGP) reappeared in 1975 and staged a number of successful operations in predominantly Indian areas in 1976 and 1977. Their activities were mainly directed against property rather than human life, and were intended as a reminder to plantation owners to treat their workers more fairly. In November 1976 the EGP destroyed ten crop-spraying aircraft on the cotton plantation of La Flora, as a protest against the uncontrolled spraying of fields without precautions to safeguard the workers and nearby communities.

The election of General Romeo Lucas Garcia in 1978, to succeed Laugerud, signalled the end of any hope of reform. In May of that year a group of Indian peasants gathered in the main square of the town of Panzos to protest against the enclosure of their lands by local landowners, but when they began to speak soldiers and civilians opened fire on them from the roof tops, killing at least 140 unarmed men, women and children in the square, and wounding another 300. Under Lucas Garcia the atrocities multiplied: the US-based Council on Hemispheric Affairs reported that in 1979 there was an average of ten to fifteen politically related murders per day, and that in 1980 this figure rose to fifteen to twenty. The Guatemalan police said that in January 1979 the death squads were responsible for five killings a day. Most of those who died were Indian peasants but no opposition sector was immune. In 1979 two social democrat politicians were gunned down, and it is estimated that over 15,000 people were killed by death squads during the four-year term of Lucas Garcia.

The union and peasant organizations were thus pushed on to the defensive and into underground forms of organization. Their best leaders had been killed or forced into exile. In these circumstances increasing numbers began to turn to the guerrilla movements which reorganized and regrouped during the 1970s and were now gathering strength. The Indians, previously noted for their passivity in the face of oppression, began to join and to offer support.

The frustration of hopes of peaceful change by means of elections, and the growing problems of landlessness and hunger among the peasantry, are the broad background to the violence which has engulfed Central America. This violence cannot be seen in isolation from the strategy of the United States for containing the spread of Communism. Besides the deleterious effects of the economic assistance component of the Alliance for Progress, there have been the training programmes for Latin American army and police officers, which aimed to transform the local armies into efficient instruments for combating subversion and at the same time provided ideological instruction, encouraging the Latin American officers to interpret all challenges to the status quo as inherently subversive. Over 17,000 Central American military personnel have been trained by the United States, mainly in the School of the Americas in the Panama Canal Zone. As the armies grew in size and technical sophistication, and were able to engage in real counter-insurgency warfare, so the opportunities for corruption and profiteering multiplied for the officer class. The armed forces changed from defensive shields for the ruling élites to institutions with their own economic goals, the clearest example of which is to be found in Guatemala, where the army even has its own bank, one of the most powerful economic institutions in the country.

In Nicaragua the turning point in the fortunes of the Somoza family was also an earthquake, and this destroyed the centre of the city of Managua on Christmas Eve 1972. The Somoza family wealth was already enormous and included some 20,000 square kilometres of land, together with interests in cattle raising, coffee plantations, gold mines, fisheries, food processing, textiles, tobacco and cement. After the earthquake Anastasio 'Tachito' Somoza, the younger son of the original dictator, appropriated much of the aid which flowed into the country and made millions of dollars in profiteering land deals and by monopolizing the production of reconstruction materials. He had by this time cowed the traditional Conservative opposition through a mixture of privilege, bribes and intimidation, and had all but wiped out the Sandinista Front Liberation Movement (FSLN) in the late 1960s. His behaviour at the time of the earthquake, however, inflamed opinion against him among the business and middle classes, which resented his control of the economy. It also alienated many of his friends in the United States whose favour he had assiduously courted. When the FSLN re-emerged in 1974 they were no longer an isolated group but a political force with support among peasants, workers and students, and they found a climate of opinion much more favourable to armed opposition to the dictatorship. Somoza struck back at them with the familiar weapon of repression, and found that he had succeeded only in bringing the different elements of the opposition closer together and antagonizing the United States. In October 1977 a group calling itself *Los Doce*, the Twelve, representing those middle sectors of Nicaraguan society which had finally lost patience with Somoza, issued a document acknowledging the sacrifices of the FSLN and calling for its inclusion in the search for a 'national solution'. In 1979 the FSLN headed a coalition which included Conservative politicians, the employers' federation (COSEP), the Roman Catholic Church and the mass of the peasantry and the workers. The United States government, under President Jimmy Carter, strove to avoid an all-out Sandinista victory by sponsoring negotiations between Somoza and the centrist opposition, but the effect of these manoeuvres was further to undermine the credibility of the centrist group, which finally threw its support behind the Sandinistas, who assumed undisputed leadership of the opposition.

The last year of fighting against Somoza was exceedingly costly. Fifty thousand people were killed and 100,000 were wounded; property damage was estimated at US $ 481 million; US $ 1.5 billion left the country in capital flight. Somoza and his allies were responsible for the lion's share of this destruction and the looting of the country's assets; before their departure they removed Nicaragua's remaining foreign currency, leaving behind only US $ 3.5 million. When the victorious Sandinistas marched into Managua on 19th July 1979 they inherited an economy in tatters.

The Sandinista victory in Nicaragua coincided with crisis in El Salvador, where the response of the government to peasant federations, urban trade unions, shanty town dwellers, students, radical sectors of the Catholic Church and reformist politicians was simply repression. In 1972 the candidate of the official governing party, Colonel Armando Molina, became president after a fraudulent election in which the real winner was José Napoleón Duarte, a Christian Democrat who had made a name for himself as a popular and reforming mayor of San Salvador. Duarte's running mate in the election was the Social Democrat (MNR) leader, Guillermo Ungo. Molina's government tried to defuse growing social tension in the rural areas by introducing a timid agrarian reform law, known as the Law of Agrarian Transformation, which affected only four per cent of El Salvador's land and provided for ample compensation. The law was welcomed by the Catholic bishops and, more cautiously, by the Jesuits who ran San Salvador's Catholic University, but Congress, controlled by large landowning interests, emasculated the law with amendments and loopholes, and Molina allowed the initiative to die.

Repression in El Salvador was in the hands of several different and sometimes competing security forces – the Army, the National Guard (a rural gendarmerie modelled on the Spanish *Guardia Civil*), the Treasury Police, the National Police and ORDEN (Organización Democrática Nacional), a network of government informers and a support group from the security forces which in 1979 was estimated to have 100,000 members. These forces were ranged against guerrilla groups which had been formed in the early 1970s, and also against peasant and union leaders, in an effort to restore order by intimidating their members into passivity. But, as the hope of peaceful change receded into the past, this attempt to set the clock back succeeded only in convincing many peasants and unionists that the armed organizations were the only realistic alternative.

The failure of Molina's agrarian reform projects signalled a hardening of attitudes on the part of the landowning élite. In 1977, in another fraudulent election, they ensured the victory of Colonel Humberto Romero, the Minister of Defence and a known hardliner, in the hope that tough, repressive measures would turn the tide in their favour. Even before Romero's election there had been a significant increase in repression. Demonstrations were fired on and the death squads became active: in April 1977 a Jesuit, Father Rutilio Grande, was shot down as he travelled to Aguilares, a country town twenty miles north of San Salvador, where he was parish priest. Shortly afterwards the armed forces occupied Aguilares in an unprecedented display of military might. In June, the entire Jesuit Order was put under threat of death if they did not leave the country, by a body calling itself the White Warriors' Union, which claimed responsibility for the killing of a second priest, P. Alfonso Navarro.

Colonel Romero assumed office on 1st July, and in November his government decreed the 'Law for the Defence and Guarantee of Public Order' which proscribed any act, doctrine or organization which could be construed as being against democracy, the constitution or public order. Although the outcry, both in El Salvador and in the United States, succeeded in forcing Romero to repeal the law a year later, there was no noticeable change in his approach to growing social tension. The number of people killed and 'disappeared' by the security forces and the death squads continued to rise: there were 147 documented political killings of civilians (i.e. not guerrilla fighters) in 1978; in the first nine months of 1979 this figure rose to 580.

On 15th October 1979 a group of colonels staged a successful coup against General Romero, in order to carry out the reforms necessary to defuse social tension and to rescue El Salvador from the international isolation which his policies had provoked. They were joined in government by reforming politicians from the ranks of the Social Democrats and the Christian Democrats. The unions, peasant federations, shanty town dwellers' groups and students – now united in large coalitions known as 'popular organizations' – took to the streets to press this new government for reforms and, above all, an end to the repression. But the security forces responded in their accustomed manner: in one demonstration alone 86 people were killed and over 200 wounded. The civilian reformers in the government were outmanoeuvred by the more right-wing colonels, García and Gutiérrez, who had been co-opted to guarantee its success. When it became clear, after three months, that they were unable to bring the security forces under their control they resigned from the government. Christian Democrats occupied the places which had been occupied by the Social Democrats. Four months later there was another series of resignations by dissident Christian Democrats, protesting against the government's inability to stop the killings and its refusal to talk to the popular organizations. The Christian Democrats in the government came to be represented by José Napoleón Duarte, back from seven years' exile in Venezuela.

The United States had been taking a more active interest in El Salvador since the presidency of General Romero. President Carter's human rights policies had been used to force the repeal of the Law for the Defence and Guarantee of Public Order, but the containment of the spread of Communism remained the principal objective of United States policy. The coup of October 1979 was greeted with a sigh of relief by the United States, which by then was actively seeking an alternative to the inept and counter-productive Romero. The new government, with its commitment to reform, provided an opportunity to make radical changes designed to undermine the guerrillas' growing base of support among the peasantry. The Sandinista victory in Nicaragua in July 1979 had come as a shock to Washington, and the first reaction there was to ensure that El Salvador did not become 'another Nicaragua'. In February 1980 President Carter dispatched Robert White as Ambassador to El Salvador; White was a career diplomat who had won a reputation as a staunch defender of human rights in his previous posting as Ambassador in Stroessner's Paraguay. He came with the stark message that Washington's continued support depended on reforms and a commitment to democracy.

The agrarian reform announced in March 1980 was more radical than the law of agrarian transformation so effectively sabotaged by the landowning élite in 1976. Their opposition had not, however, diminished in 1980; they saw the Christian Democrats as Communists in disguise, and used their influence in the security forces, especially the National Guard, the Treasury Police and ORDEN, to sabotage it again – killing and intimidating the beneficiaries. The reform itself was conceived primarily as a weapon with which to defeat the guerrillas and was implemented by a government in which few members had any commitment to reform. There was no participation on the part of the peasantry, and the reform offered no benefits to the 65 per cent of the rural population who are landless. In fact only the first stage, involving estates of over 500 hectares (just over 15 per cent of El Salvador's arable land), has ever been implemented. Phase two, which would have affected the core of the country's agricultural wealth, the coffee estates, has been suspended indefinitely. The third phase, the 'Land to the Tiller' programme – a replica of a similar initiative in Vietnam – was intended to give land titles to small tenant farmers who, with their own land problems solved, might be expected to withhold their support from the guerrillas. In April 1983, 30,000 titles out of a possible 150,000 had been granted.

The 1980 reform was accompanied by increased repression in the rural areas: civilian deaths in 1980, documented by the Legal Aid Office of the Archdiocese of San Salvador, were 8,062, the great majority of them peasants. That year also brought the death of Archbishop Romero who was assassinated in March, while in December four American women missionaries (three nuns and one lay missionary) were waylaid on the road from the airport to San

Salvador, where they were raped, tortured and killed. Roberto D'Aubuisson, a former major in the military intelligence service, who is now the leader of the far-right ARENA party, was accused by Ambassador White of having links with the death squads and having planned the assassination of Archbishop Romero.

By the time Ronald Reagan assumed the Presidency of the United States in January 1981 the conflict in El Salvador had intensified and taken on new dimensions. In April 1980 all the opposition parties, including the Social Democrats, the Christian Democrats, the Communist Party and the mass organizations linked to the guerrilla movements, had formed a political front, the Democratic Revolutionary Front (FDR). In October the guerrilla organizations came together to form the Farabundo Martí Liberation Front (FMLN), and the FDR became the political wing of the FMLN, indicating the broad agreement of all opposition forces that it was no longer possible to seek change by peaceful means. At the same time the United States was becoming more deeply involved, not only at the political level but also through its increasing military assistance to the Salvadorean army. President Reagan decided to make El Salvador a test case in what he declared was his administration's determination to halt 'Soviet subversion in the US backyard'. But his administration was unable to produce any convincing evidence to prove that the Soviet Union, Cuba or Nicaragua were in any way involved in El Salvador. In fact the White Paper produced in February 1981 to prove this assertion was found by the *Wall Street Journal* to be full of inaccuracies and false information. So unconvincing was the evidence, that opposition to US involvement in the country, led by the Roman Catholic Church in the United States, began to grow, both in North America and in Europe. By June 1981 the FMLN had control of about one fifth of the country, and in September of that year France and Mexico recognized it as 'a representative political force'.

In November the US administration began to rethink its strategy, and to lay the foundations of the policies it would pursue over the next two years. The essential elements of the strategy were revealed in a series of articles in the American press, in particular the *New York Times*, the *Washington Post* and *Newsweek*. These indicate that the commitment of the Reagan administration to the pacification of the Central American region through military means has not altered in any fundamental way. The objective is still the military defeat of the guerrilla movements in Guatemala and El Salvador, the downfall of the Sandinista government in Nicaragua, and incorporation of Honduras and Costa Rica into a co-ordinated, regional approach to counter-insurgency. The impact of US policies on each of the countries concerned is now evident.

Honduras became the lynchpin of US military strategy in Central America after the Sandinista victory. As long ago as 1980 the United States was beginning to increase its military assistance to the country, and now, under the Reagan administration, Honduras has been transformed into a base for US operations throughout the region. US military advisers have been sent to the country in growing numbers. In May 1983 there were 63, but a further 100 were to be sent to Puerto Castilla on the Caribbean coast; in 1979 Honduras received US $ 2.3 million in military assistance; this rose to US $ 37.3 million in 1983, and US $ 41 million is promised for 1984; an estimated 200 CIA agents are active in the country; increasingly frequent and large-scale joint military manoeuvres have been carried out between the Honduran armed forces and US troops. In July 1983 President Reagan announced joint exercises with the Honduran army involving 4,000 US combat troops. The effect of all this has been to strengthen the political role of the country's armed forces, particularly the most right-wing element led by General Alvarez. Although the United States encouraged the return to civilian rule with presidential elections in November 1981, the winner of those elections, Dr Roberto Suazo Cordova of the Liberal Party, has allied himself closely with General Alvarez, who holds the real reins of power. Periodic waves of repression have been known in Honduras, though never as widespread or as co-ordinated as elsewhere in Central America, but during 1982 the violation of human rights in Honduras began to increase. Thirty-one Hondurans and 50 foreigners disappeared after abductions in 1982.

A deepening economic crisis in Costa Rica, caused by raw material imports, a slump in coffee prices and a rise in the cost of oil, has been accompanied by a realignment of its foreign policy with the United States. This has been particularly apparent under the presidency of Luis Alberto Monge, of the social democratic National Liberation Party (PLN), who was elected in February

1982. It is evident that Monge was led to expect considerable US economic assistance in return, but the shift in foreign policy has alarmed many Costa Ricans. The country has a democratic tradition of anti-militarism, non-alignment, support for national liberation movements and respect for human rights. Costa Rica gave considerable support to the Sandinistas during their struggle against Somoza. Now the country is associated with the right-wing, repressive governments of Honduras and El Salvador, and has become the launching pad for US-sponsored political initiatives in the region designed to isolate Nicaragua. At the same time, the Reagan administration has encouraged Costa Rica to rearm. Already the country has agreed to the training of an 'anti-terrorist' brigade, while South Korea, Israel and Taiwan have offered to provide riot equipment and arms.

In Guatemala the first year of the Reagan administration was marked by the increasing strength of the guerrilla movement as it gained support amongst the Indians of the western highlands. The response of the Lucas García government was to intensify the repression, undaunted by the consequent international condemnation of his regime. This presented the Reagan administration with a dilemma. Close ties, in the form of business and personal links, existed between right-wing Republicans close to Reagan and members of the Guatemalan élite, and Reagan made no secret of his wish to restore close military and economic ties between the two countries. However, arms sales to Guatemala had been suspended by Congress in 1977 because of the human rights violations in the country. So, unless Lucas García improved his record, it was impossible for Reagan to restore military aid and ties with Guatemala.

In March 1982 a coup overthrew the Lucas García government before his chosen successor, elected in a notoriously fraudulent election a few weeks previously, could take office. The new President was General Efraín Ríos Montt, a 'born-again' Christian. The United States welcomed the move and a concerted effort was launched in Washington to present the new government as a significant change in Guatemalan political life that would lead to the restoration of democracy and respect for human rights. Early measures against the most corrupt figures in the previous government encouraged this view, though no one was charged for the massacres and murders which had taken place. And the claim that

Rios Montt would halt human rights violations was soon refuted. The new government launched a sophisticated counter-insurgency campaign, known as the 'Beans and Guns' programme. The objective was to pacify the Indian highlands, killing those who offered or were suspected of offering the guerrillas support, and channelling aid to those who collaborated with the government. The atrocities committed against the Indian peasantry during 1982 have been recounted by those who survived and managed to flee to refugee camps in southern Mexico. Their stories tell of burnings alive, rape, mutilations, torture and murder of men, women and children. An estimated 8,000 people died. The Guatemalan Roman Catholic bishops believe that about one million people were displaced by the government's 'search and destroy' operations, and reports produced by independent organizations provide details of the destruction of Indian communities and the killing of their inhabitants. In January 1983 President Reagan announced the resumption of arms sales to the country. The repression had brought about a reduction in guerrilla activity in Guatemala, and the widespread terror sown by the army had its effect on the peasant support of the movement. Despite the success of the counter-insurgency campaign, however, Rios Montt found himself increasingly isolated. The Guatemalan business community was alarmed by his move to introduce new taxation. The 'born-again' President had also earned himself a powerful critic in the Catholic Church, offended by his enthusiastic identification with the proselytizing activities of evangelical sects from North America. In the army, hostility among senior ranks mounted as the President resisted pressure to disband his Advisory Council of Junior Officers, in defiance of the rules of precedence set by the military hierarchy. Finally, the US Administration itself became frustrated by Rios Montt's persistent refusal to take sides in the Central American conflict. In August 1983, these tensions culminated in another coup, led by the Defence Minister, General Mejía Victores.

A product of divisions among the powerful ruling élite allied with foreign interests, the new government of Mejía Victores shows few signs of making a radical break with the past. Violence in rural areas continues and urban deaths and disappearances are once again escalating in a pattern of repression which seems set to last as long as dissent survives. A significant innovation, however, has been the move to form a triangular pact with El Salvador and Honduras in opposition to Nicaragua. This shift to an alliance with US strategy together with the temporary gains of the Ríos Montt regime in containing the guerrilla threat, has won a breathing space enabling the US Administration to concentrate on dealing with the immediate problem of neighbouring El Salvador.

In El Salvador 1982 and 1983 saw increasing guerrilla successes against the army. Despite ever-increasing amounts of US military assistance and the training of special counter-insurgency brigades in the United States, the Salvadorean army was unable to inflict any major defeats on the guerrillas. While the military situation deteriorated, the United States faced mounting difficulties on the political front. In March 1982 the United States had hoped that elections would legitimize Duarte's Christian Democrat government and its policies, but the Social Democrats and the dissident Christian Democrats, who had withdrawn from the government between January and April 1980 and were now involved in the FDR political opposition front, refused to participate on the grounds that they had figured prominently on death lists distributed by the army. They also pointed out that press freedom was non-existent, that there was no electoral register and no independent judiciary – in short, that none of the conditions for free and fair elections existed. The result of the elections was to strengthen the extreme right at the expense of the Christian Democrats. Although the Christian Democrats emerged as the largest single party in the 60-member Constituent Assembly, Roberto D'Aubuisson's ARENA party and its smaller right-wing allies managed to obtain an absolute majority. It was only by strenuous manoeuvring that the Americans managed to prevent D'Aubuisson being named President of El Salvador, and they prevented D'Aubuisson and his allies from rolling back Duarte's reforms by convincing the army that continued military and economic support depended on some degree of continuity from the previous government.

Meanwhile the violation of human rights in El Salvador continued. The civilian death toll since October 1979 now exceeds 40,000. No member of the armed forces has ever been brought to trial for any of these crimes; even the murders of American citizens, of the women missionaries and two agrarian reform advisers shot down in the bar of the Sheraton Hotel in January

1980 have gone unpunished. Continued military support for the Salvadorean government has become increasingly unpopular with the US Congress and the American public. President Reagan's six-monthly certifications that the Salvadorean government is making efforts to control human rights violations fly in the face of the evidence, even that provided by the US Embassy in San Salvador. The FDR/FMLN has offered unconditional negotiations since September 1981, but these have been rejected by the United States on the grounds that they would concede to the guerrilla forces at the negotiating table that which they had failed to win on the battlefield.

The prolonged war in El Salvador forms the background to American policy towards Nicaragua, where the Sandinista government is grappling with the inheritance of decades of dictatorship and costly civil war. It was inevitable that there should be tension within the very broad coalition which had come together with a common desire to overthrow the Somoza dictatorship. There was no common vision of a new society and many of the farmers and businessmen who backed the struggle against Somoza had little sympathy for the new economic order which, for the first time, made participation, basic necessities, health and education the main objectives of economic planning. The tension was exacerbated by shortages, caused by an economic depression which sharply reduced the prices of Nicaragua's exports – coffee, cotton and sugar – on the world market. Even so, at a time when other countries in the region are fighting guerrilla wars and cutting back on social programmes, Nicaragua has done much for the welfare of its people. Nine months after the revolution the new government organized the National Literacy Crusade: 60,000 secondary school children from the cities worked as literacy instructors in the rural areas and another 40,000 volunteers worked in the shanty towns and nearby communities. This was followed by an adult education programme and health campaigns which, by education in simple hygiene and massive inoculations, have reduced deaths caused by the traditional Third World killers such as infant diarrhoea, malaria, polio and measles. In the first three years 1,258 schools were built, and women are now equal before the law.

Detached judgement about criticisms of the Sandinista government is difficult. Some of its members are undoubtedly influenced by Marxist-Leninist ideas, and the fact that the promised elections have now been postponed until 1985 is regarded by some observers as sinister. That there is a strong Cuban influence within the government is certain, and tough action has been taken against some opposition groups. On the other hand, left-wing elements in the country have accused the government of being too soft with 'the enemies of society' and of not pursuing socialist ideals with sufficient vigour. All the government's actions have, however, to be seen against a background of diplomatic and economic pressure from the Reagan administration in the United States, and a military campaign on its northern border initiated by former members of Somoza's National Guard but now including other dissident elements, among them many Misquito Indians from Nicaragua's Atlantic coast. The Reagan administration no longer takes the trouble to deny that it is arming and financing this rebel army, the avowed aim of which is to oust the Sandinistas from Managua. A British economist, who is adviser to the Nicaraguan Ministry of Planning, made the following comments about current American policies towards Nicaragua, when giving evidence to the House of Commons Foreign Affairs Committee.

The economic difficulties faced by Nicaragua, and the degree of success in overcoming them, present valuable lessons for the rest of the region. Although there are some (including, unfortunately, the Reagan administration – at least in its first year) who do not wish it to succeed and appear to be prepared to impose sufficient external pressure to force a breakdown of the model, the result would not be a return to the free market but rather a retreat into a less pluralist strategy. It is clear that the present strategy is viewed with considerable sympathy by progressive forces in Latin America and Western Europe. Mexico, in particular, appears to believe that a socially and economically stable Central America is in her own interest, even though the form of economic organization might be more 'revolutionary' than her own. The key point is that the model should be an authentically *local* and *popular* one, as the Mexican revolution was in its time, and not imposed from outside. It is tragic that the major power in the region does not understand this, scarcely five years after the bicentenary of its own revolution. El Salvador will clearly require, sooner or later, a new economic model, for as in Nicaragua the civil war is rooted in unequal development. Much the same may be said of Guatemala, despite the illusion of wealth. Even Costa Rica, long the socio-economic paragon of the region, is now bankrupt and failing in its attempt to reduce expenditure at the expense of wages. The example of Nicaragua has raised the expectations of the poor in the region, and makes the shortcomings of existing economic models more obvious. It has also profoundly altered preconceptions as to the possibilities of private sector participation in planned economies, among both businessmen and revolutionaries; a perception that is also changing worldwide in the light of experience in socialist economies.

It is now clear that the problem for the Reagan administration is the nature of the Sandinista regime itself. The Nicaraguans do not hide their moral and diplomatic solidarity with the FMLN guerrilla front in El Salvador, but this falls far short of the massive supply of arms alleged – yet never successfully proved – by the United States government. The truth is quite simple: the Reagan administration is not prepared to accept in its backyard political change which it cannot control.

Christianity reached Central America in 1502 with the fourth voyage of Christopher Columbus. The *conquistadores* were, for the most part, rapacious pirates and fortune-seekers who had little regard for the native peoples of Central America – Maya and Aztec Indians with an advanced culture and sophisticated civilization. Priests who accompanied the first European settlers left for the colonies fired with enthusiasm for the salvation of so many Indian souls, but baptism was, all too often, the prelude to summary execution or massacre by their Spanish conquerors. That the Roman Catholic Church was closely identified with the powerful at the time of the Conquest there can be no doubt, but many Christians did take up the cause of the Indians, most notably the friars Bartolomé de las Casas and Antonio Valdivieso who became known as 'saviours of the Indians', because of their courageous stance against the authorities of their day. For the most part, however, the Catholic Church threw in its lot with the colonial rulers. Thus as the Spanish Empire increased in scope, so did the wealth and influence of the Church – amassing lands and privileges in return for providing spiritual consolation and ensuring personal salvation.

Even after independence from Spain and the growth of nation states, the Church remained at the right hand of power, but in the nineteenth century the expansion of plantation economies and the rise of the coffee oligarchies of the Central American republics called into question the comfortable relationship of Church and State. This was not brought about by any change in the Church's outlook on society, but rather by the demands of the rural oligarchy. The Church was accused of being opposed to progress, and in Guatemala, for example, archbishops were exiled and religious orders banished. This spirit of anti-clericalism explains, to some extent, the lack of an indigenous clergy and people dedicated to the monastic life which has made the Church in Guatemala in particular highly dependent on foreign missionaries. All countries of Central America were, and continue to be, evangelized to a greater or lesser extent by expatriate clergy – Spaniards, then other Europeans, and later North Americans. The Protestant denominations, too, have been dominated very greatly by their US parent churches and it is only relatively recently that local vocations have made foreign clergy less vital to the maintenance of religious life.

Today Roman Catholics in El Salvador, Honduras, Guatemala, Nicaragua and Costa Rica constitute between 90 and 96 per cent of the populations of the five countries. What this amounts to in terms of faith and practice is not always easy to tell. In El Salvador, for example, 60 per cent of the people are said to hold to a mixture of Catholic and Mayan Indian beliefs. In Costa Rica attendance at Sunday Mass in the cities is no more than 15 per cent; in rural areas it rises to 25 per cent. But each country has its hierarchy of bishops, presided over by an archbishop, and although a very high proportion of the priests and members of religious orders are from other parts of Latin America and from other continents – and this creates its own special problems – there is a strong parochial system, augmented by many educational, medical and social projects. In Guatemala City a Catholic university, founded by the Jesuits, has about 2,500 students and includes a social workers' training centre. Costa Rica, where Catholicism is still the official religion of the State, has an important diocesan centre, *Escuela Social Juan XXIII*, which is concerned with the social teaching of the Church and provides courses for community workers and trade union officials, as well as for clergy and students. In El Salvador an inter-diocesan secretariat co-ordinates the Church's social work throughout the country, and employs teams of priests and nuns on work of conscientization, using the methods of Paulo Freire. Honduras, in common with its neighbours, has a network of church-sponsored savings and credit co-operatives, and a number of community development projects and centres for rural development. Nicaragua has an acute shortage of priests, but there are a significant number of Catholic schools, a section of the Central American Catholic University, and several institutes engaged in social work.

The aftermath of the Second World War had important consequences for the Church in Central America. The prevailing Cold War mentality, exemplified by McCarthy in the early 1950s, was paralleled within the Roman Catholic Church by a militant anti-Communism, personified by Pope Pius XII, and echoed by the US-based evangelical churches. Unrest amongst the impoverished rural populations in Central America, and especially the installation of the independent progressive government in Guatemala of Jacobo Arbenz in 1949, fanned the flames of this anti-Communism. Both European and North American clergy were exhorted to counter social unrest through evangelization. The renaissance of evangelization through the influx of foreign diocesan clergy and religious orders carried the hallmark of anti-Communism, but it brought with it other distinctive features. For almost the first time, the rural areas became the target of church attention, and priests and nuns came face to face with the grinding poverty and exploitation of the rural work force. No longer were the majority of religious to be found in the well-off areas of the capital cities, mixing solely with the privileged. Their daily task became one of sharing the pain, grief and suffering of the poor, witnessing their ceaseless labour for starvation wages, the relentlessly high levels of infant mortality and their powerlessness in determining their future.

The Catholic Church in Central America thus experienced a reawakening which paralleled that of the Church throughout Latin America. While successive governments met every popular protest with ineffectual reforms and widespread repression, the Church, through its priests, monks, nuns and pastoral workers, contributed to a slow process of building an awareness among its flock of their needs and rights. It is ironic that it was this very 'crusade against Communism' in the 1950s that was a catalyst in converting the Church to an option for the poor which is often seen to be synonymous with Communism by the military rulers and oligarchies of El Salvador and Guatemala. The Second Vatican Council called by John XXIII in the 1960s served to underline what was already happening within the Church in Central America, and affirmed the essential mission of the Church in the world in service of the poor. The papal encyclical *Populorum Progressio,* which denounced the unjust maintenance of wealth by a privileged few at the expense of the mass of their fellow citizens, further vindicated the increasing involvement of the clergy, members of religious orders and laity in Central America in their search for justice.

In Honduras, Nicaragua, El Salvador and Guatemala, the Church met the 1960s with a renewed mission and vigour. Honduras, perhaps to a greater extent than any of its neighbours, pioneered the work of grassroots evangelization through the training of lay people as 'Delegates of the Word'. These were community leaders from remote rural areas whose enthusiasm compensated for the shortage of ordained priests, and who fulfilled the function of minister, guide and teacher in their own villages. Local pastoral teams attempted to find answers to concrete problems affecting the people, through Bible study and the identification of the life experience of the poor with that of Christ. Evangelization went hand in hand with the encouragement to form co-operatives. During the 1960s a new political phenomenon also arrived in Central America from Europe, creating a channel for many Christians to become active in the political arena. Christian Democracy had achieved striking successes in Chile, with its programme of reform and its 'third way' between capitalism and Communism, and was welcomed by many committed, but mainly middle-class, Christians as an authentic vehicle for social change and justice. In the countryside the identification of Christian values with the need for social reform led to the creation of an overtly Christian trade union movement, in some cases controlled by the Christian Democrat Party.

The current for renewal within the Church, which found its

articulation in the Episcopal Conference at Medellín in 1968, could not of course convert the entire Church to the cause of the poor when for centuries it had supported the rich and the privileged. Cardinal Casariego, Archbishop of Guatemala until his death in 1983, is reported to have stated that the conclusions of Medellín were optional and that he had opted out. As far as the hierarchies of the Church in Central America were concerned, the 'cry of the people' had not been heard or, rather, it had been heard and rejected. No united voice spoke out as the 'voice of the voiceless', such as happened with the bishops of Brazil, but often a prophetic voice would be raised from among the ranks of the hierarchies to echo the clamour of the 'people who suffer and who demand justice, freedom and respect for fundamental rights'. The most prophetic of these voices belonged to Oscar Arnulfo Romero, Archbishop of San Salvador from 1977, who, until his assassination at the altar on 24th March 1980, used his weekly sermons in the cathedral to denounce the deaths, disappearances and massacres carried out by the security forces. The death of Archbishop Romero is perhaps the single event which served to turn an indifferent world's attention to the oppression suffered by the majority of people in Central America. His assassination was in fact but one of a series of threats and attacks which the Church had earned for itself through its option for the poor. As one Latin American theologian noted after his death: 'Before Romero the Church tended to say: these Christians died for political not religious reasons. He was killed not because he defended the rights of the Church but because he defended the rights of the poor.'

Thus in the 1970s the Church came to share the harassment and repression of the people. The church of Olancho, Honduras, under the leadership of its bishop Nicholas D'Antonio, encouraged rural education programmes and thereby antagonized local landowners resentful of the increasing militancy of the peasants. In 1975 pressure for land reform from Christian peasant unions provoked an unequivocal response from the authorities: eleven people, including two priests, were captured, tortured and murdered by the army, and a total of thirty-two priests and nuns were arrested and expelled from the province. All church property was confiscated, and parish houses, including the bishop's residence, were ransacked. This pattern has been repeated time and again in other parts of Central America. In 1980 the Church in Guatemala took the unprecedented step of closing down the diocese of Quiché, in protest at the assassinations of catechists and clergy and the expulsion of the local bishop, Juan Gerardi.

Governments have also responded to the Church's championing of the cause of the poor with campaigns of slander, and accusations of communist infiltration. A spectacular example of this was the elaborate 'confession' by Luis Pellecer, a well-loved and able Jesuit priest working in Guatemala City, who was violently seized and arrested in the street in the summer of 1981. Attempts to discover his whereabouts and pleas for his safety went unheeded until, three months after his disappearance, the Guatemalan authorities announced a press conference to which they invited members of the foreign diplomatic corps and international journalists. The entire proceedings were broadcast on TV and radio throughout Central America. Father Pellecer was presented, a changed man, not only mentally but physically, to renounce his past links with the 'Church of subversion'. His speech linked the Church with guerrilla groups and provided the government with the justification it had been seeking to sanction a campaign of terror against priests, members of religious orders and lay Christians. Since this press conference, Father Pellecer has not been allowed to speak alone with any member of the Society of Jesus, and he is thought to be living in the Presidential Palace in Guatemala City. Close study of the tapes and the transcript of his declarations has convinced Father Pellecer's former colleagues and Amnesty International that he fell victim to an elaborate process of brainwashing. The Jesuits have been major objects of campaigns of vilification throughout Central America. In 1977 the entire Jesuit community in El Salvador was given a matter of days to abandon the country under threat of extermination from the para-military death squads. Car stickers began to appear with the slogan: 'Be patriotic – kill a priest', and newspapers often carried cartoons reflecting this message. Archbishop Romero was presented in caricature in the pro-government press with horns and denunciations of his alleged links with international Communism. His assassination came shortly after he had made an impassioned plea to the members of the security forces: 'In the name of God, I beg you, I order you, I command you, stop the repression', and only weeks after he had written to President Carter begging that no military assistance should be provided to El Salvador.

In April 1981 the Institute on Religion and Democracy was formed in the United States for the purpose of combating the infiltration of Communism in the Church and countering the evils of liberation theology. Nicaragua has been the special object of its attention. An estimated 97 per cent of Nicaraguans are, at least nominally, Roman Catholic, and since the 1960s the Church has experienced a renewal through its commitment to the poor. The bishops, who for more than thirty years had kept silent about social injustice, rallied their forces behind increasing criticism of the Somoza dictatorship until, in 1977, they strongly denounced his government as illegitimate. One month prior to the Sandinista victory, in June 1979, the bishops of Nicaragua became the first National Conference of Catholic Bishops ever to declare a revolutionary insurrection with leftist leanings to be legitimate. Religious convictions played a strong part in the commitment of many people to the revolutionary struggle, and clergy, members of religious orders and lay people became active in the conflict. They provided emergency food and medical supplies to refugees, hid people persecuted by the National Guard, and told the people how the Gospel had to become flesh in the historic conflict they were experiencing. There is no doubt that the Church played a crucial role in the overthrow of Somoza.

Since 1979, however, the church hierarchy has become increasingly opposed to the Sandinista government, and the 1983 visit to Central America by Pope John Paul II served to underline the divisions within the Nicaraguan Church. These divisions are now sharp. The bishops, while declaring their continuing commitment to the poor, are clearly unhappy about what they regard as the totalitarian tendencies of the government and the risk of an Eastern European-type state emerging. They also feel strongly that the priests should not hold political office and that the Church must be free to criticize the government whenever necessary. Yet the government continues to enjoy the support of many priests, nuns and lay Catholics, particularly those in the grassroots communities, and members of the Nicaraguan Conference of Priests and Nuns (CONFER), who believe that the Sandinistas are moving

Nicaragua towards a more just and compassionate society, and that the bishops are in danger of reverting to a traditional, conservative stance, and of becoming identified with right-wing forces concerned to halt social and political progress. Archbishop Obando y Bravo, who is often vociferous in his criticisms of the government, went to the United States in 1982 to receive a special award from the Institute on Religion and Democracy.

Four priests hold senior office in the Sandinista government, of whom the best known are Father Miguel D'Escoto, of the Maryknoll Order, who is Foreign Minister; Father Edgar Parrales, the Ambassador to the OAS; and Father Ernesto Cardenal, SJ, the Minister of Culture. Father Cardenal's poetic meditations have been translated into many languages, and his holiness is widely recognized and admired, but when he attempted to greet Pope John Paul II on his arrival at Managua Airport on 4th March 1983 the Pope seemed to raise his fingers, as if to admonish the priest, and when Cardenal tried to kiss his ring he withdrew his hand. The background to this embarrassing, and many thought unhappy, incident, is that in June 1981 the Nicaraguan Conference of Bishops issued a statement demanding that all priests holding office in the government (besides those in high office another twenty priests have senior administrative posts) should return to their vocations. This statement was said to have the 'total support and authority' of the Holy See, and today those who continue to hold government office are forbidden to celebrate Mass, either publicly or privately.

The greatest challenge to Pope John Paul in Central America was, however, in Guatemala. Only days before his visit, and in spite of urgent Vatican pleas for clemency, six people were executed for guerrilla activities. Here innumerable fundamentalist sects have sprung up since the late 1970s. These sects, such as the Church of the Word (an import from California, whose leading member was the country's former President, 'born-again' Christian General Efraín Ríos Montt), preach a message of personal salvation and offer rewards in the next world in return for virulent anti-communism in this. Even the former President's brother, the Roman Catholic Bishop Ríos Montt, fled from Guatemala in 1982 to seek protection in the Vatican. The activities of the religious sects which now proliferate in all the countries of the region seem to be fulfilling the objectives of the US Santa Fe document. This document, prepared for President Reagan by a group of his advisers even before he took office, has been very influential in determining US policy in Central America since 1982. It includes this statement:

> The United States must seize the ideological initiative. ... The war is for the minds of mankind. ... US foreign policy must begin to counter (not merely react against) liberation theology as it is utilized by the 'liberation theology' clergy. The role of the Church is vital to the concept of political freedom. Unfortunately, Marxist-Leninist forces have used the Church as a weapon against private property and productive capitalism, infiltrating the religious community with ideas that are less Christian than Communist.

The Catholic Church in Central America in the crisis of the 1980s is a Church facing an even more dramatic choice than in the past. Its present position was vividly described by a European bishop, Alberto Iniesta of Madrid, at the end of a visit to El Salvador:

> The Church of San Salvador is rooted in the renewing Church of the Council, of Medellín and of Puebla. It is that part of the Latin American Church which unashamedly has opted for the poor, which has abandoned its false mundane security, its commitment to the powerful of this world, and has begun to live and walk with the marginalized, exploited, repressed and crushed people. And it is for that reason that the Church itself is suffering in a systematic and generalized way, slander, accusations, prison, kidnapping, torture and even death in so many of its Christians, from bishops to catechists, priests and nuns. San Salvador is not an isolated case but one part of that martyred Church of Latin America which is the light of hope and a demand for the commitment of the Church throughout the world.

The gradual radicalization of the Catholic Church during years of deepening crisis and theological ferment has had its counterpart in Central America's Protestant churches. The first Protestant missionaries to arrive in the region were members of the Moravian

Church whose involvement in Nicaragua, where it is now the largest Protestant church, dates back to 1849. Most of the historical Protestant churches were founded by missionaries from the United States, with the exception of Costa Rica, where in the early days British influence was strong. American Presbyterians arrived in Guatemala in 1882, while the US-based non-denominational Central American Mission was active in Honduras and El Salvador from 1896 onwards. The Baptists, Methodists and Lutherans are also well established in the region, though their membership and influence varies from country to country. There are about 3,000 Anglicans in Costa Rica and a few in each of the other Central American countries.

The activity of the historical churches, particularly over the last few decades, has shown a keen interest in educational and health work. In Guatemala the Presbyterian Church (now about 35,000 strong) pioneered the method of Theological Education by Extension (TEE) which has since become a worldwide movement. There is also a Protestant university in Guatemala. Hospitals have been built and medical training programmes developed, notably by Baptists in Nicaragua (about 20,000 members and adherents) and the United Church of Christ and the Central American Mission in Honduras. Churches are also involved in agricultural and literacy work and, in cases like the Moravian Church in Nicaragua (working with the Misquito Indians), have provided an important social as well as pastoral ministry to marginalized groups. Frequently social ministry has been the stimulus to the formation of ecumenical organizations, such as CEPAD (Evangelical Committee for Development Aid) in Nicaragua, and CEDI (Evangelical Committee for Integral Development) in Guatemala. In particular, the catastrophic earthquakes in Nicaragua and Guatemala in 1976 brought the churches together in a massive ecumenical relief programme.

In many cases, these churches have been converted, through bitter experience, to a more radical option for the poor. Evangelical groups in Guatemala and El Salvador have increasingly spoken out against the repression and defended as Christian and legitimate the aspirations of those seeking social change. A letter from the Evangelical Confraternity of Guatemala states: 'For our ministry among these people who suffer, we affirm that these humble brothers, ours and yours, are not as the Government maintains, Communists, they are Christians in their majority and many also are members of evangelical churches who want to live a dignified life at the level which God wants and who, because of their Christian principles, do not want to support an unjust war like the one imposed by the Government.' Protestants engaged in this new and critical perspective work closely with Catholics at the grassroots level where the common element of being poor has begun to unite many Christians. A Guatemalan missionary explained in testimony before the US House of Representatives Subcommittee on Human Rights and International Organizations, Committee on Foreign Affairs, in December 1982: 'They are growing ever more aware of the close relationship in the Christian Gospel (whether communicated by Roman Catholics or Protestants) between spiritual well-being in this world and the next, and a reasonable hope to improve their impoverished lives while still on this earth. The message that the poor Christians of Latin America hear comes straight from the Bible. Isaiah 65, Amos 5, and Psalm 146 are, among many others, passages that Latin American Christians are reading as promises God holds out to them, both now and when Christ returns. Or it comes in the course of reflection sessions on the Bible led by religious workers who no longer accept the un-biblical separation between spiritual prosperity and physical misery that has been tacitly accepted and even encouraged as part of mission work for centuries.'

It is difficult to assess the extent of this movement within the Protestant denominations, as perspectives may vary even between individual churches of the same denomination. Much pioneer work in the field of theology and pastoral training has been done by the Latin American Evangelical Centre for Pastoral Studies (CELEP), with its headquarters in Costa Rica. Many pastors and lay workers have participated in the Centre's ecumenical training programmes, exploring such themes as church growth, discipleship in the local church, and social involvement, with reference to the concrete problems of their communities, and from a perspective informed by a critical social awareness. The Centre has helped plan and co-ordinate local seminar courses with partners such as CEPAD in Nicaragua.

The new approach articulated in these theological and pastoral developments finds its essential complement in the growing practical commitment of individual Christians and churches to the cause of social justice. Evangelical young people and pastors took an active part in the struggle in Nicaragua which led to the overthrow of the Somoza regime and now, with CEPAD, are contributing to the country's reconstruction programmes. In El Salvador, where there are about 10,000 Baptists, the Emmanuel Baptist Church has been closely involved in aid projects run by the Roman Catholic agency, Caritas, and more recently, with the Lutherans, has played a leading role in Diaconia, the ecumenical aid committee of the churches which runs several refugee programmes. But the cost of this commitment is high in El Salvador and Guatemala where the repression continues. Pastors and lay leaders have had to flee the country because of harassment and death threats. Some congregations have lost members in the wave of abductions and killings. Evangelicals in Guatemala write: 'Many of us have hidden our Bibles because they are considered to be sources of subversion. . . . In many villages, in Chimaltenango, Quiché and Huehuetenango, the brothers and sisters no longer meet in the church buildings to praise the Lord, for fear of being massacred.'

In numerical terms, the historical Protestant churches remain a tiny minority in Central America, though the importance of their contributions to the movements for social justice in the region have in some cases been in excess of their size. By far and away the most significant church growth, however, has been among the Pentecostal and fundamentalist churches. The earliest arrivals were the Seventh Day Adventists whose presence in some places dates back to the beginning of the twentieth century. They were soon followed by the Assemblies of God in the 1920s and 1930s, and other US-based Pentecostal churches. Now their congregations are numbered in tens, and sometimes hundreds, of thousands.

From the late 1970s onwards a new stream of fundamentalist sects have made a dramatic impact and attracted thousands of converts. Financed and directed by parent churches in the United States, their activities are regarded with deep suspicion by Protestants and Catholics alike. Their message of personal salvation, preached with charismatic zeal, is interwoven with a virulent anti-communism which conservative and repressive forces in the region have exploited – often with the willing consent and collaboration of the movement's leaders – to legitimize their violent opposition to social change. The most conspicuous example of this alliance is to be seen in Guatemala where the former President, General Ríos Montt, is a leading member of the California-based Church of the Word, and received important ideological and material support from the sect in his war against 'Communist subversion'. Ríos Montt described himself as a 'chosen man', and his weekly broadcasts on Guatemalan radio promoted his political and military programmes with frequent references to the Bible. Leading members of right-wing evangelical churches enthusiastically reinforce this image both in Guatemala and in the United States, where Pat Robertson, President of the Christian Broadcasting Network, declared 'Ríos Montt is a beautiful man. ... We're in constant battle for religious freedom and I'm very thankful to say we're winning. By the way, the people in Guatemala are thrilled that Ríos Montt is their leader. ... So let's pray. Let's pray for this man and for all of Latin America.'

The Church of the Word is a branch of Gospel Outreach which, through Operation Love Lift, pumped a million dollars of aid into rural areas of Guatemala. Supervised and co-ordinated by the government and armed forces, the aid became the cornerstone of the 'Beans and Guns' policy of the regime. This support for a government frequently accused of genocidal atrocities went hand in hand with heavy proselytizing campaigns which caused division and confusion among the Indian communities brought under its influence.

The activities of the sects seem to be fulfilling the objectives of the US Santa Fe document. In Nicaragua, where the revolutionary government has become the prime target of the US offensive against 'Communism' in Central America, there are reports of co-operatives closing down because converts to the sects have been told that participation in co-operatives is against religion. On occasions there have been proven links between armed counter-revolutionary activity and pastors of various churches, and it has been claimed in some parts that the most active areas of the Contras, right-wing guerrillas, are also the most active areas of the sects. A kidnap victim taken to a Contra camp in Honduras, who later escaped, related how the prisoners were told that if they joined the sects they would not be harmed. Reports of this kind have inflamed historical tensions between Catholics and non-Catholics, and there have been several popular invasions of Protestant churches, including those belonging to CEPAD-affiliated churches, though these have usually been restored to their pastors. Both CEPAD and the Moravian Church have taken a firm stand against the use of religion to oppose the revolution in Nicaragua, particularly in cases where their own members have been implicated. The credibility of the Gospel, as well as of the Church, is at stake.

The British Churches
and Latin America

Roman Catholic missions from Western Europe followed quickly on the heels of the *conquistadores* in the sixteenth century and played a very significant, though not always a laudable, part in the pacification of the indigenous peoples. The scale of their work, particularly that of the Spanish and Portuguese religious orders, became great and created a dependence upon European Catholicism which the Latin American Church has yet to outgrow. It was not until the middle of the nineteenth century that non-Catholic missions from Europe established a foothold, taking advantage of the more liberal political regimes, and it is only in the present century that Protestant missions from the United States have come to dominate the non-Catholic scene and been regarded, in some quarters anyway, as yet another manifestation of American imperialism.

Seen against this background, the missionary work of the British churches in Latin America is obviously quite small, reflecting no doubt the lack of general concern for this continent which characterized the British outlook until the Falkland Islands war in 1982, and still has room for expansion. The information about British missionary involvement that follows is based on facts and figures supplied by the missions, societies and agencies concerned and describes the situation during the early part of 1983.

Roman Catholic Missions

The Mill Hill Missionaries have twenty-three of their members working in Latin America. Nine are in Brazil and six in Chile, and in both countries the main emphasis is on Christian community building. The missionaries were forced to leave Chile in 1973, following the overthrow of the Allende government, but they returned in 1975. Four others are engaged in rural apostolate in Peru, another is engaged in medical work in Ecuador, two are working in the Falkland Islands, and one in Venezuela. The cost to this order is just over £25,000 a year.

The Benedictine community at Worth Abbey in Sussex have six monks engaged in parish work in a slum area of the city of Lima, with a population of 50,000. The commitment of this order in Peru began in 1968 when four monks started an agricultural and evangelizing project in the Apurimac river valley. After two years the project had 1,200 members, involved in a service co-operative of local farmers, and in 1975 this was handed over to the Peruvian Ministry of Agriculture – the monks then moving to the Lima slum to work with a local church.

The English province of the Missionary Sons of the Immaculate Heart of Mary (the Claretian Fathers and Brothers) has three of its members working, with seven American religious, in Guatemala. This work began in 1967 and has been concentrated on three parishes in the diocese of Izabal, where catechists and lay leaders are trained. Health clinics have been set up, and in one of the parishes an Indian primary school and a secondary school have also been established. The English province spends £8,000 a year on this work.

The Sisters of the Sacred Heart of Mary, in West London, established a mission in North-East Brazil in 1980. Five sisters are living among the poor on the edge of a town, where they are engaged mainly in the building of basic Christian communities. They work closely with the bishop and other religious orders, and some of the sisters are in secular employment, partly to support themselves but also as a means of solidarity with the poor. About £5,000 a year is invested in the work from England.

The Sisters of the Cross and Passion are an international Congregation which has been in Latin America since 1912. At the present time forty-nine sisters are engaged in pastoral, educational and medical work – thirty-one in Chile, fifteen in Argentina and three in Peru – with a strong emphasis on work among the poor. Just over half the sisters are Latin Americans, the rest coming from the British Isles; together they form a self-supporting Latin American province.

The Franciscan Missionaries of St Joseph have been engaged in overseas missionary work since 1883, though their involvement in Latin America dates from 1971. Now there are four sisters in Peru and another four in Ecuador – in both countries they are engaged in pastoral, catechetical, medical and social welfare work. Three sisters in Chile are part of an episcopally-led team concerned with forming basic Christian communities.

The Association of the Holy Family was founded in France during the early part of the nineteenth century and is now an international association of religious sisters with about 4,000 members working in twenty different countries. Some sixty of the sisters (mainly Spanish but including two British) are involved in pastoral, educational and medical work in rural areas of Argentina, Brazil, Paraguay and Peru. In Brazil, however, ten sisters are working in and around São Paulo.

The Crusade of the Holy Spirit has five priests engaged in pastoral and educational work in Venezuela, and two priests and three sisters similarly engaged in Argentina.

Anglican Missions

The South American Missionary Society, which began in 1844 as the Patagonian Missionary Society, has always had a deep commitment to evangelism among the indigenous peoples of Latin America and today it has six missionaries and six national workers in Argentina, five missionaries in Bolivia, fifteen missionaries and one national worker in Brazil, twenty-seven missionaries and three national workers in Chile, twenty-four missionaries and three national workers in Paraguay, and eight missionaries and two national workers in Peru. Its annual budget is £490,000. Since 1960 there has been an increasing urban emphasis in the Society's work, expressed in involvement in evangelism, leadership training, church planting and social projects in Valparaíso, Santiago, Asunción, Salta and Lima, Salvador, Rio and Recife.

The Bible Churchmen's Missionary Society, representing an Anglican evangelical tradition, has been working in Peru (where it now has three missionaries) and Bolivia (two missionaries) since the mid-1970s. In Bolivia the Society is involved in a joint church-planting project, with the South American Missionary Society, in the city of La Paz. The total Latin American budget is £25,000 a year.

The United Society for the Propagation of the Gospel, one of the Church of England's major missionary agencies, has been involved in Latin America only since 1976. It supplies church workers (mainly, but not exclusively, priests) to the Anglican diocese of Argentina and Eastern South America, and the annual budget is approximately £15,000.

The Scottish Episcopal Church has had a Latin American commitment for only the last six years and now supports a nurse in Chile, a nurse in Brazil, and a social worker in Argentina at a total cost of £5,500 a year.

In a new joint project starting in 1984, USPG, the Scottish Episcopal Church and the Church Missionary Society, in partnership with the Anglican diocese of South Central Brazil, are supporting the work of a priest in São Paulo.

The Intercontinental Church Society serves English-speaking people overseas, and has chaplains in Peru and the Falkland Islands, and associate chaplains in Brazil and Chile. The Missions to Seamen ministers to seafarers of all nationalities through its Flying Angel Clubs which are established in the ports of Santos (Brazil), Buenos Aires and Rosario (Argentina) and Valparaiso (Chile). Generally an Anglican priest is in charge, but sometimes a layman has the responsibility. Occasionally the ministry is extended to a local congregation, and the annual cost to the Missions to Seamen is £12,000.

The Churches' Ministry among the Jews has one priest and his wife working in the Jewish community in Buenos Aires. They are based on two Anglican churches in the city and have close links with the American Board of Mission to Jews.

Other Churches

The Baptist Missionary Society started its work in Brazil in 1953 when two ex-China missionaries were sent to investigate the possibility of working with the Paraná state Baptist Convention. Now it has thirty-nine missionaries engaged mainly in pastoral and evangelistic work, and a few of them involved in theological education and an agricultural project. The annual budget for this work in Brazil is just over £270,000.

The Methodist Church's Overseas Division has no missionaries directly involved in Latin America, but in 1983 it made grants totalling £28,700 to the Methodist Church in Panama and Costa Rica, and to theological education institutes and centres in Chile and Argentina.

The Salvation Army moved into Argentina and Uruguay in 1890 and now has 127 missionaries engaged in pastoral and evangelistic work in all the main Latin American countries. Most of the missionaries are from Australia and North America, but four married couples and one single person, working in Brazil, Chile and Paraguay, are British. Their work includes day nurseries and community centres, small clinics and dental care centres, and there is an extensive hospital programme in Bolivia. In most countries there are also literacy projects, and the Salvation Army's Latin American budget is in excess of £1 (US $1.5) million a year.

Evangelical Societies

The Worldwide Evangelization Crusade has thirty missionaries (one of whom is British) in Brazil, twenty (five British) in Colombia, and thirteen (two British) in Venezuela. These are engaged mainly in evangelism and church planting, with a leadership training centre at Montes Claros in Brazil, a hospital in Colombia, and two campus ministries in Venezuela. There is a publishing house in Brazil.

The Regions Beyond Missionary Union started work in Peru in 1890 and now has sixteen missionaries working there in collaboration with other evangelical agencies and churches – establishing new congregations and involved in leadership training, youth work and Bible teaching. The annual budget is £56,000.

The Evangelical Union of South America was formed in 1911 by the union of a number of evangelical agencies working in Latin America, and it now has sixty-five active missionaries (ten in Argentina, two in Bolivia, twenty-four in Brazil and twenty-nine in Peru) plus two associate workers in Argentina and in Peru, and six retired workers. These are engaged in Bible and theological training at all levels, especially in the student world, and in the production and distribution of Christian literature. There is also involvement in educational, medical and social aid services. The total budget is £250,000 a year, including administrative and support costs in Britain.

The Unevangelized Fields Mission which started in 1931 has twenty-five missionaries and two short-term workers in Brazil, most of whom serve in the autonomous Missão Cristâ Evangelica do Brasil and the Missão Cristâ Evangelica de Minas Gerais e Bahía. They are principally involved in church planting, leadership training and youth work.

OMS International, formerly the Oriental Missionary Society, is of American origin and has 500 missionaries working in various parts of the world, with a substantial commitment in Latin America. In Brazil, where one British couple are among the missionaries, the work includes training of pastors and lay leaders, telephone evangelism, four orphanages and prison ministry. In Colombia, where another British couple are working, there is 'direct aggressive evangelism', radio, film and literature work, leadership training, and church planting. Two British couples in Ecuador share in extensive work which includes an evangelical Bible seminary, a Bible institute, a youth camp, medical clinics, and evangelism in the cities and rural areas, as well as among the Quechua-speaking Indians in the central mountains.

Christian Literature Agencies

The Pocket Testament League has missionaries working in various countries around the world, and two (a married couple) are in Brazil, where the work is mainly in the hands of Brazilian Christians. The League also acts as an agency for the distribution of gospels (mainly St John's) in a variety of different languages.

The Christian Literature Crusade, founded in 1941, aims 'to take the message of salvation to all mankind through the medium of the printed page'. It is inter-denominational, with an evangelical emphasis, and serves national churches by means of literature centres and bookstalls, as well as 'literature missionaries'. In Latin America the Crusade is working in Argentina, Brazil, Chile, Colombia, Uruguay and Venezuela, though the British contribution, apart from funds, is confined to four workers in Brazil and two in Uruguay.

The Society for Promoting Christian Knowledge is an Anglican organization which provides financial support for a great variety of literature and communication projects in all parts of the world. It does not initiate its own work in Latin America but responds to requests from churches and agencies in virtually all the countries, spending from £10–20,000 a year on such things as bookshops, hymn books, a seminary library (in Cuba), and a Theological Education by Extension scheme (in Paraguay).

The United Society for Christian Literature makes grants to Christian literature and communications agencies for resource centres, mini-libraries, lay training, Theological Education by Extension programmes, book and magazine publishing, and literature for new literates. The Society supports work in Brazil, Argentina, Chile, Peru, Venezuela, Mexico and Costa Rica.

The Wycliffe Bible Translators are affiliated to the Summer Institute of Linguistics – an international organization with 4,500 members, concerned with the study and teaching of linguistics, reading and translation programmes in forty different countries. The work includes the translation of the Bible into languages requiring special expertise, and British people are working in Peru (two), Brazil (eighteen), Colombia (four) and Mexico (four).

Aid and Educational Agencies

The Catholic Fund for Overseas Development (CAFOD) is the official agency of the Roman Catholic Church in England and Wales for overseas development. It devotes approximately £600,000 a year to projects in practically all the countries of Latin America, working in collaboration with local church groups and providing financial support for a wide spectrum of activities, including community development, community health programmes, non-formal education, and agricultural projects.

Tear Fund provides financial support for development projects which are supervised by those who believe 'that the true meaning in life and fulfilment for life can only be found through a faith and trust in Jesus Christ' and wish to introduce others to the Christian faith. It has twenty-one workers in Argentina, Haiti, Honduras, Paraguay, Brazil and Peru and supports projects in almost every country in Latin America. These include vocational training schemes, relief and rehabilitation projects, health, agriculture, childcare, and evangelism and Christian education. The amount spent in Latin America and the Caribbean during the year 1981–2 was £867,000.

Christian Aid is a division of the British Council of Churches and an instrument by which the churches act together for the relief of human suffering. It has no field workers but operates through a network of church-related and secular agencies and provides financial support for development projects designed to help poor people improve the quality of their lives. Major Latin American projects are in Bolivia, Brazil, Chile, Peru and Central America, and there are links with projects in Argentina, Paraguay, Uruguay, Colombia, Ecuador, Panama, Costa Rica and Mexico. These include agricultural support, preventive health education, urban and rural development, literacy programmes, legal aid for poor farmers and workers, and community groups. The Latin America budget is about £1,100,000 a year.

The Catholic Institute of International Relations is an independent Roman Catholic lay organization working to promote issues of international justice and peace, particularly in the Third World. The Institute has two arms of operation. It recruits skilled personnel to work with small-scale development projects in selected Third World countries, and at present has small volunteer development programmes in Honduras (four workers), Nicaragua (eighteen workers), Ecuador (ten workers), and Peru (seven workers). It also has an education/action programme in the United Kingdom designed to increase awareness among British people of development issues and of the need for social justice, and to support groups in Latin America, Asia and South Africa that are working for greater social justice.

List of Useful Contacts

Roman Catholic Missions

Benedictines, Worth Abbey, Crawley, West Sussex RH10 4SB

Crusade of the Holy Spirit, St Mark Woodhill, Kentish Lane, Hatfield, Herts AL9 6EB

Franciscan Missionaries of St Joseph, St Joseph's Convent, Greenleach Lane, Manchester, M28 4TS

Mill Hill Missionaries, St Joseph's College, Lawrence Street, London, NW7 4JX

Missionary Sons of the Immaculate Heart of Mary, The Claretians, Buckden Palace, Huntingdon, Cambs, PE18 9TA

Sisters of the Cross and Passion, Brownberrie Lane, Leeds, West Yorks, LS18 5HD

Sisters of the Sacred Heart of Mary, 64 Little Ealing Lane, London, W5 4XF

Anglican Missions

Bible Churchmen's Missionary Society, Allen Gardiner House, Pembury Road, Tunbridge Wells, Kent TN2 3QU

Churches Ministry among the Jews, Vincent House, Vincent Square, London, SW1P 2PX

Intercontinental Church Society, 175 Tower Bridge Road, London, SE1 2AQ

Missions to Seamen, St Michael Paternoster Royal, College Hill, London EC4R 2RL

Scottish Episcopal Church, 21 Grosvenor Crescent, Edinburgh EH12 5EE

South American Missionary Society, Allen Gardiner House, Pembury Road, Tunbridge Wells, Kent TN2 3QU

United Society for the Propagation of the Gospel, 15 Tufton Street, London SW1P 3QQ

Other Churches

Baptist Missionary Society, 93 Gloucester Place, London W1H 4AA

Methodist Church Overseas Division, 25 Marylebone Road, London NW1 5JR

Salvation Army, International Headquarters, 101 Queen Victoria Street, London EC4P 4EP

Quaker Peace & Service, Friends House, Euston Road, London NW1

Evangelical Societies

Evangelical Union of South America, Whitefield House, 186 Kennington Park Road, London SE11 4BT

OMS International, 1 Sandileigh Avenue, Didsbury, Manchester M20 9LN

Regions Beyond Missionary Union, Whitefield House, 186 Kennington Park Road, London SE11 4BT

Unevangelized Fields Mission, 9 Gunnersbury Avenue, Ealing Lane, London W5 3NL

Christian Literature Agencies

Christian Literature Crusade, 51 The Dean, Alresford, Hampshire SO24 9BJ

Pocket Testament League, 16 Holwood Road, Bromley, Kent BR1 3EB

Society for Promoting Christian Knowledge, Holy Trinity Church, Marylebone Road, London NW1 4DU

United Society for Christian Literature, Luke House, Farnham Road, Guildford, Surrey GU1 4XD

Wycliffe Bible Translators, Horsely Green, High Wycombe, Bucks
HP14 3XL

Information and Aid Organizations

Amnesty International, 1 Easton Street, London WC1X 8DJ

Amnesty International British Section, 5 Roberts Place, Bowling
Green Lane, London EC1 0EJ

Anti-Slavery Society for the Protection of Human Rights, 180
Brixton Road, London SW9

British Council of Churches, Division of International Affairs/
Human Rights Forum, 2 Eaton Gate, London SW1W 9BL

British-Cuba Resource Centre, 29 Islington Park Street, London
N1

CARILA, 29 Islington Park Street, London N1

Catholic Fund for Overseas Development, Garden Close,
Stockwell Road, London SW9

Catholic Institute for International Relations, 22 Coleman Fields,
London N1 7AF

Central America Information Service, 14 Brixton Road, London
SW9

Chile Committee for Human Rights, 266 Pentonville Road,
London N1 9JY

Christian Aid, 240/250 Ferndale Road, London SW9 8BH

Committee for Human Rights in Argentina, 29 Islington Park
Street, London N1

El Salvador Committee for Human Rights, 20/21 Compton
Terrace, London N1

FEDEFAM (Latin American Federation of Relatives of
Disappeared Prisoners), 226 Pentonville Road, London N1 9JY

Guatemala Committee for Human Rights, 20/21 Compton
Terrace, London N1

Honduras Committee for Human Rights, 20/21 Compton Terrace,
London N1

Inter-Church Task Force on El Salvador, 19 Steventon Road,
London W12 0SX

Latin America Bureau, 1 Amwell Street, London EC1R 1UL

Minority Rights Group, 36 Craven Street, London WC2N 5NG

Oxfam, 274 Banbury Road, Oxford OX2 7DZ

Paraguay Committee for Human Rights, 29 Islington Park Street, London N1

Save the Children Fund, 157 Clapham Road, London SW9

Scottish Catholic International Aid Fund, 43 Greenhill Road, Rutherglen, Glasgow G73 2SW

Survival International, 36 Craven Street, London WC2N 5NG

Tear Fund, 11 Station Road, Teddington, Middlesex TW11 9AA

War on Want, 467 Caledonian Road, London N7 9BE

For Further Reading

Introduction

A History of Latin America
    George Pendle, Penguin 1963 (revised 1976)
The Politics of Anti-Politics: The Military in Latin America
    ed. Brian Loveman & Thomas M. Davies Jr, University of Nebraska
    Press 1978
The Latin American Peasant
    Andrew Pearse, Frank Cass, London 1975
Latin America: Geographical Perspectives
    ed. Harold Blakemore & Clifford T. Smith, Methuen 1971
The Conquest of the Incas
    John Hemmings, Macmillan 1970, Abacus 1972
The Colonial Heritage of Latin America
    Steen & Steen, OUP, New York 1970
The Open Veins of Latin America
    Eduardo Galeano, Monthly Review Press 1973
Land & Liberty
    slide/tape, LAB 1982
The Twenty Latin Americas, 2 volumes
    Marcel Liedergang, Penguin 1971

Mission in Conflict

Christology at the Crossroads
    Jon Sobrino SJ, SCM 1978
A Theology of Liberation
    Gustavo Gutierrez, SCM, London 1974
Revolutionary Theology Comes of Age
    José Miguez Bonino, SPCK, London 1975
Cry of the People
    Penny Lernoux, Penguin 1982

Frontiers of Theology in Latin America
  ed. Rosino Gibellini, SCM, London 1980
Love in Practice: The Gospel in Solentiname
  Ernesto Cardenal, Search Press 1977
Hope in Captivity
  Derek Winter, Epworth Press 1977
Theology Encounters Revolution
  Andrew Kirk, Intervarsity Press 1980
The Power of the Poor in History
  Gustavo Gutiérrez, SCM, London 1983

Cuba

Cuba: The Second Decade
  ed. John Griffiths & Peter Griffiths, Writers & Readers 1979
Cuba, the Pursuit of Freedom
  Hugh Thomas, Eyre & Spottiswoode 1971
Cuba, Order and Revolution
  Jorge Domínguez, Harvard University Press 1978
Is Cuba Socialist?
  Rene Dumont, Andre Deutsch 1974
Cuba in Revolution
  ed. Rolando E. Boachea & Nelson P. Valdes, Doubleday, New York 1972
A Man from the Interior: Cuba's Quest
  Bruce Kenrick, Epworth Press 1980

Brazil

São Paulo: Growth & Poverty
  CIIR 1978
Brazil: State & Struggle
  LAB 1982
Politics in Brazil, 1930–1964: An Experiment in Democracy
  Thomas Skidmore, OUP, New York 1967
War on the Last Frontier
  Sue Branford, Junction, London 1982
The Political Transformation of the Brazilian Catholic Church
  Thomas Bruneau, OUP 1974
Brazil Study Pack
  CAFOD 1981

For Further Reading

Exiles in Their Own Land
16mm film/VHS video, 29 mins, Christian Aid 1980

Argentina

Argentina in the Twentieth Century
ed. David Rock, Duckworth, London 1975
Argentina under Perón
Guido di Tella, St Antony's Macmillan Series 1983
Argentina: A City and a Nation
James R. Scobie, OUP 1964
Falklands/Malvinas: Whose Crisis?
LAB 1982
Prisoner without a Name, Cell without a Number
Jacobo Timmerman, Penguin 1981

Chile

Chile: The State & Revolution
Ian Roxborough, Phil O'Brien & Jackie Roddick, Macmillan 1977
The Church and Politics in Chile
Brian H. Smith, Princeton University Press 1982
The Pinochet Decade
LAB 1983
The Chilean Road to Socialism
ed. Ann Zammitt, Sussex University 1973
Audacity to Believe
Sheila Cassidy, Collins/Fount Paperbacks, London 1978

Paraguay

Paraguay under Stroessner
Paul H. Lewis, University of North Carolina Press 1980
Alfredo Stroessner (in *Political Leaders of Latin America*)
Richard Bourne, Penguin, Harmondsworth 1969
Paraguay: Power Game
LAB 1980

Indians, Missionaries and the Promised Land: Photographs from Paraguay
Luke Holland, Survival International 1980
Mbarate: The Higher Law of Paraguay
W. Wipfler & D. Helfield, International League for Human Rights, New York 1980
Paraguay – Reign of Terror
slide/tape, 22 mins, Paraguay Committee for Human Rights, London 1981

Peru

The Peruvian Experiment Reconsidered
ed. Cynthia McClintock & Abraham Lowenthal, Princeton University Press 1983
Option for the Poor
Bishop Alban Quinn, CIIR 1982
Nationalism and Capitalism in Peru
Anibal Quijano, Monthly Review Press 1971
Peruvian Labour Under Military Government since 1968
Alan Angell, University of London, Institute of Latin American Studies 1979
Sendero Luminoso
Lawrence Taylor, University of Liverpool 1983

Mexico

Mexico
G. Szakeley & D. Levy, Westview Press 1982
Mexico's Political Economy: Challenges at Home and Abroad
ed. J. Domínguez, Sage Publications 1982
Mexico: Development Strategies for the Future
D. Goulet, University of Notre Dame 1983
The Politics of Mexican Development
R. D. Hansen, Johns Hopkins University Press 1971
US-Mexican Relations: Economic & Social Aspects
C. Reynolds & C. Tello, Stanford University Press 1983
Disorder and Progress: Bandits, Police and Mexican Development
P. Vanderwood, University of Nebraska Press 1981

For Further Reading

Central America: General

Central America: A Nation Divided
    Ralph Lee Woodward Jr, OUP, New York 1976
Under the Eagle: US Intervention in Central America and the Caribbean
    Jenny Pearce, LAB 1981
Idols of Death and the God of Life
    Philip Berryman, Orbis Books 1983

El Salvador

The Long War
    James Dunkerley, Junction 1982
El Salvador, Landscape and Society
    David Browning, Clarendon Press, Oxford 1971
Oscar Romero: Bishop and Martyr
    James R. Brockman, Sheed & Ward, London 1981

Guatemala

Guatemala
    NACLA 1974
Bitter Fruit
    S. Schlesinger & S. Kinzer, Sinclaire & Browne 1982
Guatemala Study Pack
 - CIIR 1983

Nicaragua

Nicaragua in Revolution
    ed. Thomas W. Walker, Praeger 1982
Nicaragua: the Land of Sandino
    Thomas Walker, Westview Press, Boulder Colorado 1981
The Guardians of the Dynasty
    Richard Millett, Orbis 1977

Index

Index

Index

Reagan Administration, 9, 27, 67, 245f
Rega, José López, 111
Regions Beyond Missionary Union, 271
Resck, Alfonso, 163
Rocafort, Fr Juan Gomez, 172
Rockefeller, Nelson, 171
Rodríguez, Fr Lelio, 174
Rolón, Mgr Ismael, 174, 178
Roman Catholic Church, see Catholic Church
Romero, Colonel Humberto, 242
Romero, Archbishop Oscar Arnulfo, 7, 37, 226, 244, 256, 257
Rosa, St, 199
Roschmann, Eduard, 168
Rubio, Mgr Andrés, 173

Salvation Army, 182, 271
Sandinistas, 66, 73, 216, 226, 240, 244, 246, 250f
Sandino, Cesar Augusto, 10, 230
Savage, Pedro, 43
Scannone, Juan Carlos, 120
Schlesinger and Kinzer, 232
Segundo, Juan Luis, 49, 51
Seminario por Extensión Anglicano (SEAN), Chile, 150
Sendero Luminoso, 197–8
Sendic, Raul, 173
Seventh Day Adventists, 150, 203, 204, 222, 224, 263
Shaull, Richard, 98
Silva, Luis Ignacio da, see Lula
Silva, Santo Dias da, 87
Sisters of the Cross and Passion, 268
Sisters of the Sacred Heart of Mary, 268
Smith, Wayne, 65–6
Soares, Fr Francisco, 119
Sobrino, Jon, 48, 49, 51
Social Assistance Foundation of the Christian Churches (FASIC), Chile, 150
Society for Promoting Christian Knowledge (SPCK), UK, 273
Somoza, Anastasio, 22, 27, 163, 168, 230, 240, 241, 258
South American Missionary Society, 40, 179, 181, 269

Stroessner, 153, 165–8, 171
Summer Institute of Linguistics, 273
Survival International, 180

Tannenbaum, Professor Frank, 29
Tear Fund, 273
Theology of Liberation, 7, 8, 43, 46f, 145, 200, 203
  hermeneutics, 51
  and Marxism, 50–1
  methodology, 49–50
  relation to Comunidades Eclesiales de Base, 48
Third World Priests, 36, 119, 120
Thomson, James, 121, 221
Toba Maskoy, 177–8
Torre, Haya de la, 10, 187, 195
Torres, Camilo, 36
Trujillo, President, 22
Tupi-Guarani, 12

Ubico, Jorge, 22, 231
Unevangelized Fields Mission, 272
Ungo, Guillermo, 241
United Fruit Company, 19, 229, 230, 232
United Society for Christian Literature (USCL), UK, 273
United Society for the Propagation of the Gospel (USPG), 270
Uruguay, 17, 23, 24

Valdivieso, Antonio, 252
Valle, Luis del, 221
Valverde, Vincente, 198
Vargas, Getulio, 19, 77
Vatican II (Second Vatican Council), 70, 71, 143, 200, 220
Velasco, President, 194
Venezuela, 11, 27
Vicariate of Solidarity, Chile, 146–7
Victores, General Mejia, 248
Vidales, Raúl, 49, 221
Videla, General Jorge Rafael, 113–14
Villa, Pancho, 206
Villanueva, Armando, 195
Viola, General, 114

Waldensians, 121
White, Robert, 244

289